POLICY REFORM AND THE DEVELOPMENT OF DEMOCRACY IN EASTERN EUROPE

T0316130

For Ramsey

Policy Reform and the Development of Democracy in Eastern Europe

CHRIS HASSELMANN

University College, and the Program in International and Area Studies, Washington University in St. Louis

Routledge
Taylor & Francis Group

LONDON AND NEW YORK

First published 2006 by Ashgate Publishing

Reissued 2018 by Routledge
2 Park Square, Milton Park, Abingdon, Oxon, OX14 4RN
711 Third Avenue, New York, NY 10017, USA

Routledge is an imprint of the Taylor & Francis Group, an informa business

First issued in paperback 2018

A Library of Congress record exists under LC control number: 2005026472

Notice:
Product or corporate names may be trademarks or registered trademarks, and are used only for identification and explanation without intent to infringe.

Publisher's Note
The publisher has gone to great lengths to ensure the quality of this reprint but points out that some imperfections in the original copies may be apparent.

Disclaimer
The publisher has made every effort to trace copyright holders and welcomes correspondence from those they have been unable to contact.

ISBN 13: 978-0-815-39108-1 (hbk)
ISBN 13: 978-1-138-62017-9 (pbk)
ISBN 13: 978-1-351-15164-1 (ebk)

Contents

List of Tables

Preface

This project began with a basic question: what are the political consequences of privatization? Many of the economic consequences are by now fairly well understood whether in terms of the incentives facing entrepreneurs, corporate governance, the efficient allocation of resources, or the overall well being of the economy. In terms of politics, however, the subject seemed, comparatively speaking, less well developed. My interest in this question was further heightened by the unprecedented scope of the privatization process undertaken in Eastern Europe following the collapse of communism in 1989–1990. While other countries had from time to time privatized various select industries (e.g., railway service in the U.K.), the countries of Central and Eastern Europe had embarked on an endeavor the size and pace of which had never been seen before. At the same time, these countries were also undergoing a transition towards democracy. While there is no universally agreed upon definition for democracy, the myriad of proposed ones most often center around some concept of contestation, and the rules that govern it. What is generally agreed, however, is that like most competitions, resources are often critical to the outcome of political contests. So how did the redistribution of resources in Eastern Europe affect the transition to, and the consolidation of, democracy?

The process of answering this question was facilitated by the fact that each country had formulated its own unique approach to privatization that resulted in different reallocations of resources across the respective societies. With variation in the causal variable established, the tasked turned to finding a specific policy area in which to assess its impact. In this regard, the issue of pension reform offered an ideal setting. First, it is a substantively important issue that existed in every country across the region. Second, in each case, it was chronologically subsequent to the bulk of the privatization programs. Third, it introduced another interesting research question.

As described in Chapter 1, the World Bank had formulated a model of pension reform by the early 1990s, and the countries of Central and Eastern Europe were among the first to be confronted with it. In all cases, the policy advice and pressure from the World Bank was the same; however, each country adopted either slightly different versions of the model or, in the case of the Czech Republic, rejected it altogether in favor of revisions to the existing pension system How do we account for this variation? Put another way, how do domestic and international political pressures interact to produce policy outcomes?

This issue of interaction is one central to both the fields of international relations, and political science more generally. Addressing it, however, also informs the larger question of democracy raised earlier. Because the international half of the interaction can be held constant, in that the policy advice and pressure applied by the World Bank was the same in all cases, studying the interaction itself allows us to compare the status of democracy throughout the region. How able were different domestic actors to shape and recast the World Bank's policy advice into a unique set of policy reforms? How receptive were the political systems to domestic interest representation? How consolidated are these political systems in terms of democracy?

For reasons explained in Chapter 1, this research addresses these questions in the context of efforts to reform the communist-era pension systems in Poland, Hungary and the Czech Republic. In regard to privatization's political consequences, I argue that there are two. First, the privatization of state assets changes the resources groups of like-minded individuals have with which to overcome the challenges inherent in collective activity. This in-turn affects the political playing field, and can significantly affect the outcome of a political contest between groups with divergent interests. Second, because it has financial consequences, privatization also shapes individual attitudes towards each reform alternative, particularly those that promised to force retirees to rely more heavily on the market for their retirement benefits.

In terms of the interaction between domestic and international forces, I argue that international political pressures can affect domestic politics in two ways. First, they can expand the set of policy options under consideration by providing expert information and guidance. This can significantly reconfigure the political playing field. In the case of pension reform, the World Bank was able to introduce an alien policy option (pension privatization) into the mix, and endow it with sufficient credibility that seven countries in the region eventually adopted some form of it. Under any definition, this was an act of political power and influence. Second, international actors can change the costs and benefits associated with each alternative. By extending financial aid contingent on adopting a particular type of reform, the international community can alter the decision calculus made by local elites. So while the international community did not dictate policy outcomes anywhere, it certainly helped influence and structure the terms of debate, as well as the costs and benefits associated with each alternative.

Finally, regarding the status of democracy, I make two arguments; one concerning the three cases examined here, and one concerning the generalizability of the empirical test used to assess the democratic process across the region. Since 1989, the entire region, including the former republics of the Soviet Union, has been placed under the heading of transitional states. At the core of this transition lay the twin and intertwined goals of creating a more open political and economic system. What has remained unclear is exactly how we know when this transition period has ended. Both arguments are in response to this basic question.

First, I argue that as early as six to seven years into their transition, Poland, Hungary and the Czech Republic were consolidated democracies. While their status as such today is widely, if not universally recognized, at what point did they achieve this status, and more importantly, on what basis can we comparatively measure and assess their progress? Starting from the premise that democracy is ultimately an agreement about process, but not necessarily outcomes, I argue that the way in which each of these countries went about assessing, debating and constructing a major overhaul of their pension systems strongly conforms to existing standards for democratic consolidation found in the literature. In terms of how they make major public policy decisions, these three nations are not qualitatively different from the democracies found in Western Europe or North America. It is important to point out, however, that consolidated democracy does not necessarily mean either a good democracy, in some normative sense, or one that is very deep in terms of either its level of participation or contestation. What I do argue, however, is that when compared to other advanced, industrial democracies in terms of party competition, electoral turnout, or general civicness, they are not substantially different from their democratic neighbors in Western Europe. From a research perspective then, Poland, Hungary and the Czech Republic are more readily comparable than before. There is no longer a need to separate them as somehow qualitatively different in terms of how they make major policy decisions or in their level of democracy. As demonstrated by the recent events (April 2005) in the Czech Republic, where Prime Minister Stanislav Gross was forced to resign in the face of intense public outrage over a corruption scandal, there is now substantial agreement in these countries as to what constitutes acceptable public behavior and procedure.

Second, I argue that the case of pension reform offers a generalizeable testing procedure to assess the progress of democracy throughout the region. Driven by the same underlying pressures, every one of the twenty-five countries in Central and Eastern Europe, including the former republics of the Soviet Union, has had or needs to address the issue of pension reform. In the absence of changes, each faced (or faces) mounting fiscal pressures and eventual insolvency. In each case, the policy advice and pressure stemming from the international community remains a constant. Therefore, the testing procedure used here can be replicated on a significantly larger sample and used to investigate both the ability of different domestic interests to organize, defend and promote their interests, as well as to further explore the interaction between domestic and international politics.

Chris Hasselmann
Boston, MA

List of Abbreviations

AARP	American Association of Retired Persons
AWS	Akcja Wyborcza Solidarno (Poland)
BSE	Budapest Stock Exchange (Hungary)
CBOS	Centrum Badania Opinii Społecznej (Poland)
CEE	Central and Eastern Europe
CERGE	Center for Economic Research and Graduate Education (Czech Rep.)
CEU	Central European University (Hungary)
ČMKOS	Českomoravská Konfederace Odborových Svazů (Czech Republic)
CRT	Committee on the Reform of the Treasury (Hungary)
ČSSD	Česká Strana Sociálně Demokratická (Czech Republic)
DIW	German Institute for Economic Research
DŽJ	Důchodci za Životní Jistoty (Czech Republic)
EBRD	European Bank for Reconstruction and Development
ESOP	Employee Stock Option Program (Hungary)
EU	European Union
GDP	Gross Domestic Product
GDR	German Democratic Republic
HAS	Hungarian Academy of Sciences
IMF	International Monetary Fund
IPF	Investment Privatization Fund
IRAs	Individual Retirement Accounts
IRC	Interest Reconciliation Council (Hungary)
Kcs	Czech Krowns
KDS	Křestanská Demokratická Strana (Czech Republic)
KDU-ČSL	Křestanská a Demokratická Unie-Československá Strana Lidová (Czech Rep.)
KRUS	Kasa Rolniczego Ubezpieczenia Spolecznego (Poland)
KSČM	Komunistická Strana Čech a Moravy (Czech Republic)
LSU	Liberálně Sociální Unie (Czech Republic)
MDF	Magyar Demokrata Fórum (Hungary)
MN	Mniejszość Niemiecka (Poland)
MNCs	Multinational Corporations
MOF	Ministry of Finance
MOW	Ministry of Welfare
MSZOSZ	Magyar Szakszervezetek Országos Szövetsége (Hungary)
MSzP	Magyar Szocialista Párt (Hungary)
NDC	Notional Defined Contribution
NIF	National Investment Funds (Poland)

ODA	Občanská Demokratická Aliance (Czech Republic)
ODS	Občanská Demokratická Strana (Czech Republic)
OPT	Országos Takarékpénztár és Kereskedelmi Bank Rt. (Hungary)
OPZZ	Ogólnopolskie Porozumienie Zwiazków Zawodowych (Poland)
PAYG	Pay-As-You-Go
PIF	Pension Insurance Fund (Hungary)
PSL	Polskie Stronnictwo Ludowe (Poland)
RD	Regional District (Hungary)
RHSD	Council of Economic and Social Accord (Czech Republic)
ROP	Ruch Odbudowy Polski (Poland)
SLD	Koalicja Sojuszu Lewicy Demokratycznej (Poland)
SMD	Single-Member District
SOEs	State-Owned-Enterprises
SPA	State Property Agency (Hungary)
SPR-RSČ	Sdruženi Pro Republiku-Republikánská Strana Československa (Czech Rep.)
SZDSZ	Szabad Demokraták Szövetsége (Hungary)
TÁRKI	Társadalomkutatási Intézet (Hungary)
UNFE	Urzad Nadzoru Funduszy Emerytalnych (Poland)
UD	Unia Demokratyczna (Poland)
UP	Unia Pracy (Poland)
UW	Unia Wolności (Poland)
VMB	Voluntary Mutual Benefit
WGES	Working Group on Economic Strategy (Hungary)
ZUS	Zakładu Ubezpieczeń Społecznych (Poland)

Acknowledgments

I spent the dog-days of the Summer of 1989 traveling around West Germany. I still have vivid memories of sitting in my grandparent's backyard reading about the vast number of East Germans crossing over the recently opened border between Hungary and Austria on their way to West Germany. Like everyone else on the planet, I had absolutely no idea what was about to happen. I was a sophomore at George Washington University at the time and the events of that Fall had a profound impact on my academic interests and future plans. As someone interested in the politics behind economic decision-making, I was fortunate to have begun my academic career at such a moment. My subsequent career path has been heavily influenced by the extent to which the people of Central and Eastern Europe had gone to disprove almost everything we thought we knew about the region.

In conducting this research, I have been extremely fortunate to have received excellent guidance and assistance from numerous scholars and friends in Europe and the United States. At the University of Tübingen (Germany), I would like to acknowledge the assistance of Thomas Fischer, then of the European Center for Federalism Research. In Berlin, Professor Jacobsen of the Freie Universität, as well as Professor Heinrich Machowski and Deborah Bowen of the German Institute for Economic Research (DIW) provided both invaluable resources and their time, without which this project would never have gotten off the ground in the manner it did. In Prague, Professor Jan Hanousek of the Center for Economic Research and Graduate Education (CERGE) of Charles University provided insightful guidance and expert advice at the outset which helped clarify the often murky terrain of Czech privatization, investment funds and the role of state-owned banks. Ondřej Schneider of Patria Finance was kind enough to share his thoughts and writings on the Czech pension system. Vera Haberlova of STEM Public Opinion Research offered useful feedback and guidance in locating various sources of data.

In Budapest, where I spent the majority of my time abroad, the list of those who graciously offered their time and resources to an unknown "Ami" from across the pond is considerable. Eugene Spiro of the East-West Management Institute was the first to open his door. He helped me settle on the idea of using pension reform as a means to gauge both the interaction between domestic and international actors, as well as the status of democracy itself in each country. Mihela Popescu of the Privatization Project at Central European University (CEU) was instrumental in my obtaining both material and access to the university's considerable resources. Her support for my research was instrumental in my successful efforts to obtain external funding; for that I am sincerely thankful. The faculty of CEU proved to be extremely generous both in terms of the information they offered and the references they provided to other experts throughout the city. I wish to especially thank Professors

Lorand Ambruz-Lakatos, László Bruszt, Ivan Csaba, László Csaba, Mihály Laki, and Peter Mihályi. Professor Zsusza Ferge (ELTE University) kindly provided her past work on the various actors involved in the Hungarian reform effort. Julia Szalai and Mária Augusztinovics of the Hungarian Academy of Sciences each gave generously of their time and provided extremely valuable insights and information. Róbert Gál of TÁRKI greatly facilitated my understanding of his organization's survey data and research into public attitudes about pension reform in Hungary. Peter Vanhuysse of the London School of Economics offered an enjoyable and thought provoking exchange regarding our mutual research interests. Bernadett Ansca and Alex Scacco offered their friendship and much needed moments away from work.

Although fortunate to have spent a considerable amount of time living and working in Europe, my fellow compatriots in St. Louis have also contributed greatly to my experiences and this endeavor. I wish to thank Aslaug Asgiersdottir, Eliana Bala, Nina Baranchuk, Martin Battle, Zdravka Brunkova, Ricardo Da Costa E Silva, Chad Haddal, Liana Jacobi, Barbara Kinsey, René Lindstädt, Scott McClurg, Michael Popovic, Jennifer Seely, Tara Sinclair, Jeffrey Staton, Jennifer Nicoll Victor and Beth Wilner. Special thanks go to Joseph Tonon, who was always there to lend an ear or offer up a word of encouragement. I also wish to thank Randall Calvert, Lee Epstein, Steve Fazzari, Mikhail Filippov, Andrew Mertha, Gary Miller, Jack Knight, Sunita Parikh, Roger Petersen, Itai Sened, Olga Shvetsova, John Sprague and Andrew Sobel. Jan Rensing, Kerri Therina, and Pauline Farmer provided administrative assistance and much needed moments of joviality. Terry Keagan of the Olin Library at Washington University offered invaluable assistance over the years in acquiring data sets and other materials; every graduate student should be so fortunate. This research has also benefitted from discussants and participants who attend the joint meetings of the Law and Society Association and the Research Committee on the Sociology of Law (2001) as well as the annual meetings of the Midwest Political Science Association (2002), the American Political Science Association (2002), and the American Association for the Advancement of Slavic Studies (2003). In particular, I wish to thank Michael Cain, Tomaz Inglot, and Mitchell Orenstein for their extremely helpful comments and insights over the years. The faculty and staff of Tufts University, where I served as a visiting lecturer in the Department of Political Science from 2003–2005, provided an enjoyable and productive environment in which to bring this project to publication; in particular, I wish to thank Jeff Berry, Jim Glaser and Vickie Sullivan for their support and encouragement during my tenure in Boston.

As we all know, comparative research involving extended periods overseas in multiple countries can be extremely expensive. In this regard, I have been extremely fortunate and in all honesty, incredibly lucky. Over the years, I have received generous financial support from the Institute for the Study of World Politics, the German Academic Exchange Service (D.A.A.D.), the New Center for Institutional Economics at Washington University, Dean Robert Thatch of the School of Arts and Sciences, and from the department of Political Science at Washington University (Jack Knight, Chair).

In bring this research project to publication, I wish to thanks the editors and staff at Ashgate Publishing. Kirstin Howgate took the time to first explore the idea with me and offered encouragement along the way. Carolyn Court, Nikki Dines, Rosalind Ebdon, Halima Fradley, Donna Hamer, and Emily Poulton provided invaluable editorial guidance as well as administrative and technical support without which there would be no book.

Finally, I wish to thank the love of my life, Ramsey Ellis, for seeing me through this process. That I completed it while retaining some semblance of sanity is due to your patience, understanding, and kindly reminders that there is a time and a place for work, and a time and a place for fun. This effort is dedicated to you.

Chapter 1

Introduction

During the summer and fall of 1989, an extraordinary series of events rapidly unfolded in Eastern Europe that ultimately culminated in the eventual collapse and disappearance of the communist regimes that had been encamped there since their installation by the Soviet army following World War II. In the years that followed, each nation began the process of economic and political reform, a simultaneity that separates Eastern Europe from other Communist regimes such as China and Vietnam, which, while also undergoing market-based reforms, are attempting to hold onto their political control. By the late 1990s, a vast array of new institutions had been drawn up covering almost every facet of social, economic and political life. Aiding in this creation were an army of international consultants and financial experts from both academia and organizations like the World Bank, the International Monetary Fund (IMF), and the European Union (EU). While these international actors helped structure the transition, the period was also one of democratization and the supposed advent of real domestic interest representation. How have these two political forces, one international one domestic, interacted? More importantly, what does this interaction tell us about the status of the transition to democracy itself?

A Pension Crisis and the Need for Reform

This research addresses these questions in the context of efforts to reform the communist-era pension systems in Poland, Hungary and the Czech Republic. The choice of pension reform as a vehicle of inquiry is two-fold. First, the issue provides an ideal environment in which to comparatively study the question of the interaction between domestic and international politics. In order to properly examine such a relationship, one of the elements must be held constant. In this case, the policy pressure applied by the international community was the same across the board; what varies is 1) a nation's responsiveness to that pressure, and 2) the ability of domestic actors to influence the legislative process. As a result, we have a natural, controlled experiment across multiple countries. Moreover, because it is the international aspect that is constant, it is possible to comparatively evaluate the process of democracy and interest representation across the region.

Apart from methodological advantages, lies the salience of pension reform itself, one driven by two factors that combined to place the issue on the agenda of every country in the region. The first has to do with the nature of the communist labor market, and the solutions that were devised to the employment crisis that resulted from the transition to a market economy in the early 1990s. Throughout the communist-era, the incentive for managers of state-owned enterprises (SOEs) had been to employ as many workers as possible; essentially, they learned to hoard labor like they hoarded everything else. When subsidies were cut-off as part of the market and price liberalization process, firms had to bring their employment levels closer in-line with the actual requirements of producing at or near profit maximization. This entailed a massive scaling back of their labor force, and one often chosen means to this end was to offer early retirement to anyone willing to take it. As a result, most countries in Eastern Europe experienced a dramatic increase in the size of their pensionable aged populations as early retirement and generous applications of disability pensions became seen as "more humane" ways of dealing with an employment crisis in a region where people had grown accustomed to job security that "was more stable than the Japanese promise of lifetime employment" (Laszlo Bruszt 2001, personal communication).[1]

The second factor forcing states to address the issue of pension reform was the manner in which these systems were financed. Using a Pay-As-You-Go (PAYG) arrangement, current workers and employers provided for current retirees through jointly financed payroll contributions.[2] Such a system is premised on an "intergenerational covenant [whereby the current] generation of workers pay for the pensions of the generation before, with the assurance that they [will] be provided for by the generation to follow" (Noonan 1998, 2). This kind of system works extremely well where the ratio of workers to pensioners is relatively high, and as such was the standard model for communist systems everywhere as all available workers were claimed to be employed. What forced politicians to undertake reforms was the sudden collapse of this ratio in the early 1990s. As unemployment and early retirement grew, those paying into the system, and thereby supporting the current retirees, began to shrink at an ever-increasing rate. To make matters worse, gloomy demographic forecasts showed a rapidly aging population, a fact that only added to the growing sense of crisis. In short, some type of reform was inevitable as

---

1   The alternative to early retirement would have been to rely on unemployment benefits; however, by law such benefits could only be collected for up to two years. Consequently, they were of little use to the sizeable number of middle-aged workers facing what, given the economic dislocation at the time, seemed likely to be the end of their working careers. The use of early retirement took place to a much greater degree in Poland and Hungary than it did in the Czech Republic.

2   The U.S. Social Security System is also a PAYG design, and as such, is at risk from some of the same long-term demographic problems described here as the baby-boomers retire. The difference in the U.S. case, however, is that 1) the fertility rate is now actually above replacement (albeit barely), and 2) the country continues to receive an ever growing influx of immigrants who have an even higher fertility rate. Recent data for example suggests that among Hispanics in the U.S., the fertility rate is 3.0 children per women; the population replacement rate is defined as 2.1 (*The Economist* August 24, 2002, 21). The net effect of these differences is that while currently similar at around 35 years, the median age in the U.S. will be just over 36 in 2050, while in Europe it is likely to be closer to 53! (Ibid, 22).

bankruptcy and insolvency suddenly loomed large on the immediate horizon. A visual assessment of the impending doom faced by Poland, Hungary and the Czech Republic is provided in Figure 1.1; (the numerical data for each country is provided in Appendix 3).

One way in which to evaluate the viability of a PAYG pension system is through the *System Dependency Ratio*, which relates the number of pensioners to the number of contributors (expressed as a decimal in Figure 1.1).[3] Using Hungary as an example, we see that by 1995 it took the effort and payroll contributions of nearly four workers to support three pensioners (ratio: 0.748); by comparison, in 1950, almost eight retirees could be supported by the contributions of a single worker (ratio: 0.129). Figure 1.1 also clearly shows the effect of using early retirement and disability pensions to solve the employment crisis as the ratio jumped by more than 62% between 1990 and 1995! The impending demographic danger can also be seen in that the ratio is expected to reach 1:1 by 2035, all of which contributed to the projection of a pension system deficit totaling 6% of GDP by 2050 (Palacios and Rocha 1997, 12–14). While the time horizon varies, the trend is the same in all three countries. In the absence of reform, all countries would, by the middle of this century, face massive pension deficits and overwhelming dependency ratios. In short, as early as the mid-1990s, they were facing the limits of financing pensions through inter-generational means.

The World Bank to the Rescue?

The international community was quick to offer a solution to this growing problem.[4] The basic idea was to supplement, if not replace, inter-generational financing with mandatory, fully funded individual pension accounts that would be managed not by the state, but by private financial corporations. The basis for this particular set of policy prescriptions originated from the experience of several Latin American countries a decade before.[5] In 1981, Chile became the first country in the world to

---

3   By way of illustration, assume for example that pensions replace 60% of a workers wage and that all workers earn the same amount of money. A dependency ratio of 1:1 implies that 60% of every current workers salary is taxed away via payroll contributions to fund a single retired person's pension, with contributions normally coming from both the worker and the employer. A ratio of 1:2 (or 0.50) implies that two workers support every pension meaning that only 30% of their current wages need be withheld to meet current benefit requirements. In both cases, payroll withholdings are taken prior and in addition to normal income and other taxes.

4   Although the primary focus here is on the involvement of the World Bank, the IMF and the EU were also important actors. The IMF was involved due to the fiscal deficits and debt obligations faced by several of the countries involved, particularly Poland and Hungary. For its part, the EU had a clear incentive to ensure fiscal stability among its future members, ten of which joined the Union on May 1, 2004.

5   For more on the Latin American reforms, see Müller 1999, especially 18–24; Hujo 1999; Arenas de Mesa and Bertranou 1997; Mesa-Lago 1997; and Fougerolles 1996. Several

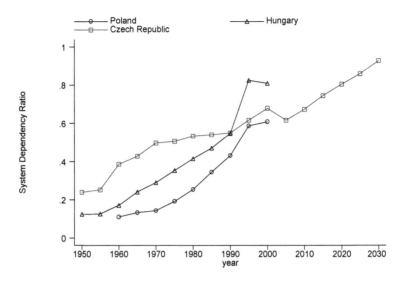

Figure 1.1   The System Dependency Ratio in Poland, Hungary and the Czech Republic, 1950–2030

The System Dependency Ratio relates the number of pensioners to the number of contributors, expressed here as a decimal. The figure reveals how widely the burden of providing for current retirees is spread among current workers. For example, in 1950, the cost of providing for 3 pensioners could be spread among 12 Czech workers (0.240), while in Hungary a single worker could provide for eight retirees (0.124). However, driven by an aging population, growing unemployment, the use of early-retirement, and generous applications of disability pensions (particularly in Hungary), these ratio began to grow substantially during the 1990s. In all cases, it is estimated that the ratio will reach 1:1 by 2050.

Sources:
Poland – Statistical Yearbook of the Republic of Poland, various years.
Hungary – Hungarian Statistical Yearbook, various years
Czech Republic
      1950–2000: Czechoslovak (Czech) Statistical Yearbook, various years
      2005–2030: Kral 2001, Lasagabaster et al 2002, own calculations.

fully privatize its pension system by shifting from a public PAYG arrangement to a system of mandatory, but privately managed pension funds that were fully funded by the individual. The only remaining role for the state, beyond supervision of the funds' investment practices, was the provision of a limited number of tax-financed

of the World Bank's publications suggest a clear preference for the Chilean model over the more mixed Argentine version; in the latter, the state continued to play a sizeable role in the provision of pensions. See for example World Bank 1997.

pensions for those who had never contributed or had failed to do so for at least 20 years.[6] In essence, the Chilean government removed itself from the provision of pensions leaving individuals to look after themselves through the marketplace. By the early 1990s, both the Chilean system and its Argentine variant had become models of the "new pension orthodoxy" and countries around the world were advised by neo-liberal institutions in Washington and Europe to follow their lead (Müller 1999, 26). In making its case, the World Bank argued that adopting a Chilean-style system "would signal the government's intention to transfer responsibility to individuals for their own well-being ... and establish a constituency for macroeconomic stability, financial sector reform, and enterprise privatization" (World Bank 1994, 286). To further spread this message, the World Bank began sponsoring a number of conferences and seminars throughout Central and Eastern Europe; it also funded the work of numerous scholars and government working groups looking at ways to implement the Latin American experience in the region. Although the individual details of their respective reforms varied, by the end of the 1990s, seven countries in the region, including Poland and Hungary, had adopted a mixed pillar model that included partial privatization.[7] The Czech Republic, however, refused and chose instead to reform its existing PAYG system.

Among those adopting the new pension orthodoxy, however, the level of adherence varies considerably. The most orthodox adoptee was Kazakhstan, a state with strong, authoritarian political institutions and control. Using these tools, "reformers in Kazakhstan set out to implement a Chilean-style pension reform, and were highly successful in pushing through their initial proposal. The Kazakh reform eliminates, over time, the current PAYG system and replaces it with a minimum pension guarantee and a mandatory, funded, second pillar" (Orenstein 2000, 29). However, most other countries in the region do not have the kind of political control seen in Pinochet's Chile and or present day Kazakhstan. In these countries, reforms have to pass through a developing democratic process, complete with multiple veto players, organized interest groups, and a multi-party system. Just how much of an effect a democratic process can have can be seen in Hungary, where the initial proposal put forth by the Finance Minister (Lajos Bakros) called for a 100% Chilean-style system. When the final package emerged several years later, it bore no resemblance to Bakros's initial proposal. While this surprised no one given the radical departure Bakros proposed, how do we explain the selection of the eventual

---

6   These state-funded pensions, however, did not even begin to approach subsistence level as they amounted to only 10.5% of the average wage (Müller 1999, 20).

7   The World Bank model includes three pillars. The first is a reformed PAYG system where the contribution-benefit link has been tightened to make it less re-distributive. The second contains the new, mandatory private accounts while the third is a voluntary one comprised of individual, privately administered retirement accounts similar in nature to individual retirement accounts (IRAs) in the U.S. In some cases, a so-called zero pillar was added which provides a tax-financed, universal flat-rate pension that acts as income floor below which no retiree can fall. This pillar is not a formal component of the World Bank's policy prescription, though it was not expressly excluded either.

reform package? Which factors account for the "paradigm choice in the area of old-age security?" (Müller 1999, 53).

In accounting for this policy choice, previous studies have focused on the influence international indebtedness and system deficits gave the Washington Consensus; a view best seen in the work of Müller (1999) and Müller, Ryll and Wagener (1999).[8] Müller makes the argument "that structural factors – notably the financial situation of the existing public retirement schemes and the degree of external debt – largely determine which actors take part in the process of pension reform, as well as their relative strength" (Müller 1999, 5). She goes on to argue that in order "for radical reform to become feasible, those actors inclined towards pension privatization – the Ministry of Finance and the World Bank – must have stakes and leverage in the local reform process, thereby outweighing the Ministry of Labor" and other actors more inclined to support adjustments to the established programs (Müller 1999, 52). Using a comparative analysis of the East European experience, these arguments are well supported. In Poland and Hungary, where the central budget stood to be immediately and significantly affected by the impending deficits of the pension system, the Ministry of Finance became a vocal and forceful advocate for the implementation of mandatory, private pension accounts. However, in the Czech Republic, where the pension system promised solvency for at least the next five years, the Ministry of Finance remained noticeably absent and no such reform took place. The experience of these three countries also points a finger squarely at the leverage large external debts gave the World Bank in influencing the reform process. Although the international community did not dictate policy anywhere, heavily indebted Poland and Hungary were forced to consider the Bank's arguments and advice to a degree that the relatively debt free Czech Republic was not.

However, these factors alone cannot explain the choice of a particular reform alternative nor the politics behind its passage. Even in Hungary, where this argument should be at its strongest given an overwhelming debt ratio and a pension system facing the financial abyss, there are serious shortcomings. Most damaging is the

---

8   The term Washington Consensus was coined by John Williamson (1990) in reference to a set of neo-liberal policy prescriptions that the World Bank and the IMF presented Latin American countries facing reform. He summarized its main features as encompassing 1) fiscal discipline, 2) a redirection of public expenditure towards education, health care and infrastructure investments, 3) tax reforms that broadened the overall base while lowering marginal tax rates, 4) the reliance on market-determined interest rates, 5) competitive exchange rates, 6) trade liberalization, 7) an openness to foreign direct investment, 8) the privatization of SOEs, 9) deregulation of the marketplace, and 10) the legal protection of property rights. He argues that "we can now develop for more consensus ... [because] we now know more about what types of economic policy work" (Williamson 1993, 1331). His original intent was to convey the lowest common denominator of advice that was being put forward. Since then, the phrase has taken on a life of its own and is now most commonly used as a cynical stereotype or caricature of inflexible policy advice that is uniformly applied to developing countries around the world by the major international institutions, primarily the World Bank and the IMF, and to a lesser extent the World Trade Organization.

inability to explain why the reformed and partially privatized system is really still a PAYG system in disguise. As described in more detail in Chapter 4, despite the creation of mandatory private accounts, the contributions contained within them are still used to provide benefits to current retirees in the PAYG pillar. Because an unexpectedly large number of people voluntary opted to join the new system rather than continue in a purely PAYG system, the government was faced with a higher than anticipated deficit in the public pillar as individuals began diverting a portion of their payroll contributions to their own private accounts.[9] To make ends meet, the government requires these private funds to invest almost exclusively in government bonds, raising revenue, which it then uses to provide benefits to current retirees covered under the public pillar. While there is some policy flexibility within the new pension orthodoxy, this was not what the World Bank had in mind as the end result is a PAYG system in disguise: the burden of paying off bond holders (i.e., the next generation of retirees) will fall on the next generation of Hungarian taxpayers. This is precisely the kind of inter-generational financing the World Bank was arguing against, particularly in light of a falling fertility rate and a rapidly aging society.

Such shortcomings are not limited to the Hungarian case. In both Poland and the Czech Republic, a reference to a lack of indebtedness and international leverage leaves a number of questions unanswered. For example, how or why were Czech opposition groups able to include a new, tax-financed, universal flat-rate pillar over the objection of Prime Minister Vaclav Klaus? In Poland, how was it that the reforms began under a left-of-center government and were continued and finally brought to fruition under a subsequent, right-of-center government? Moreover, how did over 30% of the labor force manage to exclude itself from the reforms in favor of a different paradigm altogether? In short, focusing on the role of structural factors and the influence of the Washington Consensus underestimates the significance of domestic politics. Although the debt situation and the dangers to the central budget clearly account for the origin of the Ministry of Finance's preferences, and help account for the responsiveness to international pressure, alone they cannot fully address the politics of interest representation or the choice a particular policy alternative. Ultimately, it is the ability of domestic actors to influence the legislative

---

9   Because current workers pay for current benefits, deficits are created as individuals shift a portion of their contributions to their own private accounts. Despite privatization, the government is still required to pay all current obligations under the public pillar without having collected the payroll contributions necessary to meet those obligations. The resulting deficit can be *enormous*, as it includes not only the benefits due this year, but also the benefits due each existing and future retiree each year until they die. In his review of a complete privatization of the U.S. Social Security system, Paul Krugman states that although "I haven't been able to lay my hands on a precise estimate for the real Social Security system, but I am pretty sure that the cost of paying off the overhang of obligations would be something north of $3 trillion" (Krugman, Notes on Social Security http://web.mit.edu/krugman/www/socsec. html). The estimated transition cost of the 2005 Bush proposal to divert 4% of contributions to private accounts is around $1.5 trillion dollars over the first decade (Commission on Social Security 2001).

process and have their voices heard that accounts for the unique reform packages that emerged in each country. As Gourevitch argues

> The international system, be it an economic or politico-military form, is underdetermining. The environment may exert strong pulls but short of actual occupation, some leeway in the response to that environment remains. .... Frequently more than one way to be successful exists. .... Some variance in response to the external environment is possible. The explanation of choice among the possibilities therefore requires some examination of domestic politics (Gourevitch 1978, 900).

While the current literature makes it clear that international pressure shaped the options available, I argue it does not provide an adequate explanation for the policy choice itself. So while Müller set out to "identify the factors determining paradigm choice in the area of old-age security," what she best explains is the timing of reform (Müller 1999, 53). For it is only when faced with immanent fiscal shortfalls and immense debt obligations that domestic actors in favor of radical reform gain the upper hand. Thus, she confirms what Tip O'Neill, former Speaker of the U.S. House of Representatives, suggested long ago, namely that Social Security is the electrically charged third rail of American politics. Politicians will only undertake serious efforts to reform a pension system when it is clear that failure to do so would result in system bankruptcy, something both Poland and Hungary were faced with when they began searching for a way to adopt the World Bank's policy advice. While having a better understanding of when reform will take place, this still leaves unanswered the question of *how* it will be reformed. To answer that question, "what must be illustrated is how specific interests use various weapons by fighting through certain institutions in order to achieve their goals" (Gourevitch 1978, 905). I argue that to do this, one must integrate the ability of different groups of like-minded individuals to overcome the challenges inherent in collective activity, with their ability to credibly convey an electoral threat to policy makers in an effort to have their voices heard. I begin therefore with the domestic pressure for reform and the three main alternatives considered and advocated in each country.

The Domestic Pressures for Reform

Faced with a widely, if not universally, recognized need to reform, officials in Central and Eastern Europe (CEE) considered each of the three main policy options available to them, which could be implemented either independently or jointly in a mixed pillar model. At one extreme was the option to create a universal, flat-rate pension funded by general taxation. Generally preferred by the poorer members of society, the idea was to provide a livable income for all retirees regardless of past employment history or payroll contributions. A second alternative focused on reforming, but not dismantling, the existing PAYG system. Central to this approach was an increase in the retirement age and a tightening of the contribution-benefit link. The former is designed to keep more people in the contribution phase of the program, and in light of the comparatively low retirement ages across the region (50–55 in some cases), there was generally room for such an increase. Changing the formula that linked contributions to benefits also offered a means of stabilizing the current financial arrangement. By more closely tying benefits to past contributions, the implicit deficits of the PAYG system could be minimized, thereby reducing the need for tax-financed transfers from the central budget.

The price of this approach, however, would be a falling replacement rate among the poor who had never earned as much or worked as long as some of their compatriots. Recognizing this, many governments chose to pair this with new, voluntary, individual retirement accounts (IRAs) that would be privately managed by banks and insurance companies. Designed to supplement the earnings drawn from the PAYG pillar, it was hoped that these accounts would provide individuals with a way to cushion any decrease in their replacement rate and to allow them to better prepare for their own particular retirement needs. Traditionally, such programs contain tax incentives to encourage broader participation; however, in the face of the severe economic recession of the early 1990s, some governments sought more direct methods to encourage private savings.[10] In the Czech Republic for example, a small but not insignificant matching subsidy was introduced for all individual contributions up to a certain amount.[11]

The final alternative was the adoption of either the Chilean or more mixed Argentine model being advocated by the international community. In practice, the complete privatization embodied by the Chilean approach, although proposed and considered, was ultimately deemed too extreme given both the traditions of social welfare in Europe, and the legacy of the communist-era welfare state.[12] Though radically different in terms of policy prescriptions and objective, the common thread of these historical legacies was the strong presence of the state in the provision of social welfare. The first, or so-called Bismarckian tradition, is the oldest in Europe and is designed to maintain income levels into retirement as benefits are tightly linked to earnings-related contributions.[13] The administration of such systems is

---

10   Tax incentives generally have no effect on the poorer members of society. Since many have little or no income, and hence do not owe any taxes, they have no incentive to contribute even if they could afford to so. Moreover, in the wake of the severe economic recession of the early 1990s, many households were simply either too poor to make use of tax incentives, or unable to afford to set aside even a portion of their total income (Mária Augusztinovics 2001, personal communication).

11   In practice, however, this did not fundamentally alter the savings rate as people have tended to contribute only what is necessary to gain the maximum subsidy each year (Andrej Schneider 2001, personal communication).

12   For a review of the development and typologies of different social welfare traditions, see Wilensky and Lebeaux 1965; Wilensky 1976; Flora and Heidenheimer 1981; Esping-Andersen 1990; Bonoli 1997; and Müller 1999. For an account of policy retrenchment, see Peirson 1994, 2001.

13   As the name suggests, this tradition is German in origin, having been first introduced by the Prussian elite in the late 1880s in an attempt to coopt and "appease the arising socialist

governed by a conservative, corporatist arrangement in which the pension system is jointly administered by labor, business, and government representatives. The second tradition, based on William Beveridge's 1942 report to the British government, focuses on the issue of adequate income support for retirees (Beveridge 1942). Unlike the Bismarckian model, which relies on dedicated payroll taxes to finance pensions, the Beveridgean tradition uses general tax revenue to prevent poverty among the elderly by providing a flat-rate pension below which no person can fall. Overtime, the two systems have often been intermingled into a two-tier system, such as in Sweden, where a first pillar provides a basic flat-rate pension that is individually supplemented with an earnings-related second pillar (Müller 1999, 14). A key component in both traditions, however, is the central role played by the state, either in terms of actually administering the program or having a strong coordinating role to play in a tripartite system.

Further strengthening this tradition of state involvement lies the legacy of cradle-to-grave social welfare provided under communism. While by no means a luxurious life-style, the system did provide free day-care, education, and health benefits to all citizens. Although a certain of degree of retrenchment was inevitable given the economic and financial changes taking place, expectations about never having to live in poverty remained. However, as the transition induced recessions took hold in the early 1990s, a growing number of people found themselves faced for the first time in their lives with this very real possibility, and it was into this environment that the idea of pension privatization was introduced. While the Chilean model went nowhere in Central Europe, the Argentine variant, which incorporated both a reformed PAYG pillar and mandatory private pension accounts, was ultimately adopted in seven countries throughout the region.[14]

The Politics of Interest Representation

As argued above, the existing literature does a good job of conveying a government's responsiveness to the pressure and influence exerted by the international community. By highlighting the fiscal deficits and debt obligations, it helps predict when governments will undertake far-reaching and radical reform of the pension system. Where it is lacking is in integrating this with the politics of domestic interest representation and the choice of a particular solution. In building this connection, I focus on the three avenues by which domestic actors can influence the legislative process. The first method is a restrictive one reserved for veto players, defined as actors "whose agreement is required for a policy decision" (Tsebelis 1995, 293). Tsbelis (1995) argues that the greater the number of veto players, and the greater

---

movement" (Müller 1999, 13).
14   The seven are Bulgaria, Croatia, Hungary, Kazakhstan, Latvia, Macedonia, and Poland.

the ideological distance between them, the harder it is to reform the system.[15] Consequently, veto actors play an important role in setting the boundaries within which the reform debate progresses. For example, if we wish to understand why the Hungarian reforms were ultimately optional for all current employees but mandatory for all new entrants to the workforce, we must examine the preferences of the Constitutional Court. Because current workers had established rights under the existing system, they could not be legally forced into a new arrangement; any effort to do so would have resulted in a veto by the Court. New workers by definition, however, have no such claim and therefore could be required to participate in the new financing scheme.

Beyond institutional actors like the courts, Tsebelis's framework also highlights the role of partisan veto players, who by virtue of the votes they control in parliament can block undesirable legislation. One such example is illustrated by Orenstein (2000) who shows how the Polish Peasant party (PSL) was able to shape and constrain the scope of the reform effort. Representing farmers and other agricultural sectors, which had been left farthest behind by the transition to a market economy, the PSL managed to have them excluded from a reformed system which would have forced them to accept a greater share of responsibility for their own retirement. A final type of veto player is one that is temporarily delegated veto authority on a particular issue. Though rare, and by Tsebelis's own admission "quite idiosyncratic," such delegation did take place in the context of pension reform (Tsebelis 1995, 307). The clearest example lies in the Hungarian case where the left wing of the ruling socialist party made their support in parliament contingent on the approval of the union representatives on the Interest Reconciliation Council (IRC). As a result, the government was forced to negotiate with the unions on the IRC, several of which pressed for and won a number of concessions and policy adjustments.

A second method of political influence is exercised by what Orenstein (2000) calls proposal actors. He points out that "in complex policy areas, where veto actors do not have the relevant expertise to develop their own concrete policy positions, they may rely on proposal actors to determine policy preferences for them, or to set the general terms of debate and the range of policy options in a particular area" (Orenstein 2000, 11). When it came to complicated matters such as pension reform, the record suggests that parliamentarians relied on various government ministries and social groups, like Solidarity (the Polish trade union), to provide them with both specific proposals as well as voting guidance. So the issue here is ultimately one of agenda setting and control.[16] For example, Skocpol et al (1993) show how "even before most American women had the right to vote, they were able to work through voluntary associations to set agendas of public debate over social welfare,

---

15   For more on veto players, see also Tsebelis 1999, 2002. For an analysis of veto players in the context of pension reform, see Orenstein 2000, and Bonoli 2001.

16   For more on agenda setting and manipulation see, Riker 1982, 1986; Kingdon 1984, 1993; Shepsle and Weingast 1984; Baron and Ferejohn 1989.

persuading state legislatures to enact the first explicit authorizations for social spending for mothers and children" (Skocpol et al 1993, 687).

While being able to place items on the agenda can be one source of political influence, some groups may be asked to actually draft the legislation itself. For example, due to the perceived inexperience of government bureaucrats within the Finance Ministry in matters of pensions, the financial community in Hungary was invited to draft the legislation creating the new mandatory private accounts for submission to parliament. It should come as no surprise then that the wording was such that it protected the position of the major banks and insurance companies that had temporarily lent their professional staffs to the Ministry of Finance. As a result, we must consider both actors capable of placing items on the political agenda, and those in a position to draft the terms of the legislation if we hope to make sense of the final outcome.

While both formal veto and proposal actors have been addressed in the literature on pension reform in Eastern Europe, there is a third means of influence that has not been adequately considered, namely direct action by interest groups and voters. As the above example taken from American politics demonstrates, interest groups can have a profound impact on the development of legislation. In fact, Skocpol et al go as far as to warn

> future students of social welfare politics ... to realize that political parties, elections, and bureaucratic and legislative maneuverings are not the totality of such politics. Movements and social groups that can achieve widespread social communication and can use moral arguments to set agendas of public and legislative debate may matter as much, or more than, voting and elections. (Skocpol et al 1993, 697).

I would argue that the key issue here is the question of interest representation, one whose relevance is made even more significant as some groups have been more adversely affected by the transition than others. Generally speaking, the groups hardest hit have included those most vulnerable, such as the very young and the very old, as well as those somehow deemed less essential, such as women and minorities.[17] While the true scope and prevalence of such attitudes is unknown, it raises the question how well these groups have been able to defend themselves politically, particularly in light of a transition process that has fundamentally altered social, political and economic relations.

While the notion of veto players and proposal actors gets at some of this, they cannot fully capture the democratic process that resulted in the final legislation, as Skocpol et al make clear. For example, how is it that the reform process in Poland

---

17   Reflecting the changing attitude towards women in the workforce, the Russian labor minister posed the rhetorical question of "Why should we employ women when men are out of work? It's better that men work and women take care of children and do housework" (World Bank 1996, 72, Box 4.2). In the context of Eastern Europe, one group deemed less essential has been the Roma or gypsy community, a group whose members "are almost always left out" (Milanovic 1998, 147).

began under one government comprised of political leftists, and was ultimately completed by a new center-right government several years later? Simply counting the number of veto players and the ideological distance between them cannot explain how this continuity was achieved. Such outcomes are a function of domestic politics, a process that goes beyond the number of actors with veto authority. Likewise, there are similar limits as to how far the number and variety of proposal actors can take us. What ultimately matters is the ability of like-minded individuals to place items on the agenda and collectively convey a credible electoral and/or moral threat to policy makers. It is the resolution of the resulting political conflict that accounts for the unique details of each country's legislation.

As discussed further below, one of the key determinants in such conflicts are the resources that each side can bring to bear on the political system. Therefore, the politics of interest representation must be related to the privatization and redistribution of state assets that took place during the early to mid-1990s. My central thesis is that privatization not only shaped attitudes towards pension reform, but also affected the ability of like-minded individuals to collectively organize in support of their interests. I argue that because privatization redistributes resources, it necessarily creates relative winners and losers, and consequently changes the pattern of household income. As a result, when faced with the prospect of fending for themselves in their retirement through the marketplace, the relative winners and losers formulated different preferences in regard to how the pension system should be reformed. However, the changes in income brought about by privatization changed more than just their preferences; they also changed the quantity and type of resources they had with which to organize and pressure the political process. In the context of Poland, Hungary and the Czech Republic, a variety of different privatization strategies were implemented, from the essential give-away of state assets through vouchers in the Czech Republic to cash-based sales to foreigners in Hungary. As a result, different groups of relative winners and losers were created in the three countries, each with their own set of political interests and differing abilities to organize in defense of them.

While there is empirical evidence to link preferences and privatization, the politics of interest representation is affected by a wide variety of factors; so the choice of privatization as an organizing principle requires further elaboration. The primary justification comes from a view of democratic politics where there is, at least theoretically, a link between the interests of the public and the policy outcomes that emerge from the deliberation of elected officials. However, few societies are of one mind or opinion, hence politics is the competition between competing interests over particular and divergent policy options. As the history of politics suggests, the outcome of this battle of wills is often a function of three, albeit broad, variables:

power, the ability to mobilize and effectively use it, and the structure or rules that govern the competition. While there is no universally agreed upon definition or understanding as to what power is, it is used here to mean resources such as wealth and group size. The inclusion of wealth is based on the simple fact that running for office is expensive, and parties as well as individual candidates raise the money they need by offering to represent one group of interests over another.[18] An additional resource is group size, a factor that can often offset not having tremendous amounts of wealth to help finance campaigns as the one with the most votes wins. Therefore, in order to assess how interests are represented, we must begin by taking into account the size and resources different interests possess, and given that privatization redistributed the existing resources, we must consider how it has helped reshape the current political landscape.

Regardless, however, of the type or quantity of resources a group of like-minded individuals may have, all groups are confronted with a collective action problem that may hinder their ability to organize. The nature of this problem centers around free-ridership, whereby every individual has the incentive to feed off the contributions of others in attainment of a group benefit. The obvious difficulty is that if all members act this way, there will be no benefit for either the group or individual members within it, or it will only be provided at a less than optimal level (Olson 1971). However, as even a cursory review of history suggests, there are countless examples of group action and collective behavior (the 1989–1990 revolutions in Eastern Europe for example!), suggesting that there are ways to overcome these obstacles. To do this, groups must successfully mobilize potential members and their resources. To assess the likelihood of meeting this challenge, I develop a model of collective action in Chapter 2 that generates testable hypotheses about the conditions under which groups of like-minded individuals will be more or less likely to successfully organize. The model gives the relative likelihood of successful collective action as a function of internal group characteristics, the nature of the objective sought, and the presence or absence of other actors seeking the same objective.

However, having resources and the ability to effectively mobilize them are only two of the relevant dimensions of political conflict. A third set of factors affecting interest representation are the institutional rules that govern the political process, both within elections and in the operation of the parliament. As Cox makes clear, "the laws and practices regulating electoral competition can affect the behavior of voters, contributors, candidates, factions, parties, and alliances in various and sometimes profound ways" (Cox 1999, 145). This means that the ability to act in support of ones interests ultimately depends in part on the characteristics of the political system, a fact that raises a second obstacle for those groups that do manage to successfully overcome the barriers to collective action. For once organized, they

---

18   For example, records submitted to the Polish election commission indicate that in his unsuccessful 1990 run for the Presidency, Prime Minister Tadeusz Mazowiecki spent a total of 5,669,896,103 zl. (~$600,000); this in a country whose average annual wage in 1990 was barely $1,200 (Levush 1991, 184; Wellisz et al 1993, 39; and own calculations).

must find a way to credibly signal policy makers that their demands and preferences should be taken into account. Representation does not automatically follow from organization. One type of group that has a distinct advantage in this regard are those whose memberships constitutes a credible electoral threat throughout the country as opposed to a single electoral district or region. Therefore, my model takes into account the electoral distribution of potential members, the electoral rules (such as thresholds and allocation formulas), and the party system itself to estimate the likelihood that a group, once organize, will be able to influence the legislative process and have it voice heard.

Case Selection and the Small-n Problem

As noted earlier, this research examines the experiences of Poland, Hungary and the Czech Republic in regard to pension reform and the consolidation of democracy. These countries hardly constitute a random sample; in fact, they represent the usual suspects in that they are the three most commonly researched cases in the region. That they have been selected again raises the question of selection bias and the problems that can arise as result.[19] Moreover, the fact that only three countries have been chosen raises additional concerns related to both hypothesis testing and the ability to generalize to a larger set of cases. Despite the perhaps over representation of these three countries in the literature on post-communist Europe, this research does not suffer from selection bias; however, the small-n nature of the research does require more explicit clarification of the both the unit of analysis and the generalizations that can be made.

Selection bias refers to the negative consequences or limitations that may affect research when the cases are drawn from a population in a non-random way. Put simply, any bias in how the cases were chosen may result in a sample which possesses qualities and characteristics that are no longer representative of the larger population (Collier 1995, 462). In such instances, any inferences drawn from the sample back to the larger population will lack validity. For example, if we were interested in the population of all the college students in the country, and then proceeded to select a sample that only included men, many of the inferences we might draw about the population (which includes both men and women) would undoubtedly be off the mark. Selection bias also refers to instances where one or more of the explanatory variables is endogenous to the dependent variable (Przeworski and Limongi 1993; Collier and Mahoney 1996). In such cases, what is to be explained is both a cause and consequence of another variable, which results in a biased (i.e., incorrect) estimate of the relationship between them. For example, Przeworski and Limongi (1993) demonstrate that using regime type to predict the level of economic development can

---

19   That the countries were not selected randomly does not pose a problem in terms of either hypothesis testing or inference. Nor does it automatically introduce selection bias. In fact, in small-n studies (i.e., those with a few number of cases), random sampling is likely to create more problems that it solves (King et al 1994, 124-126; Collier 1995, 463).

be problematic in that being more developed economically may make it more likely that a country is a democracy to begin with. In sum, selection bias is concerned with the introduction of systematic error into the inferences drawn from a research endeavor.

The problem of biased selection is most widely understood in the context of quantitative research, where statistical methods often depend its absence (see Achen 1986, Heckman 1976, 1979, 1990; King 1989; Long 1997; Maddala 1983). When it is present, "statistical procedures carried out on the selected cases may indicate that no relationship exists or even that the relationship is the opposite of the true one" (Geddes 2003, 93). More recently, a growing literature and debate has surrounded the issue in the context of qualitative research (see Collier 1995; Collier and Mahoney 1996; Geddes 2003; King et al 1994). While its consequences and severity in the realm of qualitative research have been questioned (see for example Laitin et al 1995), given the apparent over representation of these three countries in the literature, the issue is worth exploring in the context of this research.

There are two selection criteria that raise particular concerns for qualitative research; both focus on instances when cases are chosen on the basis of the dependent variable. In the first, cases are selected such that there is no variation in dependent variable itself. For example, in a study of war and conflict, all the cases are instances of war; in a study of democracy, all the case are democracies. Under the second criteria, only certain values of the dependent variable are selected, such as only those countries where GDP per capita exceeds $20,000 per year. As discussed in Chapter 2, democracy can be thought of as either a binary variable (i.e., democracy or non-democracy) or one with gradations where any given country is more or less democratic than the next on a continuum or ordered scale. Since all three cases here are found to be consolidated democracies (Chapter 6), and that comparatively speaking, the democratic process appears most so in Poland, one could question whether this research has introduced selection bias as a result of having used one or both of these criteria. Before arguing why this is not the case, it is worth first clarifying the potential problems associated with both forms of selection on the dependent variable.

King, Keohane and Verba argue that case selection should produce a sample where the dependent variable actually varies, ideally as much as possible (King et al 1994, 129). They raise particular concerns about research designs where no variation takes place at all (e.g., all the cases are democracies). They argue that "when observations are selected on the basis of a particular value of the dependent variable, nothing whatsoever can be learned about the causes of the dependent variable without taking into account other instances when the dependent variable takes on other values" (King et al 1994, 129). Geddes concludes that "the only thing that can actually be explained using a sample selected on the dependent variable are differences among the selected cases" (Geddes 2003, 92). When cases are selected on the basis of the dependent variable, two types of faulty inferences are possible. First, one may jump "to the conclusion that any [shared] characteristic ... is a cause; [second, one may infer] that relationships (or the absence of relationships) between variables *within* the selected cases reflect relationships in the entire population of cases" (Geddes 2003, 92 emphasis in original). The danger from the former is that one may potentially reach the wrong conclusion about causality. The danger from the second is that even if the causality is correct, the finding may be incorrectly generalized to a larger population.

While these arguments certainly have merit when the intent of the research is to ascertain causality, there are instances when such a design can be of value. For example, in devising a test of necessary and sufficient conditions, selecting on the dependent variable can be a useful way to rule out potential explanatory factors (Dion 1998; Goertz and Starr 2002). Such a design may also be necessary when using counterfactual methods to evaluate hypotheses (see Fearon 1991; Tetlock and Belkin 1996). The design can also be of utility when cases are paired or matched on outcomes, but vary widely in most other respects. This "most different design" can help synthesize a common explanation and lead to new discoveries that may never have come to light under a different design (Przeworski and Tune 1970; see also Collier 1995; Collier and Mahoney 1996; Mill 1974).[20]

A similar set of concerns arises when the dependent variable is truncated, (e.g., unable to freely assume any value). Many variables of interest in comparative politics are truncated, such as national income (truncated at zero) or the democracy index scores produced by sources such as Freedom House or the Polity data sets (see Chapter 2). Of principal concern here is when cases are intentionally selected such that the dependent variable falls above (or below) a particular value; for example, countries with Polity democracy scores above 7 on the dataset's 0–10 point scale. When selection intentionally results in a truncated sample, any causal estimates are likely to be underestimated. However, as with the no-variation design discussed above, intentionally truncated research designs can be of value in some settings despite their limitations in regard to causal inference (see King et al 1994, 141–142).

While case selection can affect the results of one's research, "it is crucial to consider carefully the research question that guides a given study, as well as the frame of comparison appropriate to that question, before reaching conclusions about selection bias" (Collier and Mahoney 1996, 75; see also Geddes 2003, Chapter 3). While the broader puzzle of this research concerns the consolidation of democracy in Eastern Europe, the specific research questions, which form the basis of case selection, are narrower. This research began by asking a simple question. What were the political consequences of privatization in Eastern Europe? While the economic

---

20   This type of research design is also known as Mill's method of agreement. For more on Mill's method of agreement and method of difference, see Mill [1843] 1974. See also Nichols 1986; Skocpol and Somers 1980; Skocpol 1986.

consequences of establishing or changing property rights (e.g., entrepreneurial incentives, corporate governance, resource efficiency...) are fairly well understood, the political effects seemed comparatively less well developed.[21]

So to be eligible for selection, a country had to have substantially completed the bulk of its privatization efforts. While many countries in the region met this requirement by the late 1990s, the goal was to draw from this pool a set of countries, each of which had utilized a different mix of privatization strategies. Although certain features can be found in every country, such as the direct sale of SOEs to foreign investors, the relative weight of each privatization technique varies considerably among three countries chosen here. For example, the Czech Republic, for reasons explained in Chapter 5, relied heavily on the essentially free give away of shares to all of its adult citizens whereas the heavily indebted Hungarians relied more on revenue-generating sales to foreign investors. In Poland, where the strength and influence of trade unions was highest, privatization entailed the setting aside and free transfer of a percentage of shares for existing employees and other firm insiders. Consequently, different patterns of resource ownership and income distribution emerged in each country. These distributional consequences form the organizing principle and key causal variable of this research. My central thesis is that privatization shaped both attitudes (preferences) regarding how to reform the pension system as well as the relative ability of like-minded individuals to collectively organize in defense of those interests. As argued earlier, if we think of democracy as the choice of a particular policy option resulting from the competition among groups with divergent preferences, then privatization (the redistribution of resources) must affect democracy as the outcome of competition often depends on the resources each side can bring to bear. So while the larger dependent variable in this study is the consolidation of democracy, these cases were chosen on the basis of the key independent variable of interest, a selection criteria which "causes no inference problems" and avoids the introduction of bias (King et al 1994, 137).

This leaves the domain restriction as the only other potential source of selection bias. If the original research puzzle concerned the political consequences of privatization, why limit the research to just Eastern Europe? Over the past several decades, many countries have undergone periods of privatization; likewise, many countries have undergone the transition from authoritarian rule to democracy. Intentionally limiting the cases to one region and one period in time may introduce adverse selection. While it is true that privatization and democratic transition are not unique to the region, I would argue that the experiences of Eastern Europe and the former Soviet Union are qualitatively different. Never before have a set countries undertaken a privatization effort of the size, scope and pace as seen here while at the same time also transforming their political, military, international, economic, and social relations. I believe this context is important to understanding the evolution each country underwent as it made its way toward democracy and a market-oriented

---

21   For more on the economics of property rights, see Alchian 1965; Coase 1960, 1988; De Alessi 1980; Demsetz 1967, 1972; and Eggertsson 1990.

economy. If context matters, then we have reason to restrict the domain. As Collier and Mahoney suggest:

> it is unrealistic to expect qualitative researchers, in their effort to avoid selection bias, to make comparisons across contexts that may reasonably be thought to encompass heterogeneous causal relations. Given the tools that they have for causal inference, it may be more appropriate for them to focus on a more homogenous set of cases, even at the cost of narrowing the comparison in a way that may introduce problems of selection bias (Collier and Mahoney 1996, 68–9).

Although I do not believe that selection bias is not a problem in this research, the small-n nature of the project does require a closer look at both hypothesis testing and the ability to generalize to a broader set of cases. The model presented in Chapter 2 involves nine variables that combine to assess the relative likelihood that groups of like-minded individuals will overcome the challenges inherent in collective activity, as well as the likelihood that once organized, the group will wield political influence. So at first glance, the project suffers from the "many variables, small N" problem (Lijphart 1971, 686). It is methodologically impossible to estimate nine parameters with only three observations. For all their power, statistical models require that the sample size be greater than the number of parameters to be estimated. In short, because the solution rests on solving a system of simultaneous equations, there have to be at least as many equations (e.g., observations/cases) as there are unknown parameters to estimate. However, this study does not rely on statistical methods, nor are there only three observations to work with.

Although only three countries have been selected, the nation-state is not the unit of analysis. As indicated above, the model presented in Chapter 2 is based not on countries, but on groups of like-minded individuals; and within each country, there are multiple groups providing observations. So the degrees of freedom problem is not a concern; there are sufficient observations across the three countries to evaluate the hypotheses presented in Chapter 2, even if statistical techniques were to be used. While such methods would be useful in addressing, for example, which of the nine variables provides significant leverage in overcoming the collective action problem; they are less useful in addressing the types of questions posed in this study. The primary goal here is not to test a theory of collective action, which it nonetheless does, but rather to assess the political consequences of privatization, how domestic and international forces interact to produce policy outcomes, and ultimately, what these events tell us about the democratic process in each country. I would argue that these questions are best addressed using qualitative techniques.

Avoiding the degrees of freedom problem, however, does not resolve of all the concerns related to small-n hypothesis testing. The chief remaining concerns relate to indeterminacy and over fitting (Lieberson 1991; King et al 1994; Geddes 2003). Lieberson makes perhaps the most vehement case against small-n designs arguing that "small-n studies operate in a deterministic manner ... [and] ... have difficultly in evaluating probabilistic theories" (Lieberson 1991, 310). He goes on to argue that another shortcoming to such data analysis is that the conclusions are extremely volatile if it turns out that a multideterministic model is appropriate. Moreover, with a small-N study, although it is possible to obtain data that would lead one to reject the assumption of a single-variable deterministic model (assuming no measurement error), it is impossible for the data to provide reasonable assurance that a single-variable deterministic model is correct, even if the observed data fit such a model (Lieberson 1991, 314).

While Lieberson's arguments and logic have been challenged (see for example Savolainen 1994), a certain degree of caution is warranted. It is not that hypotheses cannot be tested with only a small number of cases, but rather that an additional set of risks are encountered. Similar to the concerns about selection bias, Geddes notes that among the "problems identified with the use of case studies include the inability to recognize or ignore idiosyncratic features of the cases chosen" (Geddes 2003, 133-134).[22] In a similar vein, King, Keohane, and Verba raise concerns over indeterminacy and the degree of leverage smaller samples offer; in fact, they go as far as to argue that "we should always observe as many implications of our theory as possible" (King et al 1994, 122–123). Although leverage, or the confidence in the soundness of the test may increase as more cases are added, it is not necessary to do so. As Eckstein (1975) demonstrates, a single, crucial case is at times all that is needed to test and definitively falsify a hypothesis. Innumerable studies in comparative and international politics have demonstrated how even a small number of cases can readily test hypotheses. Moreover, they have done so using a variety of methodologies such within-case designs (Putnam 1993), comparative historical analysis (Skocpol 1979), or process tracing (George and Mckeown 1985; George and Bennet 2005). The underlying concern, however, is that "in small-N analysis ... findings may be seriously distorted by a single observation that is greatly in error" (Collier 1993, 114). This risk holds regardless of whether the test involves quantitative or qualitative methods. While careful case selection can help minimize the danger any single case may bring, it highlights perhaps the greater difficultly resulting from small-n hypothesis testing, name the ability to generalize the findings.

Some scholars argue that such "conclusions are often wrong because a small number of cases is an inadequate basis for generalizing about the process under study" (Lieberson 1991, 311). Even small-n enthusiasts such as Skocpol and Somers freely admit that "comparative-historical causal arguments cannot be readily generalized beyond the cases actually discussed" (Skocpol and Somers 1980, 195). Generalizeability, however, is crucial the scientific endeavor. According to King, Keohane and Verba, "research should be both general and specific: it should tell us something about classes of events as well as about specific events at particular places. We want to be timeless and timebound at the same time" (King et al 1994, 43).

---

22   A distinction can often be found in the literature between case studies and small-n research; for example, Ragin (1987) sees small-n studies as offering "a middle ground between case studies and [large-n] statistical models" (Collier 1993, 111). As the methodological challenges are essentially the same, and as there is no clear dividing line, I use the terms here interchangeably.

Nonetheless, while generalizeability ought to be a consideration in any research, it is equally necessary to consider appropriate limits on the range of our conclusions. As the above justification of the domain restriction suggests, I find Satori's (1970, 1984) work on conceptual stretching to be a useful guide. Satori warns us that "while a general concept is conducive to scientific 'generalizations,' mere generalities are conducive only to vagueness and conceptual obscurity" (Satori 1970, 1041). He goes on to add that "even though we need universals, they must be empirical universals, that is ... somehow amenable ... to empirical testing" (Satori 1970, 1035). This focus on what can be empirically extended, rather than conceptually stretched to cover other cases, forms the basis for the generalizations drawn from this research.

As discussed below and further in Chapter 6, the out-of-sample generalization relates to the testing procedure used here, not to the empirical finding themselves. That Poland functioned as a consolidated democracy as early as 1997 has no extension beyond Poland itself. However, the way in which this conclusion was generated is generalizeable to the twenty-five remaining countries of Eastern Europe and the former Soviet Union. I argue that the case of pension reform offers a useful critical-case test of democracy throughout the region. It is a policy issue that was on every country's agenda for largely the same reasons, although not necessarily with the same degree of urgency.[23] In each case, it was subsequent to the privatization of state-owned assets; and in each case, the policy pressure from the international community was the same.[24] What varies is the responsiveness to that pressure, and the way in which the domestic political process formulated a unique set of policy reforms to confront a specific situation. If one accepts the conception of a consolidated democracy as argued here (Chapter 2), then this policy issue offers a generalizeable way in which to evaluate the democratic process across the region, and possibly beyond.

Plan of the Book

The remaining chapters are largely self-contained, meaning the reader is free to jump around. Chapter 2 reviews the three relevant literatures upon which this

---

23   Every country in former communist region was faced with similar demographic pressures and had inherited roughly the same type of pension system from the Soviet-era. Where they varied most was in regard to their relative use of early retirement to address the rise in unemployment early in the transition, and, consequently in part, the relative fiscal viability of the existing system in the short-run.

24   It should be noted, however, that not all countries, particular some of the former Soviet Republics had made significant progress in the privatization of the their state-owned enterprises. However, all of them were forced to adjust to new economic realities following the collapse of COMECON and the former financial support handed out by Moscow during the communist era. In this sense, there was also a relative degree of economic distribution, even among those states of the Soviet Union that attempted to resist to development of a market economy.

research draws. The first considers the issue of democracy itself in terms of its definition, measurement and idea of consolidation. The second concerns the debate about the conditions under which politics is likely to be dominated by losers seeking compensation for their losses, or winners using their winnings to enact policies favorable to themselves. The third concerns the challenge of collective action faced by both groups if they are to influence policy decisions. Focusing on the interaction between a group's internal characteristics (e.g., size, potential resources, geographic concentration....) and the nature of the group's objective, I present a model which describes the conditions under which groups of like-minded individuals are expected to be more or less successful in advancing their interests.

Chapter 3 examines the case of Poland. After much debate and political infighting that lasted several years, the Polish pension program was converted into a three-pillar system (PAYG; mandatory private accounts; voluntary supplemental insurance). What makes the Polish reforms unique is 1) that the reforms were designed and carried out under two consecutive but different governments, 2) the way in which the reformed PAYG first pillar is now financed, and 3) the remarkably open and democratic fashion in which the legislation was drafted. The chapter begins by outlining the several puzzles these features raise. It then follows an outline used in all three case studies. First, I describe and discuss the distributional consequences of privatization in terms of how it reshaped household income and assets. Briefly reviewing the key features of the Polish experience, I present the relative winners and losers that this process of redistribution created. In Poland and Hungary, I do this using household panel data to track individual households overtime; however, as such time-series data was never a high priority for the Czech statistical office, I am forced there to rely instead on yearly surveys of economic expectations and attitudes to chart similar developments.

In Section II, I describe the set of actors and derive their preferences over reform alternatives using survey evidence and the available literature. I show how the process of privatization not only created relative winners and losers in terms of income changes, but in doing so, also shaped attitudes and preferences over pension reform alternatives. Section III combines these preferences with the model presented in Chapter 2 to yield testable hypotheses about the ability of like-minded individuals to collectively organize in support of their interests. These hypotheses are then tested in Section IV by tracing the process of legislative design and passage. The analysis demonstrates how domestic political actors shaped the pressure exerted by the World Bank into a unique reform package.

Chapter 4 examines the Hungarian case, which represents the strongest case for the arguments presently contained in the literature. Given its overwhelming indebtedness and a pension system on the verge of financial collapse, the World Bank was able to significantly influence the reform debate. The mounting fiscal pressures also gave the Ministry of Finance a vocal stake in promoting privatization of the pension system. However, the final legislation contains a number of features not readily reducible to these actors. The chapter begins by discussing the two most obvious inconsistencies. First, why, if the idea was to protect the state budget, was a guaranteed rate of return added to the new private accounts that was backed by that same state budget? Second, and more importantly, why does the final legislation actually represent a PAYG system in disguise? After presenting these puzzles, the chapters again follows the outline described above; it concludes by showing how each of the shortcomings identified at the start can be accounted for by examining the ability of domestic interest groups to influence the design and passage of the legislation.

Chapter 5 examines the case of the Czech Republic, the only country in the sample to not enact mandatory private pension accounts. The obvious chapter puzzle is why? While I do not attempt to refute the existing explanations, which point to the limited indebtedness and consequentially limited influence of the World Bank, I do show their shortcomings in terms of their ability to account for the choices made in terms of the final legislation. For example, why was a universal flat-rate pillar added over the initial objection of Prime Minister Václav Klaus? The case shows how the relative losers of the transition (i.e., those left financially behind during the early years) were able to block the unwanted mandatory private accounts and at the same time reveals why the relative winners, who in part favored such a move, proved so unsuccessful in the context of the Czech Republic. It also explains the chapter puzzles set out at the beginning regarding the form of the final legislation.

Chapter 6 pulls the three cases together, draws conclusions, and suggests refinements and areas for future research. This research has both a specific and a general claim to make. First, it addresses a shortfall in the existing literature by providing a clearer image of how domestic politics interacted with international pressures to produce policy reform. Because of the natural, controlled experiment offered in this case, it is possible to isolate how different domestic environments responded to a common international pressure to make individuals more responsible for their own retirement needs through privatization of the pension system. By linking the distributional consequences of privatization to the politics of interest representation, this research helps us better understand how and why each crafted their own unique policy responses.

The broader claim of this research is that these cases make the argument for treating Poland, Hungary and the Czech Republic as consolidated democracies.[25] Since 1989, the most common adjective used to describe the countries of Central and Eastern Europe has been transitional, having been applied to both their economic and political systems. What has never been clarified, however, is exactly how we know when the transition period is over? This research provides an empirical test that helps answer this question.

The starting point is Przeworski's (1991) argument, which says essentially that what distinguishes democracies is that the losers do not wreck the playing field when they lose; rather, they agree to continue in the existing framework because they believe that they might win the next political contest. These cases collectively show

---

25   For more on the debate about democracy with and without adjectives, see Collier and Levitsky 1997.

that only six to seven years into their transition, the losers in Eastern Europe were able to do just that. Those left financially behind during the early years of the political and economic transition were able to block unwanted reforms; they were also able to extract concessions and push for the inclusion of measures not originally conceived of, or wanted, by the government. Moreover, a political culture had formed whereby interest competition, negotiation and compromise had been accepted by all. I argue that as a result, these cases are more readily comparable for political scientists, and that there is no need for an asterisks, footnote, or label such as "transitional" to distinguish them as somehow different from other advanced, industrial democracies. Their experiences with pension reform suggest that, although relative winners and losers were created by the earlier process of privatization, the former do not necessarily always win, nor do the latter always necessarily continue to lose. The political process has proven itself susceptible to influence and interest representation by both, and that contestation means that they are simply democracies with no special need to identify them as transitional or East European. Their transitional status is over, and appears to have been so for several years now.

I conclude with an out-of sample generalization. As noted earlier, I argue that the case of pension reform provides an extremely useful critical-case test of democracy in Eastern Europe and the former Soviet Union. Given the fact that every country's system, if left unreformed, would have collapsed either almost immediately or within a few years time, the issue should have been on every nation's political agenda. The pressure and interests of the World Bank and other international actors remain a constant in every case. What varies is 1) the responsiveness to such pressure as argued by the present literature, and 2) the ability of domestic political actors to influence the process as argued here. Therefore, it is the testing procedure itself that is most generalizable. How well were domestic actors able to collectively organize? What avenues of access to the political process existed for groups that did successfully organize? Finally, and most importantly from an evaluation standpoint, were those left behind or injured by earlier reforms (marketization, liberalization, privatization) able to influence the process and have their voices heard? If we accept Przeworski's basic premise about democracy, then social welfare reform provides an ideal and comparable test case to evaluate the development of democracy and better understand how domestic politics interacts with international forces.

Chapter 2

Democracy and the Politics of Reform

> No one pretends that democracy is perfect or all-wise. Indeed, it has been said that democracy is the worst form of Government, except all those other forms that have been tried from time to time.
>
> Winston Churchill (1947)

What constitutes a democracy? At one level, the answer appears rather intuitive; we all seem to know one when we see one: Norway is a democracy; North Korea is not. If a group of people were handed a list of countries and asked to place each into one category or the other, the evidence suggests there would be a high degree of correlation or agreement among them (see for example Przeworski et al 1996, 52). Japan, Costa Rica, and Canada yes; Cuba, Zimbabwe and Turkmenistan no. This apparent consensus suggests that there are some underlying concepts and characteristics that we all agree upon, even if we cannot agree upon a precise definition for the term itself. Nonetheless, one of the goals of this research is to assess the development of democracy in the region; therefore, it is necessary to examine and clarify, at least to a degree, what is meant by democracy and the process of democratic consolidation.

When I ask my students what constitutes democracy, their responses reflect this underlying consensus as they consistently respond with a near identical set of characteristics. Elections, various freedoms (of association, of speech, from oppression), checks and balances, and separation of powers are among the most common responses. Scholarly accounts of democracy zero in on the same set of characteristics. When pressed to posit a definition, almost all scholars since the early 1970s have offered a derivation based on Dahl's (1971) notion of polyarchy, which combines civil and political rights with fair, free, and competitive elections.[1] Where the divergence occurs perhaps most substantively is in regard to whether or not democracy is a binary condition, or whether the concept is best measured as a matter of degree.[2]

Reflecting our ability to immediately distinguish the likes of Norway and North Korea, many scholars strongly advocate for a dichotomous definition. Sartori (1987) argues that democracy and non-democracy are natural contradictions; a country is

---

[1]   On defining democracy, see also Schumpeter (1950) and Schmitter and Karl (1991). On procedural minimums, see Dahl 1982, 11; O'Donnell and Schmitter 1986, 8; and Valenzuela 1992, 60–62.

[2]   For an excellent introduction and some sound advice on this debate, see Collier and Adcock 1999.

either one or the other (see also Sartori 1962, 1991). Echoing this sentiment, Alvarez et al argue that:

> while some regimes are more democratic than others, unless offices are contested, they should not be considered democratic. The analogy with the proverbial pregnancy is this that while democracy can be more or less advanced, one cannot be half-democratic: there is no natural zero-point (Alvarez et al, 1996, 21).

Such arguments in favor of a dichotomy are relevant here as it suggests that democratizing countries cross an absolute threshold somewhere in their transition from authoritarian rule. If true, then the task here would be to posit and defend the choice of a particular threshold, and then compare each country against it. Numerous such democracy-qualifying thresholds have been offered, most of which again can be traced back to meeting Dahl's basic conditions. For example, Przeworski and Limongi posit a two-part threshold arguing that "what is essential to considering a regime as democratic is that two kinds of offices are filled by elections, whether directly or indirectly: the chief executive officer and the seats in the effective legislative body" (Przeworski and Limongi 1997, 178).[3] Likewise, Geddes uses a similar "decision rule for determining whether a political system has crossed the threshold to democracy" (Geddes 1999, fn 3; for additional thresholds, see for example Huntington 1991; Linz 1975; and Przeworski et al 1996).

The alternative view holds that "democracy is always a matter of degree" (Bollen and Jackman 1989, 618). Adherents argue that "the concept of political democracy is continuous [and that we] unnecessarily compromise the concept by considering it a dichotomous phenomenon" (Bollen 1990, 13). Reflecting on the spread of democracy beyond Western Europe and North America, both Huntington (1996) and Diamond (1996) argue that it has become increasingly necessary to view democracy on a continuum rather than a stale, binary condition that is largely based on the western experience. Further justification for using a graded scale is found in Dahl's original work, which begins by considering the democratic ideal-type, and then uses it as reference point "for estimating the degree to which various systems approach this theoretical limit" (Dahl 1971, 2). He concludes that there is "an underlying, hypothetical continuum that extends from the greatest to the least opportunity for" opponents to challenge the government (Dahl 1971, 231).

There may also be methodological advantages that come with using a graded approach. For example, Elkins (2000) demonstrates that such gradations can reveal effects that the more blunt dichotomous approach misses. In essence, by aggregating all types or levels of democracy into one block, many of the nuances in the relationship under study can be washed out. In addition, Coppedge (1997) and Geddes (1999) show how divergent the results can be depending on which cut-point is used. This raises concerns over arbitrary or gerrymandered thresholds that may

---

3   Operationally, they define democracy by the absence of a violation of any of four rules concerning the election of the executive, legislature, party competition, and the removal of incumbents.

bias whatever conclusions are reached. Some of the methodological advantages stemming from using a graded scale are reflected in the dominant data sets currently in use relating to democracy. Both Freedom House's *Freedom in the World*, which measures political rights and freedoms often found in definitions of democracy, and the Polity data sets (I–IV) provide graded measurements. Freedom House measures political rights and freedoms on 1–7 point scale, where 1 represents the highest degree of freedom and 7 the lowest (Freedom House 2004). The Polity IV data set measures democracy on an 11-point scale (0–10) designed to capture the general openness of the political institutions in each country (Marshall and Jaggers 2005).[4]

However, while gradations may offer more nuanced empirical findings, they do come at a price. As the use of such graded data sets has grown, so too has the use of adjectives to describe democratic subtypes. Demonstrating the patience of Job, Collier and Levitsky (1997) finally gave up counting the number of adjectives used to describe and distinguish democracies when they reached 550. The fact that there are only about 200 countries on the planet, and that we can subdivide them into at least 600 nominally distinct types strongly suggests the field is at risk of falling into a semantic black hole. This is not to say that democracy with adjectives has no merit; on the contrary, they correctly argue that the use of subtypes can be of considerable value, as for example in the work on presidential versus parliamentary democracies (see for example Stepan and Skach 1993; Linz and Valenzeula 1994; Baylis 1996). The danger, however, is the loss of conceptual and analytical clarity (see also Sartori 1970).

The particular adjective of concern here is the use of consolidating. Much like democracy itself, the term has no clear definition or accepted measurement. One review of its use finds that

> the study of democratic consolidation, at its current state of conceptual confusion, is condemned to stagnation. The aspiring subdiscipline of 'consolidology' is anchored in an unclear, inconsistent, and unbounded concept, and thus it is not anchored at all, but drifting in murky waters. The use of one and the same term for vastly different things only simulates a shared language; in fact, the reigning conceptual disorder is acting as a powerful barrier to scholarly communication, theory building, and the accumulation of knowledge (Schedler 1998, 92).

This distortion has led some authors to reject the word altogether as "an empty term" when used to describe democracies (Przeworski et al 1996, 50). In its place, they focus on survival as the critical feature. Many countries have successfully held a democratic election; however, as Huntington (1991, 1996) suggests, the real test is whether or not the country manages to have a second or a third. Przeworski et

---

4   There also exists a methodological counter-argument which notes that "if the distribution of true observations is unimodal and close to symmetric, [then] a more refined classification will have smaller error, but in fact observations on all the polychotomous scales tend to be U-shaped, which advantages a dichotomous classification" (Przeworski et al 1996, 52).

al argue that democracy is likely to endure if the country is affluent, has moderate inflation and declining income inequality, faces a favorable international climate, and has parliamentary institutions (Przeworski et al 1996, 39). While this focus on stability or durability is an important component, it does pose a number of shortcomings for present purposes. First, while survival is a characteristic of well established democracies, "the retention of democratic government after a process of transition does not necessarily ensure the consolidation of a democratic regime;" for example, a long standing democratically elected government may owe its longevity to its reluctance to challenge or confront "actors whose power escapes democratic accountability" (Valenzuela 1992, 59). In the history of Latin America, for example, true civilian control of the military has often remained outside the hands of democratically elected governments, leaving the degree of consolidation in question.

A second shortcoming is that while these factors may predict regime survival, they do not capture the political process that ultimately produces policy outcomes. For that, one must combine institutional features with attitudinal and behavioral changes within society. From the institutional perspective, one must begin with procedural minimums for a democracy: "secret-balloting, universal adult suffrage, regular elections, partisan competition, associational recognition and access, and executive accountability" (O'Donnell and Schmitter, 1986, 8; see also Dahl 1971, 1982; Przeworski 1991; Valenzuela 1992). Democracy implies some agreement about the rules, norms, and procedures used to make policy decisions. Thus, one part of the test for consolidation is that such institutional arrangements are in place. The focus on a minimal standard is necessary because "even long established democracies rarely have all the attributes that can be ideally associated with such regimes" (Valenzeula 1992, 60). Too rigid an adherence to an ideal-type is empirically impractical. From this perspective then

> democracy is consolidated when under given political and economic conditions a particular system of institutions becomes the only game in town, when no one can image acting outside the democratic institutions, when all the losers want to do is try again within the same institutions under which they have just lost. Democracy is consolidated when it become self-enforcing, that is, when all the relevant political forces find it best to continue to submit their interests and values to the uncertain interplay of the institutions (Przeworski 1991, 26).

Implicit in this view, however, are behavioral and attitudinal changes that go beyond the rules and procedures. Diamond argues that consolidation requires both

> behavioral *and* institutional changes that normalize democratic politics and narrow its uncertainty. This normalization requires the expansion of citizen access, development of democratic citizenship and culture, broadening of leadership recruitment and training, and other functions that civil society performs (Diamond 1996, 238 emphasis added).

In other words, the consolidation of democracy requires, to some degree, the resurrection of civil society (see O'Donnell and Schmitter 1986, 48–56). The adoption of formal rules and procedures alone is insufficient, for while democracy is in part an agreement about process, it is also an agreement about inclusion and the active participation of non-state actors in that process. The quality of a democratic process rests not in its formal mechanisms, but rather the way in which society animates those mechanisms (see for example Almond and Verba 1965; Bernhard 1993; Putnam 1993; Muller and Seligson 1994). In pulling these components together, I follow the work Linz and Stepan (1996) who integrate behavioral, attitudinal, and what they call constitutional (e.g., institutional) elements into a definition of consolidation. They argue that

> behaviorally, democracy becomes the only game in town when no significant political groups seriously attempt to overthrow the democratic regime or secede from the state....
> Attitudinally, democracy becomes the only game in town when, even in the face of severe economic and political crises, the overwhelming majority of the people believe that any further political change must emerge from within the parameters of democratic formulas. Constitutionally, democracy becomes the only game in town when all the actors in the polity become habituated to the fact that political conflict will be resolved according to the established norms and that violations of these norms are likely to be ineffective and costly. In short, with consolidation, democracy becomes routinized and deeply internalized in social, institutional, and even psychological life, as well as in calculations for achieving success (Linz and Stepan 1996, 5).[5]

These three dimensions are measured according to eight benchmarks (Linz and Stepan 1996, Table 16.1). First, the basis of action revolves around competing interests. Second, the units of analysis are groups of like-minded individuals attempting to support and defend their interests. Third, such groups accept as normal some degree of internal difference. Fourth, the response to the conflict of ideas within the democratic community is an effort to organize, aggregate, represent, and defend one's interest. Fifth, actors view compromise as a positive and necessary aspect of the political process, even if this means not always seeing one's preferred option incorporated into the final policy. Sixth, actors are positively disposed toward routinized use of existing institutions as opposed to reinventing new procedures and institutions at every turn. Seventh, actors are negatively disposed to what Linz and Stepan call antipolitics or efforts to disrupt or destroy existing arrangements. Finally, the attitude toward to the state (government) is that one ought to strive to direct it; in other words, to make it respond to one's interests.

---

5   They also posit six necessary pre-conditions for consolidation. First, the country's borders must be largely uncontested. Second, there must be a social and political environment that allows for the growth of civil society (i.e., actors not formally linked to the state). Third, the presence of political parties and other institutions capable of choosing leaders and policies. Fourth, the establishment of the rule of law. Fifth, a bureaucracy that is capable of executing these policy decisions; and sixth, a functioning market economy with sufficient laws and institutions regulating it to allow for profitable endeavors.

With consolidation so defined, the question remains whether to use it as a threshold separating democracies from non-democracies, or a as a graded scale comparatively measuring the degree or depth of democracy in each country. In deciding, Collier and Adcock's (1999) pragmatic advice offers useful guidance. They argue that "specific methodological choices are often best understood and justified in light of the theoretical framework, analytical goals, and context of research involved in any particular study" (Collier and Adcock 1999, 539). They go on to reject "the idea that there is a single correct, or 'best,' meaning for all concepts" and that how such a concept is defined and measured "should depend in part on what [researchers] are going to do with it" (Collier and Adcock 1999, 539). So what is the purpose of assessing the development of democracy in the region? What does one do with such an assessment? My intent is to determine whether these countries are now more readily comparable with other advanced democracies. Do they make major policy decisions in similar manner? If they do not, then we must continue to exercise caution when including them along side such countries in future research. This may entail the continued use of adjectives such as transitional, or including either dummy variables or interactive terms in our regression equations. While these measures may have independent utility, at what point are they no longer required? At what point can the countries of Central and Eastern Europe simply be included along side Japan, Australia, Canada and other full, mature, consolidated, advanced democracies? When are the adjectives no longer needed? If they make major policy decisions, such as an overhaul of their pension systems, in an equivalently democratic manner, then they should be included along side the latter in future research, greatly expanding the sample size and allowing for more refined and robust conclusions.

This focus on procedure conforms to the general view of democracy as an agreement about process, not necessarily policy outcomes. It also corresponds to using the above definition of consolidation as a threshold, or minimum criteria establishing a binary distinction. Either we can include these countries in our sample without introducing a qualitatively different political process, or we cannot. However, this does not preclude subsequently using a graded approach to measure the relative depth of democracy in each country (Collier and Adcock 1999; Przeworski et 1996; Sartori 1987). In Chapter 6, I endeavor to provide such a relative assessment of the three countries considered here.

This threshold definition of consolidation needs to be measured against a concrete, substantively important policy decision, like pension reform, and integrated with the broader process of political and economic transition. What we are interested in is the politics of policy reform in the context of regimes attempting to consolidate their democracy. The World Bank's 1996 *World Development Report* focuses on the transitions from centralized economic systems to market economies underway in Eastern Europe, Asia and other parts of the world. It argues that one of the major challenges

> is to relieve poverty and address the other ill effects of transition on particular groups. Many gain from transition, and depending again on the starting point and context for

reforms, transition can be accompanied by declining poverty from day one. But the vast adjustments involved in a change of economic system can also have adverse implications for many. The losses they suffer need to be addressed through effective social policies that encourage sustained growth. (World Bank 1996, 8)

Unfortunately, while the study makes several policy recommendations to aid in this endeavor, it completely ignores the collective action challenges inherent in its advice. How able are the losers to organize behind their political objectives? Under what conditions are the winners able to use their additional resources to gain political favor? The answers to these questions depend in part on the how well individuals are able to overcome the challenges inherent in collective activity. Despite this omission, however, by highlighting the gains of some and the "adverse implications" for others, the report does suggest a way to conceptualize the groups facing these challenges, and integrating it with the threshold definition of consolidation used here.

The key lies in the relative winners and losers created by earlier aspects of the transition to a market economy. We know that these programs (i.e., marketization, price liberalization, and especially privatization) had distributional economic consequences, and there is a great deal of evidence to suggest that these programs have also had significant political effects as well. However, there is disagreement as to just what these effects are. The debate centers around two alternative perspectives of interest representation, one which holds politics to be loser-centered, and one which sees political conflicts as being more often dominated by the winners of recent changes in policy or economic well-being.

Two Views of Politics

Loser-centered Politics

The loser-centered view draws heavily on the Latin American experience with reform and crisis. It suggests that "the sharp declines in consumption following the onset of [market-oriented adjustments will] lead to a political backlash against reform" by those financially injured (Gould 1999, 2–3). Frieden (1991) offers one such instance of loser-centered pressure in his account of the reactions to the emerging debt crisis in Latin America during the mid-1980s. He argues that in response to the withdrawal of credit by international bankers, some domestic groups were either favorably or neutrally affected; consequently, they had no incentive to pressure the state for new policies or relief. Essentially, these winners were content to sit back and be winners while the losers were "expected to pressure policymakers for government support" and relief in the wake of severe financial hardship (Frieden 1991, 36). He goes on to argue that any resulting policy adjustments are likely to alleviate the pleas of some but not all of the initial losers. Those left unsatisfied are likely to then "consider working for a change in *policymakers* to some more favorably disposed" to their plight (Frieden 1991, 3, emphasis in original). In the end, this can result in sweeping institutional reform or even a change in the regime itself.

Part of the logic behind such losers-centered accounts is offered by Nelson (1993) who argues that when faced with such reforms, "losers know who they will be; gainers [meanwhile] are much less certain. Moreover, losers include powerful vested interest groups (not least those from within the state apparatus) that are organized and vocal, whereas potential winners are often neither" (Nelson 1993, 434–5). This sentiment is echoed by Haggard and Kaufman (1995) in their examination of democratic transitions. They contend that one characteristic of such reforms "is that the costs of reform tend to be concentrated, while the benefits are diffuse, producing perverse organizational incentives; losers are well organized, while prospective winners face daunting collective actions problems and are not" (Haggard and Kaufman 1995, 157). They also add that "institutional arrangements may amplify the veto power of losers by effectively granting them a disproportionate weight in policy considerations" (Haggard and Kaufman 1995, 157).[6]

One example of this kind of institutional enhancement in regard to pension reform is offered by Orenstein (2000) in his study of Kazakhstan, Hungary and Poland. He demonstrates that while most interest groups simply attempt to minimize the affects that the reforms will have on them, "there are some cases of interest groups threatening to play a veto role, as in Hungary, or formulating their own [counter] proposals, as in Poland" (Orenstein 2000, 62). In both cases, it was the institutional access granted to unions by way of their membership on Tripartite councils that accounted for their added influence. Existing institutions, therefore, can amplify the voice of those injured by providing a direct avenue of access to decision makers.

The role of losers is also seen as important for the very continuation of democracy itself. As discussed in earlier, Przeworski (1991) argues that if democracy is to survive such transitions, the losers must be willing to continue playing within the existing political framework rather than choosing to try and rewrite the rules. This requires, among other things, a belief that they might win (i.e., see their policy preferences implemented) in the future, and that it is therefore worth continuing, and complying with, the current political system and its decisions. A similar focus lies at the heart of Hirschman's seminal look at how individuals respond to deteriorating circumstances. *Exit, Voice and Loyalty* examines the conditions under which the withdrawal of support (exit) will prevail over the expression of dissatisfaction (voice), and vise versa (Hirschman 1970, 5). In the context of a democratic system, one of the principle exit options is a withdrawal from the political process itself. In practice, this often entails either no longer registering or bothering to vote in elections, a move which can lead to winner-dominated politics, as they remain the only group actively electing the decision makers. As we shall see in the cases examined here, the non-involvement of the very poor in the electoral process is a

---

6   For more on veto players in political contests, see Tsebelis 2002, 1999, 1995. For specific applications of veto players to the issue of pension reform, see Bonoli 2001, and Orenstein 2000.

fact that has not been lost on politicians, and one which raises the alternative view of political life where the relative winners are the primary focal point.

Winner-centered Politics

The case for focusing on the relative winners of earlier reforms is put forth most strongly by Hellman (1998) who argues that

> the politics of postcommunist economic reforms has not been dominated by the traditional short-term losers of economic transition - striking workers, resentful former state bureaucrats, impoverished pensioners, or armies of the unemployed. Instead, the most common obstacles ... have come from ... enterprise insiders ... commercial bankers ... local officials ... and mafioso.... These actors can hardly be classified as short-term losers in the overall reform process. On the contrary, they were its earliest and biggest winners (Hellman 1998, 204).

Hellman argues that the key in completing such difficult reforms lies not in "insulating the state from the short-term losers," but in "restraining the winners in the early stages of reform" (Hellmann 1998, 205).[7] Focusing on the concentration of income, he depicts "the reform process as a sequence of decisions on separate components of reform that is continuous over time and in which the winners who gained from earlier decisions [principally privatization] have the decisive voice" (Hellmann 1998, 223). Thus it is the winners who have both a strong incentive, as well as the political ability and resources to stall the reform process in mid-course in order to extract rents or financial gains. Echoing this line of reasoning, Robinson (2001) points out that

> the ability of losers to do anything about their disproportionate shouldering of the reform burden is low since they do not have resources to support political organization or overcome the collective action problem of organizing to achieve redistribution. Winners, on the other hand, have the power and the incentive to block reforms that might create more equitable distribution and the provision of public goods by the state to society as opposed to the private goods that they enjoy (Robinson 2001, 428–429).[8]

One reason for this winner-success in Eastern Europe is that many of the traditional losers "were themselves discredited or in disarray" as result of their ties to the communist past (Nelson 1993, 437). In the aftermath of 1989, trade unions, government bureaucrats and other vestiges of the past were all severely tainted. As a result, both union membership and influence began to fall off rather rapidly, and

---

7   For more on the need to insulate political leaders from the losers in order to pursue reform, see Haggard and Kaufman 1992.

8   Robinson does, however, question the ability of winners to maintain so-called partially reformed systems. He argues that in order to do so, winners must be "prepared to countenance the transfer of resources from themselves to the state sufficient for it to replicate itself" or else "run the risk of the state taking action against them" (Robinson 2001, 432).

the legitimacy of former party officials and institutions was called into question at almost every level. Under these circumstances, it was relatively easy for the short-term winners to step into the political vacuum.

The Twin Challenges of Political Influence

Empirically, it appears that each perspective has something to offer; however, regardless of which perspective one subscribes to, both winners and losers face two hurdles if they are to influence the political process and have their voices heard (Gould 1999). First, they must overcome the challenges inherent in collective activity. Discussed in more detail below, groups of like-minded individuals must do more than simply recognize and communicate their shared interests; they must also find a way to control the free rider problem whereby every individual have an incentive to free ride on the contributions of other members in obtainment of the collective interest. When aggregated across all individuals, this micro-level incentive to cheat suggests that no collective action will take place or will do so only to a less than optimal degree (Olson 1971). Overcoming these obstacles, however, is only half the battle for once organized, each group must find a way to convey a credible electoral threat to policy makers if they hope to have their interests taken seriously (Lohmann 1993). As the ability to overcome these twin hurdles (organizing and signaling) is a function of different variables, I deal with each in turn.

Collective Action

In developing his theory of competition and political influence, Becker (1983) argues that "the political effectiveness of a group is mainly determined not by its absolute efficiency – e.g., its absolute skill at controlling free riding – but by its efficiency relative to the efficiency of other groups" (Becker 1983, 380). This relative efficiency is influenced by factors that are both internal and external to the group itself. The model outlined below combines five measures internal to the group, three measures concerning the nature of the objective sought, and one variable which accounts for the presence of other actors working towards the same objective. This last measure answers the question of whether individuals are alone in their efforts to acquire the collective benefit, or whether there are organizations and institutions, such as trade unions, social movements or political parties, seeking the same benefit. If there are, then these actors may be able to assist in the organization and mobilization of potential members and resources, thereby increasing the probability of collective action. While the assistance of other actors may be critical, the ability to organize is primarily a function of the group itself and the nature of the objective sought. Each variable's hypothesized effect is summarized in Table 2.1 on page 41.

Group Characteristics   One factor affecting the ability to organize is the geographic concentration of potential members. The key here is the intuitive role that proximate geography can play in helping groups overcome the barriers to collective action, a case made clear by Busch and Reinhardt:

> Geographic concentration bolsters an industry's capacity for collective action. In particular, as a wide variety of literatures insists, spatial proximity facilitates greater 'face-to-face' communication, aids in the diffusion of specialized political knowledge, provides the basis for denser social networks, and enables more effective monitoring and sanctioning of those who might free-ride on the political contributions of others. In short, individuals in geographically concentrated groups are more likely to recognize and act upon their collective interests (Busch and Reinhardt 2000, 703).[9]

So we would expect the probability of collective action to be higher among groups with a denser concentration than among those where members and resources are diffusely spread out across the country. To measure the scope of this diffusion, I rely on the same survey data used to construct the relative winners and losers of the transition (described below) as each of the national survey instruments contains data on the residential location of the respondent. In the Czech Republic for example, which has eight administrative regions, I define a group to have a densely concentrated membership if 40% of the group is located in two or less of these eight regions; otherwise the group is deemed to be geographically diffuse. The coding scheme for all variables is provided in Appendix 2.

A second factor affecting the probability of successful organization are the resources a group of like-minded individuals has at its disposal. *Ceteris paribus*, having more resources is better than having less as collective action normally entails some sort of cost, either in terms of time, money or some other unit of measure. For example, Olson (1971) argues that large groups must often offer selective incentives in order to induce members to both join and contribute towards collective activities. In this way, large groups, like nation-wide trade unions, are able to elicit support and contributions by selectively offering these private benefits to members who contribute and withholding them from those who free ride. This allows the collective benefit to be achieved "as a byproduct of individual contributions aimed at the selective rewards" (Bendor and Mookherjee 1987, 130).

Beyond providing private incentives for members, resources are also a useful tool for eliciting cooperation from other political actors, be they politicians running for office, or bureaucrats administering an established program. As western experience demonstrates, especially in the United States, groups spend a great deal of time and money lobbying on behalf of their interests. While nowhere near as pervasive as the beltway bandits, the lobbying activity of interest groups in Eastern Europe has been steadily increasing over the past decade as groups adjust to the new realities of life

---

9   For more application of geography to the economic and political behavior of firms and actors, see also Busch and Reinhardt 1999; Schiller 1999; Audretsch 1998; Schiller and McGillivray 1998; and McGillivray 1997.

in a democratic system. Therefore, one would expect the probability of successful collective action to increase the greater the quantity of resources a group has to work with. While there are different types of resources, I focus here on physical resources such as the number of potential members and the total financial resources that could be marshaled; other resources, such as an existing institutional infrastructure or highly motivated and tireless advocates, are captured by some of the other measures used below.

While the quantity of available resources is critical, not all assets are equally mobile. For example, highly liquid assets such as money are fairly easy to mobilize; whereas wealth defined in terms of real estate holdings or a large but widely diffuse membership is often more constrained. Therefore, a third factor affecting the probability of collective action is the mobility of the assets a particular group has to work with. One way to think about mobility is in terms of transaction costs which measure the difficulty in mobilizing the resource: the higher the transaction costs, the less mobile the resource. There are several factors which can reduce these costs including pre-existing, centralized organizations (such as trade unions and business organizations) as well both formal and informal institutions which help structure the rules of the game; by reducing uncertainty, they help enable otherwise costly transactions.[10]   For example, one common solution for larger groups has been to form a hierarchy, such as a trade federation, or some other contractual arrangement that has certain rights of authority over the collective membership, such as a constitution.[11] While this too has many organizational challenges, in the end, groups with a more institutionalized structure are more likely to effectively mobilize both potential members and their resources (Salisbury 1984). Therefore, one would expect wealthier groups to have an easier time mobilizing resources than poorer groups, and that groups either possessing or being associated with a larger organization will be more likely to successfully mobilize the resources they have than individuals who must coordinate this aggregation on their own.

A fourth group characteristic affecting collective action is the heterogeneity of resources within the group (Hardin 1982, Oliver et al 1985). Its importance lies in the free rider problem: one can only free ride if someone else is actually paying for the ride (Oliver et al 1985, 548). The probability that such a benefactor will exist depends on the distribution of resources within the group. If it varies considerably (i.e., has a high variance and/or is positively skewed), then it is more likely that such a person will exist (Oliver et al 1985, 529). If, however, all members have exactly the same amount to contribute, then the likelihood that any one of them will act differently is fairly low. To illustrate this point, Hardin (1982) cites a 1975 example of a then-unknown Texas billionaire (Ross Perot) who individually provided a lobbying effort that would have benefited taxpayers to the tune of $150 million;

---

10   See Coase 1937, Williamson 1979, and North 1990.

11   For an excellent introduction to the nature of organizing and administering collective associations, see Miller 1992. On constitution formation, see Buchanan and Tullock 1962; North and Weingast 1989; and Powell 1989.

Perot himself stood to pocket $15 million (Hardin 1982, 78–79). Although the so-called Perot provision was ultimately defeated, the example illustrates the effect of having one really wealthy person in the group upon whom everyone else can free ride in the attainment of a collective benefit. A similar story could be told regarding his 1992 run for the presidency, and the formation of the Reform Party. This third party movement did not really get off the ground until Perot joined the group and put cash on the table.

The fifth and final group characteristic is the related notion of interest heterogeneity, which captures the advantage of having someone who is deeply committed, interested and motivated to acquire the benefit in question. Such people are more likely to man the picket-lines, staff the phone-bank, and burn the midnight-oil, all of which raise the probability that the group will successfully organize. In the extreme, Olson (1971) argues that one person may have such an intense preference for the good that they will provide the collective effort all by themselves, such as Perot did in 1975 and 1992.[12] The origin of such an intense preference is often the asymmetry of benefits to be received under the proposed action. In essence, if the demand for the collective benefit varies within group members, then it is more likely that there will be someone willing to take on an added burden to bring about its provision. However, if there is a uniformity of interest, because each person either values or demands the benefit equally, then it is much less likely that any one person, or a subgroup, will undertake the added burden. In effect, the group is paralyzed into inaction as each waits for someone else to step forward.

Each of the cases examined here illuminates the critical importance of such entrepreneurs, defined as an actor (or group of actors) who takes the lead in mobilizing the larger group. These individuals serve as focal points around whom others can align themselves. In doing so, they help sharpen the terms of the debate and channel the efforts of many into a single, coherent and ultimately more effective political force. In Poland for example, it was Andrezj Bączkowski, an original member of Solidarity and the extremely well respected chairman of the Tripartite Commission, who recognized the need for a single office to create a reform package that was both substantive meaningful and politically acceptable. The resulting *Office of the Government Plenipotentiary* provided the forum in which groups could express their voice and negotiate the details of final reform package. Although Bączkowski died before this process was complete, participants on both sides of the debate have acknowledged that the reforms may never of gotten off the ground had it not been for his considerable efforts and talents.

---

12   In 1975, Perot was motivated by the potential "windfall rebate" this provision would have allowed him to collect (Hardin 1982, 78). The proposed amendment he had inserted into the tax law (the "Perot provision") would have allowed retroactive reporting of personal capital losses to 1974 to offset current capital gains liabilities; 1974 just happened to be a year in which Perot suffered substantial capital losses.

The Nature of the Objective Sought   Beyond these five internal characteristics of the group lies the independent influence of the objective itself, and the incentives it creates for individual members. The first of these has to do with whether or not the objective offers a benefit in joint supply (Frohlich and Oppenheimer 1970; Hardin 1982; Oliver 1993). Such a situation means that "one person's consumption of [the collective benefit] does not reduce the amount available to anyone else" (Hardin 1982, 17). The effect this has on the probability of collective action is variable and depends on the size of the group. This is where Olson's (1971) notion that size matters enters the equation. Olson argues that although the free rider problem exists for every group, some groups are more likely to overcome it than others. Small groups he claims have an advantage in that they are, in a sense, privileged. In such a group, each member, "or at least some one of them, has an incentive to see that the collective good is provided, even if he has to bear the full burden of providing it himself" (Olson 1971, 50). Larger groups he argues are more problematic and, therefore, more latent in nature.

In the years since, it has been shown that these arguments logically rest on nature of the objective sought.[13] If the benefit cannot be provided in joint supply, then Olson's argument about large groups being likely to fail is correct. The logic is that with each additional member, the per capita share of the total benefit falls. Therefore, if each member must pay some part of the total cost of providing the collective benefit (e.g., membership dues), then there will come a point with increased membership where the per-capita reward is no longer worth its price. Consequently, no member would want to contribute and the collective good will go unprovided.

However, if the objective *can* be provided in joint supply, then Olson's argument is wrong, and the effect of added membership will be increasingly positive (Oliver 1993, 275). The logic of this assertion is twofold. First, individuals are expected to rationally calculate the expected value of contributing: if the private sunk cost of contributing exceeds the expected value of the benefit, then the individual will *not* join in the collective effort.[14] Second, a good that offers joint supply "costs the same no matter how many people enjoy it" (Oliver and Marwell 1988, 2). This is simply a restatement of the more standard definition of joint supply given by Hardin earlier; however, it becomes clearer that the per-capita cost of provision is dependent on group size. As the size of the group increases, those per-capita costs will fall while the individual benefit will remain unaffected. As a result, it is more likely that any one individual will choose to contribute.

---

13   For critiques of Olson's size argument, see Frohlich and Oppenheimer 1970; Frohlich et al 1975; Schofield 1975; Hardin 1982; Schelling 1978; Kimura 1989; Oliver, Marwell and Teixeria 1985; Oliver 1993.

14   Formally, an individual will contribute if: $C_i - (P_i * B_i) > 0$ where C_i equals the per-capita cost of the contribution, P_i equals the probability that the collective benefit will actually be provided given the added contribution and effort of the individual, and B_i equals the individual's portion of the collective benefit. The probability is essential as the provision of the benefit is in question, and must therefore be discounted by the likelihood that it will actually be realized.

Therefore, the hypothesis has two parts. If the benefits of the proposed reform cannot be jointly supplied (i.e., the per-capita benefit will fall as the number of beneficiaries increases), then larger groups are less likely to successfully organize. However, if the benefits can be jointly supplied, then larger groups have an advantage. In the context of pension reform, this clarification is of crucial importance as some proposals offer a benefit that is in joint supply while others do not.

A second characteristic of the objective sought to consider is whether or not the benefits can be excluded from those who free ride (Olson 1965, 1971; Frohlich and Oppenheimer 1970; Hardin 1982, Oliver 1993). If one cannot be denied the benefits of a collective good once provided, then a strong incentive to free ride is introduced. However, this incentive disappears if the good will only be available to those who contribute. So again, this incentive is variable and dependent on the specific reform proposal being advocated.

A third factor concerns the presence of an incentive for a sub-group to undertake the initial costs of organizing the collective and their resources. A great deal of research has shown that this incentive depends on whether or not the objective sought offers increasing returns (Schelling 1978; Hardin 1982; Oliver et al 1985). The key here are the per-capita costs members must pay to obtain the collective benefit, either in terms of financial contributions or simply time spent working towards the objective. While these per-capita costs will be precipitously high in the beginning when few members are contributing, if there are enough potential members available, the presence of increasing returns makes it possible to eventually drive down the average cost to the point where it is worthwhile for "an entrepreneur or subgroup of fixed size to organize the group for collective benefit" (Hardin 1982, 43).[15] Thus, for a large group, an objective possessing increasing returns makes collective action more likely; however, for smaller groups, such a characteristic poses a hindrance, as the high initial costs are unlikely to ever be overcome. So again, the role that size plays is variable and dependent on characteristics of the collective benefit, not only in terms of whether it can be provided in joint supply or not, but also whether or not it exhibits increasing returns to scale.

The Environment   A third dimension to consider is the presence of existing institutions and other means of organizing. One would expect collective action to be more likely when groups of like-minded individuals are able to draw on pre-existing institutions, symbols, or other types of structures. The presence of civic organizations (Putnam 1993) or a shared language (Laitin 1998) can greatly facilitate face-to-face monitoring and the recognition of a shared preference, both of which increase the likelihood of collective action. In the cases examined here, actors such as the Catholic church (Poland), the trade unions, and organized business communities

---

15   A similar logic lies behind the application of tipping-game models where, after some number of people of acted, the scales suddenly tip in favor of everyone else joining in; see Sen 1967; Schelling 1978. Such models are often used to explain protests, riots and rebellions, see for example Kuran 1991.

offered existing structures upon which to piggyback collective efforts to reform the welfare state. Beyond providing organizational capacity (e.g., office space, phone lines, material resources), these entities also provided a means of communication between the elites who sat around the negotiating table and the broader public. One such channel which proved particular critical was offered by the trade unions. For example, Czech elites were able tap into the existing union membership base and means of communication to mobilize 60,000 demonstrators in response to a breakdown in negotiations over the inclusion of a new, universal flat-rate pension.[16] Similarly in Poland, the Catholic Church provided an opportunity to regularly communicate with working-class Catholics, many of whom held reservations about privatizing the pension system.

Creating such organizations, however, is costly, so one would expect new issues to be incorporated into existing structures wherever possible. I argue that this helps explain why pensioner parties struggled to carve out a niche for themselves. From an electoral standpoint, such single-issue parties are often easily incorporated into larger parties, particular in areas such as pension reform, which ultimately effects all age groups and regions of the country. This issue was such that almost every party took a position on it, and in doing so offered pensioners a more competitive chance at representation (in that their vote was more likely to result in parliamentary representation).[17] From an advocacy standpoint, organizations such as the Council of the Elderly (Hungary) already had a seat at the negotiating table. As such, there was little incentive for retirees to create a new vehicle for themselves.

In sum, the likelihood that a group of like-minded individuals will successfully organize increases as the number and diversity of pre-existing means of organization increases. Whether they are cultural in nature (e.g., a shared language or religion) or more institutional (e.g., trade unions, civic groups, business communities, advisory boards), their presence greatly facilitates collective action. In the cases examined here, both supporters and opponents of the World Bank model had a correspondence of interest with at least one such actor, thereby increasing the likelihood of successful organization.

The individual hypotheses which result from these three areas (group characteristics, the nature of the objective, and the broader environment) are summarized in Table 2.1. Taking their combined affect provides a good assessment of the likelihood that a group of like-minded individuals will successfully organize for collective action. However, as argued above, organizing is only half the battle for once organized, the group must still find a way to send a credible signal to politicians

---

16   Note that such communication is not limited to the union's membership. The channel is actually much broader in practice as it reaches all employees (union and non-union) as well as all the individuals with whom these workers interact (e.g., friends, family, neighbors) through their social networks.

17   The only parties that failed to express a particular policy stance on pension issues were the small, right wing nationalist parties, most of which had a questionable commitment to democracy in the first place.

that its policy demands ought to be acted upon. Therefore, I also assess the likelihood that a group will be able meet this challenge, given that it has organized.

Table 2.1   Hypotheses Regarding Collective Action

Group Characteristics

H1:   The more dense the geographic concentration of potential members, the higher the probability of successful collective action

H2:   The greater the quantity of potential resources available, the higher the probability of successful collective action

H3:   The lower the transaction costs (difficulty in mobilizing) potential resources, the higher the probability of successful collective action

H4:   The greater the heterogeneity of resources within the group, the higher the probability of successful collective action

H5:   The greater the heterogeneity of interest within the group, the higher the probability of successful collective action

Nature of the Objective Sought

H6a: If the collective good offers a benefit in joint supply, then the probability of successful collective action will increase with the size of the group

H6b: If the collective good does not offer a benefit in joint supply, then the probability of successful collective action will decrease as the size of the group gets larger.

H7:   If the collective good offers non-exclusionary benefits, then an incentive to free ride will be introduced thereby lowering the probability of successful collective action.

H8a: If the collective good offers increasing returns to organization, then the probability that a sub-group will undertake the added burden of organizing the collective will increase with the size of the group.

H8b: If the collective good does not offer increasing returns to organization, then the probability that a sub-group will undertake the added burden of organizing the collective will fall as the group gets larger.

The Broader Environment

H9:   The probability of successful collective action will increase as the number of other organizational actors (trade unions, business federations, political parties....) increases.

The Politics of Interest Representation

Since the primary focus here is on groups of like-minded individuals and voters, I argue that expected influence is a function of the electoral appeal of the group, a variable which comprises the potential voting block represented by members, and the electoral rules and allocation formulas used to translate votes into seats. I combine these effects into a single measure of electoral appeal that assumes the group has successfully organized.

I argue that the voting potential of a group is the result of the geographic distribution of members across electoral districts. As noted above, geographic concentration increases the likelihood of overcoming the barriers to collective action by facilitating greater face-to-face communication and monitoring. However, it also has a direct impact on the appeal groups have to political parties and electoral entrepreneurs. As suggested earlier by Cox (1999), the electoral rules defining minimum thresholds and seat allocation formulas play an important role here: a group that represents 3% of a district in an environment with a 5% electoral threshold is not the same as one facing a 2% threshold.[18]

Beyond electoral thresholds, however, the wider political distribution is also a factor. The case of the American automobile industry helps illustrate the point, as one significant resource this group has been able to draw upon over the years has been the fact that it has strategically located its factories and suppliers in almost every state.[19] This distribution gives the industry a constituency in almost every representative's district, and consequently its members are far more effective politically than had they just been located in districts in and around Detroit, Michigan. By spreading the collective benefit to the industry around a broader jurisdiction (i.e., the country as a whole), the industry is able to increase its chances of gaining sought after policy objectives and benefits.[20] Therefore, success in extracting policy concessions from a legislature is enhanced by the degree to which the benefits extend across the political arena. Going back to Olson, we see much the same argument, only slightly more abstracted: "when a collective good reaches only a minority of those in a jurisdiction, … it will not (in the absence of some lucky bargaining) get majority support, and will be provided, if at all, only to a less than optimal degree" (Olson 1971, 171). In context of social welfare reform, the relevant jurisdiction is the nation as a whole as retirees and contributors can be found everywhere, a fact which poses an added

18   Electoral thresholds define the minimum percent of the vote that must be received in a given jurisdiction in order to receive a seat in parliament. In the Czech Republic the threshold was 5% for single parties and from 7–11% for coalitions depending on the number of parties contained. The threshold in Hungary was 4% in 1990 and 5% in 1994 (and thereafter). In Poland, the threshold was 5% for single parties and 7% for coalitions.

19   See Schiller and McGillivray 1996a, 1996b, 1998.

20   A similar strategy has been employed by American defense contractors, thereby making it much harder for politicians to cut a specific defense program as almost every district stands to be affected.

challenge for small, politically concentrated groups favoring policies which benefit themselves at the expense of the general public.

The measurement of this variable varies slightly from country to country depending on the number of districts (see Appendix 2). In the Czech Republic for example, I define groups to have a high electoral appeal if they could deliver at least 10% of the vote (twice the threshold) in six or more of the eight districts, medium appeal if they could do so in only four or five districts, and low appeal if they could manage that level in only three or less of the districts.

While potential electoral appeal is important, it is also necessary to formulate an expectation about the response of politicians to that threat. A group may represent 25% of the vote in district, however, that does not mean that all these voters will necessarily vote in the same fashion. In short, a link is required between the theoretical threat posed by a mobilized group, and the empirics of being voted out of office. I argue that this link has to do with issue salience. Essentially, politicians must consider whether or not mobilized voters will actually respond negatively to their revealed legislative behavior in matters relating to pension reform. By 1996, when the pension reform efforts began in earnest, the evidence from Central and Eastern Europe was clear and unmistakable that politicians, parties and governments can and would be voted out of office. Every country had experienced at least one post-communist change in government, and several had seen the reelection of former communist parties. So losing an election was clearly possible, if not likely. Therefore, the question was whether or not pension reform would trigger such a backlash. The evidence suggests that politicians believed (or acted as if) it could. In all cases, they repeatedly surveyed public attitudes about the issue and its salience. While in no case was it the number one priority for a majority of the population, it was consistently listed as a concern and a salient issue. Backing up those surveys was a palatable sense of frustration with *ad hoc* changes and the continual redirection of pension surpluses to fund other government activities. This was particular true in Poland where over 15 separate changes and adjustments were made to the pension system between 1989–1995.

The evidence also suggests that politicians undertook extensive public relations campaigns to win support for their actions. In all cases, the message was largely the same: current retirees would not be adversely effected and younger workers would benefit in the long-run. Taken together, this suggests that politicians could reasonably assume that they would be held accountable for their actions in regard to pension reform. In practice, they would have done well to recognize this as in all three cases examined here, the government that passed the reform legislation lost the next election, albeit for a variety of reasons not necessarily related to their actions on pension reform. What does seem clear is that in what was likely to be a close race, every politician should have taken any credible electoral threat seriously. Therefore, groups that did mange to successfully organize, *and* constituted a genuine electoral threat as defined above, should have been listened to by all concerned.

Measuring Winners and Losers

Central to the above arguments are groups of like-mined individuals with divergent preferences over policy outcomes. Although there are numerous groupings around which political conflicts may be waged (e.g., ethnicity, religion, or in light of the diversity found in some East European countries, language), I focus here on socioeconomic status. Implicit in this is an assumption that individual preferences over pension reform alternatives are derived from one's financial position. As discussed in Chapter 1, the logic behind this assumption is that for those at the bottom of the income distribution, the potential move to mandatory private pension accounts was seen as threatening as it left each individual financially responsible for his own well being in retirement. Moreover, by identifying the relative losers and focusing on their ability to gain political representation, it allows a test of Przeworski's (1991) notion of what constitutes a democratic process. It also allows testing the broader question of democratic consolidation.

Given my thesis that the process of privatization shaped both individual preferences over reform alternatives and the collective ability of individuals to mobilize in support of those preferences, I begin with the changes in household income brought about by the privatization process. After briefly describing the different strategies employed in each country, I examine the distributional consequences of those choices. To measure these effects, I first construct household income quintiles using individual-level survey data.[21] The use of quintiles provides a simple, intuitive measure of privatization's effects as the expected percentage of households in each quintile, if there were no relationship between income and privatization, is 20%. Therefore, when we see for example that in 1990 only 3.5% of the Hungarian households where at least one member worked for a joint stock company (a form of privatization) were among the bottom 20% of household, we have evidence that this method of privatization produced a disproportionate share of relative winners. By investigating the ownership status of an individual's firm, the degree of foreign ownership, the occupation and the type of residence across household income quintiles, the pattern of relative winners and losers quickly emerges and the distributional consequences of privatization are revealed.

While household income is an appropriate measurement tool given the study of pension reform, two refinements are required before a working definition can be stated and the politics of pension reform explored. The first concern is time. In short, anyone can have a bad year, particularly in a transition environment. So the argument has been made that "only persistent positions over a longer period should be counted" (Habich and Spéder 1998, 14). While there is a litany of panel-data based research supporting this argument, a strong case can also "be made against

---

21   To account for the large number of extended families in Eastern Europe, household incomes are adjusted according to the total size and composition of the household (i.e., the number of adults and the number of children). See Appendix 4 for more on the adjustment and the survey instruments used.

an excessive emphasis on stability in time," as one's final position may matter more than one's position a decade before (Habich and Spéder 1998, 15).[22] Consider for example a household that was at the top of the income distribution in 1991, but at the bottom of it from 1994 onward. Its earlier status probably has very little to do with the family's economic interests in 1997. Balancing these competing tensions, the relative winners and losers in Poland and Hungary are defined here in terms of their household income over the two-year period in which the pension reform legislation worked its way through the political process.[23] The data for these countries are drawn from Household Panel surveys, which tracked approximately 8000 individuals and their households from 1991 to 1997. However, because such times series data was never a high priority for the Czech Central Statistics Bureau, I am forced there to use the annual surveys of *Economic Expectations and Attitudes*. As a result, I define the relative winners and losers there using a one-year snap-shot.

The second refinement concerns the actual measurement by which a household is defined to be either a relative winner or a loser of the transition. While the use income quintiles provides an intuitive baseline for measuring the distributional consequences of privatization across types of households, they cannot be used to assess the size element of the collective action arguments outlined above as their size does not vary (they always contain 20% of the observations). Following the work of Habich and Spéder (1998), I therefore define winners and losers in percentage terms relative to the mean household income. Again using a five-fold classification, groups are defined in Table 2.2.

Table 2.2   Defining the Relative Winners and Losers of the Transition

Group	Definition
Big Losers	Households with an income less than 50% of the mean in both years.
Little Losers	Households with an income less than the mean, but more than 50% of it in both years.
In Flux	Households whose relative income position fluctuated from year to year.
Little Winners	Households with an income more than the mean, but less than 150% of it in both years.
Big Winners	Households with an income in excess of 150% of the mean in both years.

One potential criticism of this classification is that those at the bottom of the income distribution, the Roma or gypsy communities for example, have always been at the bottom of the distribution. This raises the question of the extent to which they are really losers of the transition. While it is true that this ethnic group in particular was at the bottom of the income distribution in both 1955 and 1995, and appears set to be so in 2005 and beyond, I would argue they are real losers of the transition

---

22   See also Spéder 1998; Headey, Habich & Krause 1994; and Duncan 1984.
23   For Poland, this period is 1996-1998; for Hungary, it is 1995–1997.

in two ways. First, given their lower level of income, they and others like them were disproportionately affected by the price liberalization and ending of subsidies during the early years of the transition. Whatever their relative position under state-sponsored socialism, it was clearly lower as a result of the movement to a market-oriented economy. Second, they are real losers of the privatization process itself as they lost their guaranteed right to employment in a state-owned enterprise. What they got out of privatization was unemployment and a lower standard of living.

For Poland and Hungary, another group requiring clarification includes those defined as *In Flux*. These households are a consequence of using a two-year time period; inevitably some experienced a fluctuation in relative position from year to year. In most cases, the change is negligible as the household moves from slightly above the mean one year to slightly below it the next. However, there are always a small number of households that experience substantial changes. In Hungary for example, two of the poorest households in 1996 found themselves among the wealthiest the following year, while over 25% of the wealthiest households in 1996 that experienced a change in status saw their incomes suddenly fall below the 1997 mean.

In what sense then is this really a group with a common identity or interest? I would argue very little. Although they would appear to share a high degree of uncertainty given their changing financial situation, they do not constitute a group of like-minded persons in regard to pension reform. It is more reasonable to assume that some members identified themselves with the consistent winners, while others shared the interests of the consistent losers. This inherent fragmentation and their wide-spread, almost uniform geographical distribution suggests that those *In Flux* did not play a significant independent role in the reform process in any country. Rather, some added their voices to those pushing for mandatory accounts while others joined the chorus for the preservation and reform of the existing system; however, in no case do they appear to have swung the balance for either side. Consequently, I focus my analysis on the four remaining groups.

With groups so defined, their preferences over policy alternatives are derived from either survey data or the available literature. Given this, my model then generates testable hypotheses about both 1) the likelihood that each group would successfully organize, and 2) the likelihood that once organized, the group would represent a credible convey an electoral threat to policy makers. Since the central question here concerns the ability of domestic actors to influence the policy making process, the testing procedure used is a qualitative review of the legislative and lobbying history in each country. Using archival research and interviews conducted in the region, I examine the legislative and lobbying record surrounding the efforts to reform the pension system in each of these three countries; the evidence collected is then compared against the group hypotheses derived from the model.[24] In doing so, each of the research puzzles presented in Chapter 1 are addressed. First, the political consequences of privatization are more fully explored. Second, the interaction between domestic interest groups and international organizations pressing for

---

24   This type of analysis is akin to process tracing; see George and McKeown 1985 and George and Bennet 2005.

particular types of reform is clarified. Third, the overall experience of instituting a major policy reform helps assess both 1) whether these countries are consolidated democracies, and 2) the relative (comparative) extent of that consolidation among the three countries examined here. Finally, this testing procedure provides a template with which to examine the remaining countries of Central and Eastern Europe, including the former Soviet Union.

Chapter 3

The Case of Poland

Though still fiscally sound at the end of the communist period, the Polish pension system soon began suffering the affects of a declining birthrate, a rising life expectancy, and the increased burden caused by program expansions undertaken in the 1980s (Hausner 1998, 9).[1] While these changes helped make pension reform an important issue in the 1990s, two other factors combined to make it a virtual necessity.

The first was the growing use of early retirement in the face of rising unemployment. As the unemployment rate grew, fueled by more than 90,000 new applicants a month, a number of employees took the opportunity to retire early rather than face the prospect of living on temporary unemployment benefits. Seeing the logic in such a move, the government actually went as far as to encourage such behavior by easing the restrictions attached to it (Müller 1999, 101). The obvious consequence for the Pay-As-You-Go (PAYG) system was a substantial increase in the number of people collecting benefits with an equivalent drop in the number of contributors.[2]

The proverbial straw that broke the camel's back, however, was the widespread tax evasion that, while always present to a degree, exploded following the imposition of hard-budget constraints in the early 1990s. Confronted with the removal of subsidies and grants from the state budget, many public and private firms decided to continue collecting the mandatory payroll contributions, but to withhold them from the Social Insurance Institute (ZUS). Given the government's relative inability to enforce the rule of law so early in the transition, firms could do this with relative impunity. As a consequence, ZUS was owed almost 4.76 billion (new) zloty by the end of 1996, or the equivalent of 13% of the total benefits it paid out that year (Cain and Surdej 1999, 154). This, when combined with the long standing tradition of allowing certain privileged sectors (e.g., mining, railway workers) to accumulate substantial arrears to the pension system, effectively made the existing system financially unviable.

---

1   The agricultural sector, which to this day employs about 25% of the population, was added to the pension system only in the 1980s. Unlike most other communist systems, agriculture had remained mostly a private sector activity and had never undergone a period of forced collectivization. As such, it had remained outside the state pension system.

2   Further complicating matters was the fact that program "backfired" as "many people took early retirement and then continued to work, often in the same jobs as before, [effectively] using their retirement income as a supplemental wage" (Cook and Orenstein 1999, 81).

Realizing this, over a dozen, small piecemeal changes were made to the pension system between 1989 and 1995. Included among these was the "practice of periodically and temporarily suspending a portion of the state's commitments to pensioners for fiscal reasons" (Hausner 1998, 14). Not surprisingly, the Constitutional Tribunal eventually ruled such ad hoc changes unconstitutional and "forced the government to repay any lost benefits" (Orenstein 2000, 40). Despite its rulings, however, the Court

> clearly stressed that this did not preclude the possibility of a permanent change in the regulations, provided that such a change was preceded by appropriate legislation. *Thus, it was only when the legal and political factors prevented ad hoc manipulation of the pension system that the warnings of experts and the idea of major reform came to be taken seriously* (Hausner 1998, 14 emphasis in original).

Although the Court had laid clear a path for politicians, a combination of personal and inter-ministerial rivalries stalled the process from late-1994 until 1996; it was only following a change in personnel that real progress began (Hausner 1998, 15-16). By that point, however, electoral politics loomed large on the horizon as party leaders looked towards the elections scheduled for September 1997. Realizing that there was insufficient time to reform the entire system, the decision was made to focus on creating a new mandatory second pillar (i.e., fully-funded, individual, private accounts) before the election, leaving reforms to the existing PAYG pillar until afterwards (Orenstein 2000, 42). That effort led to three pieces of legislation passed in the summer of 1997.[3] Although the subsequent change in government delayed reforms to the existing first pillar until late 1998, the new right-of-center coalition continued the process that ultimately created a mixed pillar model along the lines being advocated by the World Bank. The new system came into effect in 1999.[4]

While the end result broadly conforms to the new pension orthodoxy, I argue that both the long-delay, and the particular characteristics of the reforms, suggest that the Poles took what was a standard set of policy prescriptions from the World Bank, and fashioned themselves a unique set of reforms. In doing so, they reveal a functioning democratic system wherein both the relative winners and losers from earlier reforms could have their voices heard. However, before examining their abilities to influence politics, I begin with the privatization process that gave rise to these groups, and helped shape their respective interests over how to reform the pension system and influence the political process.

---

3   The three acts covered 1) the application of privatization revenue to the pension system (June 25, 1997); 2) employee pension programs (August 22, 1997); and 3) the organization and operation of pension funds (August 28, 1997).

4   Technical problems, primarily with the new computer system ZUS was supposed to implement, delayed the launching of the second pillar until April 1999 (Orenstein 2000, 46).

Privatization

As in all countries, the way in which state owned enterprises (SOEs) were privatized can best be understood in the context of the environment into which the process was introduced. In Poland, this requires consideration of the sizeable private sector that already existed prior to 1989, and the very strong position of organized labor within each firm. In regards to the former, almost 20% of the economy was already in private hands when Solidarity took over in 1989, a stark contrast to the Czech Republic where almost 99% of the economy at that time was still owned by the state (Akov 1997, 32). Although this private sector was largely confined to the agricultural sector, by the late 1980s, there had already been some degree of movement towards private enterprises as well. The most significant feature of the Polish SOEs, however, was "the dominant role of the workers" in the management and decision-making of the firm (Frydman et al 1993, 159). Following the debt-induced crisis of the early 1980s, Solidarity (the then illegal independent trade union) was able to demand and receive a significant degree of authority over the management of state owned firms. Encapsulated in the 1981 Law on State Enterprises, employee councils were given the right to "hire and fire the director" as well sell or lease state property while keeping all profits in excess of book value (Frydman et al 1993, 159–160). In addition, most major decisions affecting the enterprise could not be made by state officials without the consent of the council and the existing management, which had often been put in place by organized labor.

It was into this environment of very independent, essentially labor-managed firms that privatization was introduced in 1990. While there were numerous programs over the next several years, some successful others not, the three most important ones were the sale of small and medium sized retail outlets, the liquidation of enterprises, and a mass privatization program involving the free distribution of shares through National Investment Funds. The latter would prove to play a critical role in maintaining the solvency of the PAYG pillar after the introduction of mandatory private accounts.

Small Privatization

Driven by widespread public resentment of the "hopelessly substandard businesses run by the socialist domestic trade sector," the government decided to transfer the title to the real estate on which the shop or restaurant was situated rather than try to sell an unwanted, unpopular and unproductive business (Earle et al 1994, 176). In practice, this meant that titles were transferred to local governments and cooperatives, which then worked with the existing employees to undo the damage caused by the former employers, usually a centralized founding organization or ministry (Akov 1997, 38). In most cases, the new owners leased the property to one or more of the employees, or less frequently an outside entrepreneur, who then undertook the task of running the business. Overall, the program proved both successful and popular as the move not only removed an inefficient and unpopular distribution system, but also helped stimulate the further development of the private sector and entrepreneurship. While the public as a whole benefited from a better series of retail shops and restaurants, the primary beneficiaries were the firm insiders who leased the property and assets to start what were essentially new businesses. Their dominance can best be seen in the different types of transfers that took place as 61% were the result of direct negotiations with employees, and only 27% the result of an open, competitive auction; the remaining 12% were dispersed through auctions that were either limited to or gave special preferences to existing employees (Earle et al 1994, 215). So began a privatization process that consistently privileged organized labor and the existing employees, a scenario which stands in stark contrast to either Hungary, which privileged foreign investors and wealthier citizens who could afford to pay for assets, or the Czech Republic where the center-right government of Václav Klaus was adamant that employees receive no special advantages. Consequently, the Polish experience would result in a comparatively better financial standing for traditional blue-collar employees than seen in the rest of Central and Eastern Europe, a result than can be seen in Table 3.1 on page 55.

Liquidation   These privileges were further expanded during the process of privatizing larger enterprises. Initially designed around cash-based sales to generate income for the state, a combination of political instability and poor results eventually led to liquidation as the preferred method of privatization. The term, however, is somewhat of a misnomer as it was applied to both insolvent and solvent firms. For the former, the process was "a covert form of ownership transformation, with the assets of the 'bankrupt' sold at an auction, most often to enterprise insiders" (Frydman et al 1993, 168–169).[5] For financially viable enterprises, the decision to liquidate rested with the founding organ (i.e., the appropriate government ministry or local authority) that nominally owned the firm and assets in question. The process involved creating a successor organization that could sell, lease or combine the assets with another firm. The most common variant involved leasing "to a new company specially created [to lease the assets] by the employees of the liquidated state enterprise" (Frydman 1993, 188). The law actually required any corporation that leased liquidated assets to make the majority of its shares available to the employees of the liquidated enterprise; if they failed to purchase these allotted shares within two months, the lease could proceed without them. So again, as with the privatization of the retail sectors, one can see the power and influence of organized labor in drafting procedures favorable to its members.

The extent of this preferential treatment also extended to the financing of the lease itself. As with most leases, they could be written with or without a purchase option; however, the law also allowed for leases under which the lessor was required

---

5   Bankruptcy in the socialist sense is somewhat confusing as the creditor, the state (as owner of the banks), is most often also the nominal owner of the enterprise (Frydman et al 1993, 168). That said, there were legal procedures for what we would normally understand as bankruptcy protection from creditors. In Poland, these statutes were updated by the Insolvency Act in February 1990.

to cede title to the lessee at the end of the period if all payments had been made and certain other conditions satisfied (Frydman et al 1993, 189). This arrangement amounted to an installment-plan purchase of the assets; a useful device given the lack of capital in the country. Essentially, the lessees ended up owning an asset outright that they did not have the up-front capital (or credit history) to purchase at the beginning of the lease period. They also benefited from a fixed interest rate, which in a high inflationary environment like Poland, was "significantly negative in real terms" (Frydman et al 1993, 190).[6]

Mass Privatization   The Polish experience with mass privatization sought to avoid many of the pitfalls witnessed in the Czech Republic. As described in Chapter 5, Czech reformers essentially gave away shares in their largest SOEs for free. In brief, all adult Czech citizens living in the country could, for a nominal fee, purchase a voucher booklet worth 1000 points. These points were then used to bid on blocks of shares in SOEs that had been converted into joint-stock companies. When it was over, 80% of the adult population had become a shareholder of some sort in the national economy (Coffee 1996, 114). While this was exactly what Prime Minister Klaus wanted, the situation led to numerous problems involving corporate governance. For although only individuals could purchase voucher booklets, there was no restriction on their subsequent sale or transfer. As a result, several large Investment Privatization Funds (IPFs) ended up holding over 70% of the voucher points, having bought them in exchange for shares in one of their own mutual funds. Many of these IPFs were owned by state-owned-banks. Consequently, the Czech government was now the new owner of a recently privatized company.[7] Beyond this seemingly circular process, there were other problems that effectively blocked efforts to fundamentally restructure the management and governance of these new, nominally private, firms.

Hoping to avoid this scenario, Poland created 15 National Investment Funds (NIFs) with a different one being designated the lead fund for each enterprise.[8] Each lead fund received 33% of the enterprise's shares while the other fourteen divided 27% equally among themselves. The lead NIF was responsible for overseeing the restructuring of the firm. Of the remaining 40%, the enterprise's employees received

---

6   In 1990, the Consumer Price Index (CPI) measure of inflation was 240%, while the GDP deflator for the year rose 538% (EBRD Transition Report; Frdyman 1993, 152.) The interest rates contained in the lease agreements did not approach anywhere near these levels.

7   For a more detailed discussion of the numerous corporate governance problems stemming from the Czech experience, and privatization in Eastern Europe more generally, see Frydman et al 1996.

8   Not all large enterprises were covered by this program as "the stated policy of the Ministry of Privatization [was] to exclude from the program all enterprises which [could] be realistically expected to be privatized through other means, those that [were] potential or actual monopolists, and those in poor financial condition" (Frydman et al 1993, 1994). Eventually, 512 SOEs were selected and privatized through the program.

fifteen percent free of charge, while the state claimed the remaining twenty-five.[9] In order to avoid one of the Czech pitfalls, these government shares were non-voting so long as they remained in state hands; if resold to a private entity, they would become standard voting shares (Frydman et al 1993, 195).

The NIFs themselves were established and licensed by the government as closed-end joint stock companies, where the management of each was awarded on the basis of competitive bids received from companies around the world (Akov 1997, 42). Although it was intended and expected that experienced international financial intermediaries would submit the most competitive bids, the funds themselves were to be closely governed by a Supervisory Board comprised of Polish citizens (Frydman et al 1993, 196–7).[10] In addition, the actual ownership of the NIFs was to remain private and exclusively in Polish hands. So following a similar strategy as the Czech Republic, all Polish citizens over the age of 18 were eligible to purchase a certificate of ownership giving them a share of one of the fifteen NIFs. The cost of a certificate was only 20 zlotys (~$7), which led to a very high participation rate among the public as over 90% of those eligible purchased a certificate (Kapoor 1997, 13). Those shares became tradeable on the Warsaw stock exchange in June 1997. While this marketization benefited the average Polish citizen, it also created "an enormous windfall for the employees" who had received 15% of the former enterprise's shares for free (Frydman et al 1993, 195).

In sum, the Polish experience with privatization was one that extended certain privileges to existing employees while at the same time managed to avoid many of the governance problems that plagued the Czech Republic. In doing so, the Polish government fundamentally altered the socialist-era income distribution. The figures in Table 3.1 provide an assessment of its variance across different occupational and education categories. The bases for the comparison are the quintiles of adjusted monthly household income. If there were no relationship between these quintiles and the categories listed to the left, then 20% of the observations should fall in each quintile. When we look across the respondent's professional status, this is precisely the distribution we see, with the notable exception of the agricultural sector. Reflecting the advantages and privileges extended to labor, almost 20% of all blue-collar workers could expect to fall into each of the income categories. While white-collar workers had a 45% chance of belonging to the richest 20% of the households, certain blue-collar workers, such as miners or electrical workers, were almost as likely to belong to one of these upper income households. Turning to education, we see that although those with a university degree were the ones most likely to belong

---

9   The original plan called for employees to receive 10% and the state to hold 30%. This violated the guidelines set forth in the Privatization Law that guaranteed employees the right to purchase 20% of an enterprise's shares at up to a 50% discount. Ultimately, a deal was struck whereby employees received 15% for free. The state's shares were ultimately linked to financing the pension system as described further below.

10   The current international management teams include Barclays PLC, Dresdner Bank AG, Chase Manhattan International Finance, Creditanstalt Investment Bank AG, and the Japanese firm Yamaichi among others.

to one of the wealthiest households, those with lower levels of education were not significantly more likely to belong to a lower income quintile. Somewhat surprising is the relatively sound position of pensioners. Overall, 57% of the retirees belonged to one of the upper income households, due in part to the widespread practice of retirees continuing to work either part or full-time, often in the informal shadow economy where no taxes were paid and the income went unreported. If we separate those retirees living alone from those living in an extended household, we see that the former are much more likely to belong to a higher income quintile. The most likely explanation is that extended families have several adults living in the home who were non-financial contributors. Given the way in which household incomes were adjusted to account for size and composition, such individuals would significantly lower the household's quintile standing.

Table 3.1   The Relative Winners and Losers Following Privatization, 1995

	Percentage of Individuals working for or as a ...	*Household Income Quintile (%)*				
		1st	*2nd*	*3rd*	*4th*	*5th*
Professional Status	White-collar Employee	2.6	9.4	17.2	25.9	45.0
	Blue-collar Employee	12.4	22.0	23.5	23.3	18.9
	Self-employed	11.7	11.0	15.5	27.9	33.8
	Farmer	34.8	18.8	14.1	13.8	18.5
Industrial Sector	Agriculture	33.0	14.5	16.0	15.4	16.2
	Utilities (gas, electric, ...)	7.8	12.5	17.3	28.9	33.7
	Manufacturing	10.5	19.0	23.4	21.8	25.3
	Mining	3.8	8.7	16.8	31.4	39.5
	Real Estate, Finance, Insurance	5.5	12.3	12.9	21.5	47.9
Type of Employer	Public Employer	7.5	16.2	20.4	24.2	31.7
	Private Employer	22.1	18.8	18.4	19.7	21.0
Highest Level of Education	Elementary	23.2	22.2	22.0	19.9	12.8
	Secondary or Vocational	17.0	19.3	20.7	21.4	21.8
	University	4.8	7.6	11.4	23.2	53.0
Retirees	Overall	6.6	15.0	21.3	26.9	30.2
	Living in all-retiree household	0.7	13.8	20.2	29.2	36.2
	At least 1 non-retiree in home	11.7	16.0	22.2	25.0	25.1

Sample size: Individuals (15,693); Quintiles 1,3,5 (3,139), 2 and 4 (3,138); Total number of households (4,858). Quintiles based on net monthly household income, adjusted for household size and age composition.

Source: Polish Household Panel Survey, 1995.

The Income Consequences of Privatization

While the above figures suggest that, unlike Hungary or the Czech Republic, labor was not left significantly behind in terms of financial gains, the process did create relative winners and losers. Although some of this can be seen using the above quintiles, their size invariance prohibits the testing of some of the hypothesis spelled out in the preceding chapter. Therefore, the relative winners and losers of the Polish transition are defined below in terms of relative household income across the two-year period 1995–1996, and presented in Table 3.2.

The first thing to notice is that very few Polish households (6.5%) were left significantly and consistently behind financially. By the same token, less than 8% of the households consistently earned more than 1.5 times the mean. What also stands out is the significantly large number of households whose financial standing fluctuated from year-to-year. Unpacking this category reveals that the situation was roughly evenly split between those households whose standing improved (47.0%) verse those whose position deteriorated (53%). In any given year, the ratio of losers to winners was about 60/40. The figures in Table 3.2 represents the new Polish income strata.

Table 3.2   The Relative Winners and Losers of the Transition, 1995–1996

Category	Definition	1996 Average Monthly Income	Number of Households	Percent of Sample
Big Losers	Households with an income less than 50% of the mean in both years.	182.98 Zlty	306	6.5%
Little Losers	Households with an income less than the mean but more than 50% of it in both years.	376.81	1609	34.2
In Flux	Households whose relative position fluctuated from year to year.	503.29	1727	36.7
Little Winners	Households with an income more than the mean but less that 150% of it in both years.	605.96	711	15.1
Big Winners	Households with an income in excess of 150% of the mean in both years.	1,113.35	349	7.4
	Average/Total	499.97 Zlty	N=4,702	

Average net household income is in new Polish Zloties, adjusted for household size and age composition. In 1996, the official end-of-year exchange rate was $1=2.87 Zloty.

Actors and Their Roles

Individuals

One of the central premises of this research is that attitudes towards reforming the pension system are in part a result of one's financial standing. One basis for this can be seen in a 1998 survey conducted by the Centrum Badania Opinii Spolecznej (CBOS), a publicly funded but independent research center in Warsaw, the results of which are presented in Table 3.3.

The data shows that there was widespread support for creating private, individual accounts rather than continuing the purely communal PAYG arrangement. While this support extended across each income grouping, and the population in general, 90% of the wealthiest households preferred such a change as opposed to less than 60% of the poorest. This suggests that the opposition to the World Bank's pension orthodoxy largely rested with those left financially behind by the transition, a proposition further supported by examining those who had the choice of joining the new pension arrangement (with private accounts) or opting to remain in a purely PAYG system. This choice stemmed from the legislation that mandated that those under 30 join the new scheme, and that those over 50 remain in the PAYG arrangement. The logic was that the latter did not have enough time until retirement to build up a sizeable nest egg in their private accounts, while the former had several decades to amass sufficient funds to retire. Those in the middle (aged 30–50) could choose which version they preferred to work under. Although a majority (57.6%) indicated they would choose the new system, only 40% of the transition's relative losers were so inclined as opposed to over 76% of its biggest relative winners. It should be noted, however, that three times as many of the transition's biggest losers were uncertain of what they would do as opposed to those with higher household incomes, a ratio that was fairly consistent throughout the survey. Also of note is the fairly uniform agreement that the new system would largely benefit younger workers and those 10–15 years from retirement.

Organizations

The Elderly and Trade Unions　One group with a clear, vested interest in the reform process was the elderly; however, while it would make sense to expect some degree of collective organization, there is no equivalent of the American Association of Retired Persons (AARP) anywhere in Central or Eastern Europe. That said, two separate pensioner parties were created in Poland, however, neither managed to break the 4% electoral threshold (later raised to 5%) needed to gain representation.[11]

11　　Although pensioners comprise 40% of the electorate, the figure is somewhat misleading given the heavy use of early retirement. In 1996, almost 39.5% of men and 28% of all women collective pensions had not yet reached their official retirement age (Müller 1999, 101).

Table 3.3   Relative Winner and Loser Attitudes Toward Pension Reform

	Big Losers	*Little Losers*	*Little Winners*	*Big Winners*	*Overall*
Public vs Private Accounts					
Each person's contribution should be set aside in a special, personal account, and they should be informed of its condition.	58.8%	72.1	72.4	90.3	72.2
All contributions should be combined in one common pool; individual pensions should be paid from this central fund.	27.8	15.1	17.1	5.5	16.8
Hard to say / do not know	13.4	12.4	10.5	4.1	11.0
Total (N)	194	445	152	145	936
Voluntarily opt for the new system (those 30–50 were free to choose)					
Would participate in the new system, where part of the pension will be paid out by social insurance and part from a capital retirement fund (private account).	40.6%	61.6	48.5	76.6	57.6
Would remain in the current system only, and would not divert contributions to a capital retirement fund.	29.0	20.6	33.3	12.8	22.7
Hard to say / do not know	30.4	17.8	15.2	10.6	19.3
Total (N)	69	146	33	47	295
Believe that new system will be advantageous for: (could answer more than one)					
The growth of the Polish economy	43.3%	49.7	48.7	66.0	50.7
Current retirees	23.2	18.0	11.8	13.1	17.3
Those retiring in 10–15 years	46.4	47.2	38.2	53.8	46.6
Young people starting to work	61.3	67.4	67.8	84.8	68.9

Source: CBOS 1998-9825, Government and International Relations, 1998. N=936

Instead, it has been the labor unions throughout Eastern Europe, which have been "far more involved than pensioners in negotiations over pension reforms" (Nelson 1998, 21). Poland was no exception as both Solidarity and the post-communist confederation (OPZZ) were deeply involved in the designing of the new system. However, following the collapse of communism in 1989, organized labor was replete with internal divisions and tensions as it sought to create a new political identity for itself. As a result, members of the same organization often professed support for different, if not contradictory, objectives. For example, many of Solidarity's more left-wing members were "deeply skeptical about diluting the [PAYG] system, partly on grounds that fully funded, individual accounts would destroy the redistributive and solidaristic character of the system," while the union's leadership both called for and actually proposed their own version of a system with such accounts (Nelson 1998, 21). Both aspects of this fragmentation found their way before the *Plenipotentiary for Social Security Reform* (described below) through consultations it held with the Tripartite Commission. Similar to corporatist structures found in Germany, Hungary and elsewhere, the Commission brought together labor, management and government in order to discuss not only wage contracts but also the marketization of the economy and issues like reforming the welfare state.

The Commission contains five groups (the government, the Confederation of Polish Employers, Solidarity, OPZZ, and the other unions which had signed earlier social pacts with the government), each with one vote and, effectively, a veto in that all members must be present for a decision to be "legally binding" (Hausner 1996, 115).[12] To speed the development of a reform package, a special working group was created comprised of policy experts and trade unionists. Through this venue, the unions added "the final details to certain elements of the reform programme, and at the same time also created the belief that reform was a joint undertaking, a fact which the government plenipotentiary systematically referred to" (Hausner 1998, 33).

Substantively, Solidarity's main concern was how to use the proceeds from privatization. It had long proposed that the proceeds from the sale of *all* state assets be transferred as "seed money" into every individual's private account (Hausner 1998, 26). Although the government strongly opposed this complete form of empropriation, it did consent to the idea in part through the creation of the NIFs described above.[13]

---

12   The OPZZ effectively has multiple representatives on the Commission through its own seat and that of some of the separate union signatories (such as the Machine Industry Union and the Confederation of Energy Workers) that are part of the larger OPZZ. Although the unions collectively held three of the five votes, there existed fundamental differences of opinion over policy alternatives, particularly between the left-of-center OPZZ and Solidarity (right-of-center), two groups that regularly failed to find common ground.

13   Empropriation is a process whereby recipients receive ownership rights not by purchase but by "recognized eligibility;" the primary advantage is that it does not require financing or "even a precise estimate" of the asset's true value (Hausner 1998, 25). Given the immense difficulty in the later and the lack of the financial resources, such programs were particularly appealing to many actors.

Having received 15% of the shares in each NIF at no charge, employees could use this windfall fund their own retirement accounts if they wished. The 25% stake the government initially held would be used to finance the deficits created in the public pillar as individuals began diverting a portion of their contributions to their own private accounts. In doing so, Poland became the only country considered here to directly link the proceeds from privatization to the funding of the pension system. In reaching this compromise, the government "signaled that the dispute with Solidarity was not over doctrine, but was purely technical in nature, and that the union's proposal had been accepted by the government as a supplementary measure" (Hausner 1998, 27).

The other principle union, the OPZZ, was closely linked to the left wing of the Democratic Left Alliance (SLD), the senior coalition partner from 1993–1997. Their primary interest was expanding and protecting the position of employees, and by extension had the strongest reservations against the move to mandatory private pension accounts. Throughout the early transition, the OPZZ had continuously sought to stipulate a Charter of Social Guarantees that it hoped would protect those left relatively behind by the transition to a market economy (Hausner 1996, 117).

The Plenipotentiary for Social Security Reform   The initial stalemate between the Ministry of Labor and the Ministry of Finance was eventually broken by appointing Andrezj Bączkowski, the chairman of the Tripartite Commission, as the new Labor Minister. An original member of Solidarity, Bączkowski was widely respected by both government and opposition parties. It was his idea to create a single office to oversea the process of reforming both the pension and health insurance systems; the plan was for the office to act as both the drafter of the proposals, and the forum for bringing together the myriad of interests and organizations that would have to be involved if the projects were to be successful (Hausner 1998, 19). Although he had previously come out in favor of radical reform (i.e., mandatory private accounts), his personal reputation as a fair and skilled negotiator assured opponents that they would have an opportunity to not only have their say, but influence policy as well.

The Office also extended a hand to the World Bank, which provided both the funding for the Plenipotentiary as well as its day-to-day office manager in the form of Michal Rutkowski, a polish national who worked for the Bank (Orenstein 2000, 42). This move ensured proponents of the new pension orthodoxy that they too would at the very least have their ideas heard and considered. To that end, the World Bank funded a number of study trips to Latin American for reformers, union representatives and journalists alike.

With funding and organization secure, the Plenipotentiary began drafting the new pension system, called "Security Through Diversity," in September 1996. Sadly, Bączkowski died suddenly of a heart attack in November before the drafting and negotiations were complete. While his death was a tremendous blow to all concerned, forceful intervention and backing by the Prime Minister kept the project moving (Orenstein 2000, 43). Jerzy Hausner, the Secretary of State in the Council of Ministers, was appointed the new Plenipotentiary. In his own account of the reform process, Hausner makes clear that he understood Bączkowski's vision and the need to include and consult with both supporters and opponents. Writing in 1998 when most of his work had been done, he stated that, "I am convinced that a radical reform of the pension system (involving the abandonment of the PAYG-system in favour of a multi-pillar system) could [only be implemented through a combination of] strategic leadership with dialogue and social partnership" (Hausner 1998, 36). Under the leadership of Bączkowski, Hausner, and Ewa Lewicka, who took over following Solidarity's electoral victory in 1997, the Plenipotentiary effectively served as the forum for that dialogue (Chlon et al 1999, 15).

Parties and Electoral Factors

The Sejm and its Electoral Rules   The Polish Sejm contains 460 seats, 391 of which are awarded on the basis of multi-member constituencies. The remaining 69 are distributed among competing lists of nation-wide candidates. In order to qualify for one of these compensation mandates, a party must be registered in more than half of all the constituencies and receive at least 7% of the national vote. Single parties are confronted with a 5% threshold while coalitions of parties face an 8% barrier. Following the immense fragmentation of the 1991 election, where 24 different parties won seats, a new electoral formula (d'Hondt) was introduced for the 1993 lection.[14] The net effect of the change to was to drastically decrease the number of parties at the cost of increasing the vote-seat disproportionality. For example, the Alliance of the Democratic Left (SLD) only won ~20% of the vote in 1993, but was awarded more than a third of the seats; for its part, "the Polish Peasant Party (PSL) obtained twice as many seats as it would have obtained under the old electoral law" (Gryzbowski 1998, 172). Politically, this consolidation prevented either of the two pensioner parties, along with over a dozen other small parties, from gaining representation; almost 5 million votes, ~35% of all the votes cast, "were wasted in the sense that they did not go towards representation in the Sejm" (Gryzbowski 1998, 172). In the end, only seven parties were awarded seats in Parliament, and the three largest accounted for 82% of the seats. The SLD-PSL coalition held 65.9% of the seats, so as long as it could maintain some degree of party (and coalition) discipline, it had the votes to pass its legislative agenda.[15]

The Party System and Social Cleavages   Analysis of the social cleavages in Poland identifies two central dimensions of political conflict. The first, and strongest, "pits socio-economic protectionists against market liberals," while the second sets secular

---

14   For an account of different allocation formulas and their consequences, see Cox 1997.

15   The Union of Labor (UP) initially took part in the cabinet formation discussions, but eventually elected not to join the coalition. It did, however, support the government "informally" until June 1994 (Gryzbowski 1998, 173). The party held 8.9% of the seats in the Sejm.

liberals against religious, more authoritarian and nationalist elements (Kitschelt 1999, 231). These cleavages, along with the electoral rules described above, supported five main political parties that must be considered in regard to pension reform in each Parliament, the seat distributions of which are provided in Table 3.4.[16] As the task of reform was divided between two consecutive but different governments, I discuss the constellation of parties within each in turn.

The 1993–1997 Parliament The 1993–1997 Parliament provided opportunities for those both for and against the idea of radically reforming the pension system. This equal opportunity also extended to both the ruling coalition and the SLD itself, which suffered from deep internal schisms. At one extreme, former Prime Minister Oleksy (1995–1996) led a fairly pragmatic group of followers who were supportive of reform. At the other, lay a more conservative group led by Lezek Miller, later Prime Minister himself from 2001–2004, that was more leftist and socialist in its policy preferences (European Forum 2000b, 1). This latter element had severe reservations about mandatory private accounts. It was Miller who, as Minister of Labor and Social Affairs, had helped cause the year and a half long stalemate from 1994 to 1996 (see Hausner 1998, 15–18).

Further adding to the diversity of opinion was the SLD's coalition partner. With its support base largely in the conservative, agricultural areas of the country, the PSL's primary concern was protecting the position of farmers, a group that had been granted special privileges upon joining the pension system in the 1980s. From a fiscal standpoint, the farmers pension system (KRUS) "was heavily indebted and kept afloat by government subsidies" (Orenstein 2000, 40). Aware that the PSL could derail the entire process, the SLD decided to focus exclusively on the employee portion of the pension system in creating the new second pillar, consciously bypassing "those arrangements that dealt with farmers and agricultural labourers as well as the military sector" (Hausner 1998, 34). Despite this, serious differences of opinion remained between the coalition partners, so much so that three different cabinet formations took place between October 1993 and February 1996. Things grew so bad that "members of the SLD leadership, including the Prime Minister, [eventually tried] to establish a dialogue with the opposition" (Hausner 1998, 16). His choice of Andrejz Bączkowski to replace Miller as the Minister of Labor and Social Affairs was just one of the olive branches he extended to Solidarity. Although these moves were ultimately unsuccessful, that gesture, as well as the establishment of the Office of the Plenipotentiary, went a long way to "winning the trust of the opposition" (Hausner 1998, 16). However, they also served to further alienate the reform-resistant elements within the PSL. In the end, the coalition tensions proved too much and the PSL itself introduced a vote of no confidence in July 1997 that brought down the government.

---

16   The two others represented in Parliament from 1993–1997, the German Minority Party and the Confederation for an Independent Poland, are not directly relevant for this issue.

Table 3.4   The Polish Parliament 1993–1997, 1997–2001

1993–1997		1997–2001	
Government	*Seats*	*Government*	*Seats*
Alliance of the Democratic Left (SLD)	37.2%	Solidarity Electoral Alliance (AWS)	33.8%
Polish Peasant Party (PSL)	28.7	Freedom Union (UW)	13.4
Opposition		*Opposition*	
Freedom Union (UW)	16.1	Alliance of the Democratic Left (SLD)	27.1
Union of Labor (UP)	8.9	Polish Peasant Party (PSL)	7.3
Confederation for an Independent Poland (KPN)	4.8	Movement for Rebuilding Poland (ROP)	5.6
Non-Partisan Bloc (BBWR)	3.5	German Minority (MN)	0.4
German Minority (MN)	0.9		

The primary opposition party started out as the Democratic Union (UD), which held 16.1% of the seats following the 1993 election. However, it soon merged with the Liberal Democratic Congress, which having won only 4% of the vote had received no seats in parliament. The resulting merger in April 1994 created the Freedom Union (UW) which drew "its main support [from] those people who [were] able to profit from the socio-economic developments since 1989, such as the emerging Polish middle class, the business community and the urban intelligentsia" (European Forum 2000a, 1). As a representative of the transition's relative winners, it was a strong supporter of the new pension-orthodoxy. Recognizing this, "the Office of the Government Plenipotentiary also included individuals who had close personal contacts with the UW leadership" (Hausner 1998, 32).

The other main party represented was the Union of Labor (UP). A rival to the SLD, it had attempted to position itself "as [the] main defender of the interests of the ordinary working people" (Grzybowski 1998, 171). Although it participated in the cabinet negotiations following the 1993 election, it decided to remain as an outside supporter. In terms reforms, the party was reluctant to support endeavors that entailed a high social cost, and where it did favor reform, it did so in the name of increasing the redistribution of income. As such it was generally opposed to the idea of shifting to a more fully-funded pension system.

The 1997–2001 Parliament   The second parliament under consideration here was marked by the return of Solidarity, which was voted out of office and parliament in 1993. The party returned as the leader of the Solidarity Electoral Alliance (AWS), an amalgamation of over thirty moderate and right wing parties and trade unions. Not surprisingly, there was a considerable degree of diversity within its ranks. In terms of pension reform, as with most legislation, it sought to balance the need for reform with the equally necessary but painful social costs (European Forum 2000a, 1). Thus the party was open to compromises necessary to ensure legislative passage, both from its own members and opposition groups.

Its coalition partner was the Freedom Union (UW) described above. It was the only party that "was unconditionally in favour of full liberalization" (Grzybowski 1998, 176). The SLD and PSL were regulated to opposition parties following the election. While the latter continued to oppose the idea of fundamental reform, and any measure that promised to limit or erode its occupational preferences, the SLD remained committed to the completing the task of reforming the pension system. The two other parties represented in parliament, the Movement for Rebuilding Poland (ROP) and the German Minority party (MN) are not relevant to this discussion, as the former was largely a right-wing, nationalist protest party and the later was a party dedicated to ethnic minority representation.

Other Organizations/Institutions

The Constitutional Tribunal   The Tribunal's impact on pension reform has already been highlighted. For although the World Bank had been actively pressing for fundamental reform for a number of years, it was ultimately the Court that put a stop to seemingly unless series of *ad hoc* changes and helped put Poland on the path of reform. While not as powerful in scope as the Hungarian court (see Chapter 4), lawyers were traditionally supporters of the existing PAYG system, while economists primarily filled the ranks of those favoring a mixed-pillar model. This occupational divide was not lost on reformers who realized that "the legal doctrine of social insurance does not recognize funded pension insurance as being social in character.... [Enforcement of this doctrine would be] a serious problem, because if the Constitutional Tribunal were to adopt such a position, it could block radical reform" (Hausner 1998, 16). Fortunately for reformers, the Court never did adopt such a stance, leaving the government free to implement privatization while "arguing that the 'social character' of the pension system related to the whole system and not to its individual parts" (Hausner 1998, 17).

The Legislative Council   A key advisor to the Prime Minister is the Legislative Council, a group which is comprised of "established, mainly older lawyers [most of whom] opposed the proposed reforms, particularly the mandatory fully-funded second pillar, which they regarded as contrary to the basic principles of solidarity and state guarantees underlying a pension system as they understood it" Nelson 1998, 28). In part to allay their fears, and to co-opt any future rulings by the Constitutional Tribunal, the state agreed to guarantee the mandatory accounts by "underwriting any deficits" they may encounter (Nelson 1998, 28). Furthermore, a compromise was "worked out with a key member of the Council" whereby the PAYG pillar would receive more than half (5/8ths) of an individual's contribution, while diverting the remainder to the individual private account (Nelson 1988, 28; Hausner 1998).

ZUS The final actor to consider is the management of the existing PAYG system. Clearly, the proposed reforms would have significant financial and bureaucratic consequences for the ZUS. However, unlike its opposite number in Hungary, ZUS never opposed the development of mandatory private accounts. As Hausner, the Plenipotentiary, makes clear, "cooperation with the management of [ZUS] ... played a key role ... for both substantive and personnel reasons" (Hausner 1998, 22). Orenstein (2000) attributes ZUS's willingness to cooperate to both institutional features and the nature of its leadership. In terms of the former, ZUS was assured a significant role in the new system, and hence "was not threatened institutionally by reform plans ... as the Pension Insurance Fund [PIF] was in Hungary" (Orenstein 2000, 43). As for leadership, he argues that ZUS was far more agreeable as its president was a political appointee of the Prime Minister, whereas in Hungary, the PIF "was an independently-elected body with substantial trade union representation and intransigent leadership" (Orenstein 2000, 43). The bottom-line is that there was no real opposition to overcome from the existing system; so long as it was consulted and included in the new arrangements, ZUS cooperated with the plenipotentiary in designing and, despite technical delays on its part, implementing the new system.

Theoretical Expectations

With the actors and their preferences so described, I turn now to the model of collective action and the ability of like-minded individuals to influence the reform process. The first challenge facing any such group is to overcome the barriers inherent in collective action. The second is to influence the political process through democratic means. While corruption and bribery offer one route to groups that lack a sizeable electoral base but do possess significant financial resources, the goal here is to assess the level of democratic consolidation. So while such activities were part of the political scene to a degree, the real question is whether or not voters and interest groups could influence the political process *without* having to purchase what they wanted. Put simply, to what degree does the political process functions in a democratic fashion? Can interest groups, which overcome their own internal barriers to collective action, influence the political process without having to rely on bribery or corruption? If so, under what circumstances? To assess these questions, I begin with those who sought to create mandatory, individually fully-funded, private pension accounts.

Implementing a Mixed Pillar Model

Table 3.5 summarizes both the likelihood of collective action and of subsequent influence for those seeking to adopt the new pension orthodoxy. It suggests that while little was to be expected from the poorest element of Polish society, wealthier individuals and households, who were also the biggest proponents of radical reform, were very likely to overcome the barriers before them. The biggest relative winners of the transition were aided by a dense membership concentration that facilitated the twin tasks of recognizing their common interests, and coordinating their activities. Likewise, they benefited from both their large quantity of disposable income, and the presence of some members with incomes well above the group average. Groups with positively skewed resource distributions are more likely to contain a sub-group willing undertake the cost and challenge of organizing the masses. In this regard, the wealthier winners not only benefited themselves, but the aggregate of those seeking to introduce mandatory private accounts as well.

The largest segment of pro-privatization support was comprised of the Little Losers, that is those left slightly behind financially by the transition to a market economy. At 34.3% of the total population, this portion of the transition's Little Losers constituted a large but geographically dispersed group, as members could be found in all but one of the forty-six regions for which data is available.[17] Further lessening the likelihood of their successful organization was the lack of easily mobilized resources (financial or personnel), and the absence of resource heterogeneity within the group. The latter is particularly onerous for larger groups, which often require a political entrepreneur to get the ball rolling.

In terms of the nature of the benefit sought, I would argue that jointness of supply is irrelevant. Private pension accounts are essentially private goods, not public or collective ones. While there would be definite spillover effects, particularly to the capital market and the supply of savings, such features did not play a prominent role in the debate over how best to reform the system. What remains relevant, however, are the non-exclusionary benefits offered by their collective efforts and the increasing returns to organization offered by their objective. Although the accounts would be individual in nature, and hence exclusionary, the issue in terms of collective action is whether or not the objective sought creates an incentive to free ride. In this regard, creating mandatory private accounts does because if an individual were in favor of their introduction, one could free ride on the contributions and efforts of others to bring them about. Because they were to be mandatory, one could not be denied the benefit of their existence simply because she had failed to contribute to their creation. This incentive to free ride lowers the probability of successful collective action for all groups.

---

17   Until 1999, there were 49 voivodships (regions/provinces) in Poland that were broken up into 52 electoral districts; most districts corresponded to a single voivodship. Following reforms passed in 1998, the 49 areas were collapsed into 16 administrative provinces as part of new 3-tier administrative system. The 52 electoral districts were maintained. The 1998 CBOS Government and International Relations Survey (#9825), used to measure attitudes over pension reform alternatives, only contains data on 46 of the 49 voivodships.

Table 3.5   **The Likelihood of Collective Action in Support of Mandatory Private Accounts**

	Big Losers	Little Losers	Little Winners	Big Winners	Aggregate
Group Characteristics					
Geography	Diffuse (-)	Diffuse (-)	Diffuse (-)	Dense (+)	Diffuse (-)
Resource Quantity	Low (-)	High (+)	High (+)	High (+)	High (+)
Resource Mobility	Low (-)	Low (-)	Moderate (0/+)	High (+)	Moderate (0/+)
Resource Heterogeneity	No (-)	No (-)	No (-)	Yes (+)	Yes (+)
Interest Heterogeneity	Yes (+)	Yes (+)	Yes (+)	Yes (+)	Yes (+)
Electoral Appeal	Moderate	Very High	Moderate	Moderate	Very High
Nature of the Objective					
Joint Supply	Moot	Moot	Moot	Moot	Moot
Exclusive Benefits	No (-)	No (-)	No (-)	No (-)	No (-)
Increasing Returns (group size)	Yes (-) (small)	Yes (+) (large)	Yes (-) (small)	Yes (-) (small)	Yes (+) (large)
Environment					
Other Actors	Yes (+)	Yes (+)	Yes (+)	Yes (+)	Yes (+)
Likelihood of Organizing	Low	Moderate	Low to Moderate	High	High
Likelihood of Influence	Moderate	Very High	Moderate	Moderate	Very High

A more variable effect was caused by the increasing returns to organization offered by such accounts. If there are enough potential members to drive down the initially high per-capita cost of organizing the group, then a positive incentive is introduced for political entrepreneurs to get the ball rolling. In the aggregate, this was not a problem, however, within each of the income groupings, size matters. For small groups, the presence of increasing returns (i.e., a decreasing cost function) makes collective action less likely. Therefore, only the Little Losers as a group, independent of the other income classifications, were in a position to take advantage of this incentive.

For those groups that did manage to organize, the likelihood of political influence was either moderate or very high (the coding scheme of all variables is provided in Appendix 2). Measured as the number of districts where the group constituted 10% or more of the vote, the results ranged from 26 (the Big Winners) to all 46 (the Little

Losers) districts for which data was available. In the aggregate, supporters of private accounts could deliver between 50–100% of the votes in every district. Put simply, if they managed to organize and lend their collective voices to the process, it was incredibly unlikely that politicians would fail listen.

Rejecting the Mixed Pillar Model and Mandatory Private Accounts

Table 3.6 provides a similar summary for those interested in maintaining the PAYG system without the addition of new individually fully-funded private accounts. While collective action seems somewhat likely in the aggregate, the subdivision into the relative winners and losers suggests that no group was overly likely to organize or yield sufficient influence by itself. In other words, without collaboration across income levels, it is very unlikely that opponents of the mixed pillar model would be able to influence the process, much less prevent its adoption.

Table 3.6   The Likelihood of Collective Action in Support of Reforming and Maintaining the PAYG System

	Big Losers	*Little Losers*	*Little Winners*	*Big Winners*	*Aggregate*
Group Characteristics					
Geography	Dense (+)	Diffuse (-)	Dense (+)	Dense (+)	Diffuse (-)
Resource Quantity	Low (-)	Low (-)	Moderate (0/+)	High (+)	High (+)
Resource Mobility	Moderate (0/+)	Low (-)	High (+)	High (+)	Moderate (0/+)
Resource Heterogeneity	No (-)	No (-)	No (-)	No (-)	Yes (+)
Interest Heterogeneity	Yes (+)	Yes (+)	Yes (+)	Yes (+)	Yes (+)
Electoral Appeal	Very Low	Low	Low	Low	High
Nature of the Objective					
Joint Supply (group size)	No (0/-) (small)	No (0/-) (small)	No (0/-) (small)	No (0/-) (small)	No (-) (large)
Exclusive Benefits	No (-)	No (-)	No (-)	No (-)	No (-)
Increasing Returns (group size)	Yes (-) (small)	Yes (-) (small)	Yes (-) (small)	Yes (-) (small)	Yes (+) (large)
Environment					
Other Actors	Yes (+)	Yes (+)	Yes (+)	Yes (+)	Yes (+)
Likelihood of Organizing	Low to Moderate	Low	Moderate	Moderate	Moderate to High
Likelihood of Influence	Very Low	Low	Low	Low	High

On the positive side of the ledger, opponents benefited from an overall resource base that included lots of potential members, some with a sizeable degree of disposable income. The aggregate was also marked by a resource distribution that was both positively skewed (in the sense of being statistically significantly), as well as a degree of interest heterogeneity among members. Both of these factors increase the likelihood that a subgroup will act differently from the rest of the group and undertake the added burden of organizing the masses (Oliver et al 1985).

As for the nature of the objective, things were less promising. Unlike supporters of radical reform, those seeking the maintenance of the current system had to face the issue of joint supply. Barring a soft budget constraint, a PAYG pension system cannot be supplied jointly. If a hard budget constraint is imposed, meaning that no deficits are allowed to accumulate within the system, then the total amount of funds available for benefits is limited by the contributions made. As a result, one person's consumption of the public good automatically reduces the amount available to everyone else. Such a constraint was part of then Labor Minister Miller's 1995 plan to rationalize the existing system.[18] In the long-run, the country's aging population meant that without subsidies from the state budget, the per-capita benefits available under a purely PAYG system would have to fall, or alternatively, that the per-capita contribution rate would have to rise beyond its current level of 45% of gross income. This lack of jointness lowers the probability of collective action as the size of the group gets larger. Also hindering their efforts was the possibility of members free riding. Since the PAYG system was mandatory for all, each individual had an incentive to let others extend the resources and effort to maintain it in its current form. If they were successful, the individual could not be denied the benefit of their success.

What did work in their favor were the increasing returns offered by proposals that included an increase in the retirement age. By increasing it to 65 for both men and women, which Miller's proposal called for, it was possible to reverse, albeit temporarily, the upward trend in the system dependency ratio. With each one-year increase in the retirement age, the number of contributors to the system would rise while at the same time decreasing the number of recipients. This provided a strong incentive for both the young and the old to raise age limit as much as possible. By increasing the number of contributors, it became theoretically possible to lower the monthly payroll withholdings of each worker without changing the total amount of funds available, effectively lowering the per-capita cost of the system for each young person. Likewise, reducing the number of claimants would make it possible to maintain the per-capita benefits received by pensioners, or even increase them, without effecting the overall fiscal balance of the system. Although the long-term stability of this arrangement would ultimately depend on demographic trends and the fertility rate of future generations, in the short-term, these increasing returns to organization created a positive incentive to organize collectively.

---

18   For a summary of Miller's 1995 proposal, see Orenstein 2000, 41.

The chief problem facing this group of like-minded individuals is that collectively they comprised less than 17% of the population. While in the aggregate, the group could deliver 10% of the vote in 33 of the 46 districts, the electoral threat posed by any one of the income groups alone was not credible. This was particularly true of the transition's relative winners as the richest Poles opposed to private accounts constituted 10% of the vote in only one district, while the Little Winners did so in only two. This is perhaps the strongest evidence yet that the opposition to a mixed pillar system would have to work collectively if it was to have any influence on the process.

The Politics of Pension Reform

The 1993–1997 Government

Despite its internal cleavages, the SLD had committed itself to reforming the pension system along the lines laid out by the World Bank, the Argentine experience, and the new pension orthodoxy. As noted above, the center of activity was located in the Plenipotentiary for Social Security Reform, which was initially focused on creating the new private accounts while expressly leaving reforms to the existing PAYG pillar until after the 1997 election. From public opinion surveys, government officials knew that most people "wanted more radical reform" than what was being proposed by the Labor Minister (Orenstein 2000, 41). What public opposition did exist largely rested with the transition's relative financial losers (see Table 3.3), and the nation's trade unions. Given a correspondence of interest and membership, the unions became the organizing force for opposition to the new fully funded individual pillar.[19] Consequently, the Tripartite Commission became one of the major focal points for discussion and negotiation.

According the government Plenipotentiary, "most discussions concerned the plan to use revenue from privatization to finance future [system] deficits" (Hausner 1998, 22). While Solidarity wanted to ensure that people "would gain something specific from privatization," particularly those left behind financially by the transition to the market economy, the government was unwilling to adopt the plan in full (Hausner 1998, 26). The resulting compromise involving the NIFs described above satisfied both parties. From the union's perspective, the transition's relative losers would able to acquire share certificates which they could, if they were under the age of fifty, voluntarily deposit in their new, private pension fund as seed money.[20] From the

---

19   Many retirees were also members of the trade unions through such bodies as the Council of Labour Veterans contained with the OPZZ (Müller 1999, 114). In the early 1990s, it was the unions and pensioners that fought the piecemeal and *ad hoc* changes implemented by the various governments, a battle that ultimately ended in the formers victory before the Constitutional Tribunal.

20   To further appease concerns that the elderly would be adversely affected by the proposed changes, those over 50 were entitled to purchase up to three share certificates in the

government's perspective, the plan allowed them to cover the deficits that would be created in the pubic pillar *without* having to divert scarce resources from the general budget or raise the contribution rate. This was critical as it had previously pledged publicly that the reforms would not lead to 1) an increase in taxes, 2) an increase in the mandatory contributions, or 3) a reduction in the level of benefits provided (Hausner 1998, 30).

A further result of these negotiations was the choice offered to those between 30–50 of entering the new system or remaining in the purely PAYG arrangement, something "which had not initially been anticipated" by anyone (Hausner 1998, 31). The choice evolved as a negotiated solution to the problem of determining the actual pension amount for different age groups. Satisfied that their concerns, and those of their members, had been taken seriously and incorporated, the unions voted in April 1997 to send the resulting proposal to parliament with their unqualified support.

With the union's approval won, the government undertook a major public relations campaign to both inform the public about the proposal, and to highlight the broad consensus that had been marshaled behind its creation (Orenstein 2000, 47). It was heavily supported in this endeavor by the media, which in the eyes of the Plenipotentiary played "an enormously positive role" by not only providing extensive coverage of the problems facing the pension system, but doing so "for the most part ... in a competent and fair manner" (Hausner 1998, 30). Assisting with the funding of this public relations effort, including several of the informational study trips to Chile and Argentina for politicians and journalists alike, was the World Bank.

The other source of opposition came from special interests. At one level, numerous actors attempted to protect special privileges already contained in the new system. Chief among them were miners who were entitled under the law to more than double the average pension and to retire anytime after having worked 25 years (Cain 1999, 162; Hausner 1998, Table 1). At another level, however, some domestic actors were sufficiently powerful to choose a different paradigm for themselves altogether. The most powerful of these was the agricultural sector, forcefully represented at every step by the PSL. The party was able to credibly threaten a veto of any legislation that attempted to encroach on the privileges of its members. It further used its position to demand and receive a separate system for the nation's farmers that was heavily subsidized and only required participants to contribute 10% of the gross income; the standard rate is 45% among industrial workers (Cain 1999, 162). This conforms to Orenstein's hypothesis that "the impact of interests groups depends on their relation to ... important veto players...," as the agriculture community was the backbone of the PSL (Orenstein 2000, 11).

Another group to exclude itself from the new reforms were segments of the legal community, which was always suspicious of individually funded accounts. Working through the Minister of Justice, they submitted a private member's bill to the legislature ensuring that employees of the court and the public prosecutor's

---

NIFs (Hausner 1998, 27).

office were not only excluded from the new system, but that they would also enjoy a separate pension system fully funded by the state budget (Hausner 1998, 23). Between the farmers and lawyers, over 30% of the labor force managed to exclude itself from the new system in favor a different paradigm altogether. So while the state, along with the World Bank, set out to create a universal system, powerful domestic interests forced it to compromise on the scope and nature of the reforms.

While unions and special interests were critical in shaping an acceptable reform package, "the main unofficial mechanism for achieving consensus took the form of systematic consultations ... with parliamentary deputies" which were coordinated through an "extraordinary parliamentary commission" (Hausner 1998, 33). This working arrangement, which included opposition party members, was critical to the reform continuity that took place following the change in government in 1997. In the end, with farmers and lawyers having exempted themselves and the unions and special interests having won concessions and adjustments, 90% of the parliament voted to create new, mandatory private accounts (Orenstein 2000, 45; Hausner 1998, 31).

The 1997–2001 Government

Although the new Solidarity-led government attempted to distance itself from the SLD and considered revisiting the arrangement on using privatization funds, its coalition agreement with the UW "recommitted the government to pension reform as part of an aggressive package" of reforms covering social welfare and local government administration (Orenstein 2000, 46). Adding to the pressure for continuity were "powerful constituencies [created by the private pillar legislation] that would force the next government to complete reform legislation" (Orenstein 2000, 45). These included not only existing government agencies like ZUS, but also new a bureaucratic agency (UNFE) to regulate the private funds, as well as private actors within the banking and financial community who expected to manage those funds. Continuing the process of consultation and negotiation through the Office of the Plenipotentiary, work began on reforming the retirement age, occupational privileges and the funding of the PAYG pillar.

When the new right-of center government took office, the existing plan, contained in the *Security Through Diversity* proposal, called for equalizing the retirement age for men and women at a uniform 62 years. This idea was quickly challenged by "conservative politicians ... [who] were attached to a more traditional view of women's role in society and proposed differential pension ages of 60 for women and 65 for men" (Chlon 1999, 15). In justifying their position, they pointed out that the effective retirement age was due to increase anyway as incentives for early retirement were already scheduled to be withdrawn. This provoked vigorous opposition from most (left-of center) trade unions and the various occupations with special privileges allowing them to retire even earlier, such as miners (after 25 years), teachers (after 30 years), or ballet dancers (at age 38!) (Chlon et al 1999, fn 13). Adding to the bargaining power of such groups was a Constitutional Tribunal ruling that forced the government to recognize acquired rights to early retirement under the old system. As a result, the government agreed not to change the retirement rules for anyone who was within eight years of becoming eligible for early retirement. Although this meant that the existing early retirement options would stay in effect until 2006, some of the unions continued to press for an even longer extension (Chlon 1999, 16).[21]

While the UW, a party of mostly young urban professionals, supported the idea of increasing the retirement age, the coalition-leading AWS opted to retain the existing retirement age of 60 for women and 65 for men. However, in an effort to raise the ages indirectly, and thereby increase (decrease) the number of contributors (pensioners), an incentive scheme was added under which retirement benefits would increase by 9–10% annually for each year worked beyond the retirement age (Müller 1999, 117). While the left of center trade unions were disappointed at the decision not to lower the retirement, they "did not mobilize to oppose the pension reform" legislation, although they did send "qualified negative opinions to parliament" (Orenstein 2000, 47). However, by not lowering the retirement age for men to 62, the AWS-UW coalition was acting in the interests of its core, right of center, urban constituents.

Closely related to the issue of the retirement age were the various occupational privileges that covered more than half the work force (e.g., miners, farmers, teachers, railroad workers, military personal). Recognizing that the challenge involved in curtailing these special interests could derail the entire process, "a pact was reached between the government and the trade unions to allow the legislative process to go ahead, with the thorny issue of how to adapt special privileges to be negotiated with union representatives starting in the middle of 1998" (Orenstein 2000, 47). However, with local elections scheduled at about the same time, those negotiations were eventually put off until 1999. In the end, the government opted to enact necessary reforms to the current pillar without tackling the problem of its uneven application directly. It did, however, try to equalize the system by more indirect means such as tightening the contribution-benefit link contained in the public pillar.

To do this, reformers drew on the experiences of Sweden and Latvia in adopting a notional defined contribution system (NDC) in which each employee's contribution to the PAYG system was treated as if it had been deposited into an individual account that would accrue interest at a fixed rate until they retired. In reality, the system was still PAYG as current contributions were used to pay for current benefits, however, by using NDCs, the contribution-benefit link is significantly strengthened and the

---

21   A 1999 Constitutional Tribunal ruling finally settled the matter by setting the minimum vesting period for acquiring a right to early retirement under the old system at one third of the required tenure. This meant that a teacher who had worked for ten years (one third of the required 30 years) could not have her right to early retirement taken away, but one that had only worked for nine years could. By extension, this provided the government with the legal backing to eventually phase out occupational early-retirement privileges. To date, however, no government has been able to pass legislation ending the occupation privileges as almost the entire workforce is covered by at least one special privilege (early retirement, a lower contribution rate, higher benefits...).

transparency of the PAYG pillar was greatly increased. Furthermore, it was hoped that the increased transparency "might ease the [subsequent] elimination of privileges for particular groups" (Nelson 1998, 26).

Under the new NDC system, individual pensions were a function of the virtual capital contained in one's PAYG account and the average life-expectancy (of both men and women taken together) at retirement (Müller 1999, 117).[22] To function properly, this required a calculation of a beginning balance based on the employment history of everyone born after December 31, 1948. Unfortunately, ZUS had never maintained individual records of past contributions, as there was no need for such information in state-sponsored socialism. Therefore, the agency was charged with calculating everyone's so-called "starting capital" based on the old pension formula and all the acquired rights an individual may have accumulated under the old system. The resulting amount would be credited to each persons PAYG account to which their subsequent contributions (plus interest) would be added.[23]

Conclusion

By the late 1990s, the Polish pension system was in dire need of reform. Hampered by a fiscal crisis brought on by an expanding pool of recipients and a declining pool of contributors, the PAYG system had become financially unviable as means to secure the well being of future generations. While both international and domestic actors had advocated a Latin American-style solution since as early as 1991, the idea was initially met with extreme skepticism, particularly by most legal experts.[24] Eventually, however, the fiscal strains grew to the point that Ministry of Finance (MOF) became a vocal and forceful advocate for radical reform. Faced with a large international debt obligation and impending negotiations with the European Union over enlargement, the MOF could ill afford the fiscal costs of an unreformed pension system.[25] Although this too was insufficient to break the domestic deadlock, rulings

---

22   A mathematical simplification of an individual pension calculation (P) can be defined by the formula $P=C/E$, where C equals the total notional capital contained within a persons PAYG account, and E equals the average life-expectancy at the time of retirement (Müller 1999, 117).

23   It was estimated that it would take ZUS until 2004 to determine the millions of individual starting balances. Though past experience suggested delays were likely, the first cohort to retire under the new system will not do so until 2010, which should leave ZUS sufficient time to make the necessary calculations.

24   In 1991, two Polish social security experts, the former ZUS president Wojciech Topiński and Marian Wiśnieski, proposed reforms closely modeled on the Chilean experience. The proposal went nowhere as it was "deemed too radical a departure from the status quo" (Müller 1999, 105-106).

25   Poland, Hungary and the Czech Republic joined the EU on May 1, 2004. While a date has not been set for joining the Euro-zone, the primary conditions for membership in the Union's common currency are fiscal discipline and a balanced budget. Currently, members

by the Constitutional Tribunal and the removal of a hard-line opponent in the Labor Ministry, eventually brought the proposal to the negotiating table in 1995–1996.

What followed was a remarkably open and consensus driven effort to fundamentally reform the pension system in manner that promised to provide security for the next several generations. Though supported by a majority of the public, which had generally lost its confidence in the existing system by 1996, the reforms were not without opposition. The bulk of this opposition was comprised of those left financially behind by the transition to a market economy, particularly the middle-aged who no longer had thirty years to save for their retirement. In what amounted to a correspondence of both interest and membership, these actors found their voice through the trade unions that were formally represented on the Tripartite Commission.

As a result of their collective pressure, the draft legislation was amended to give those aged 30–50 the option of entering the new arrangement or staying in public PAYG system. In addition, those over fifty were allowed to purchase extra ownership certificates in the NIFs as an added source of income when they retired. Recognizing that many of the transition's relative losers would opt to remain in the current system (see Table 3.3), the unions also sought to ensure that the divergence of contributions to new private accounts would not affect the level of benefits they received. Likewise, the government was aware that "without the support of the middle-aged population - which has the most to lose if reform [did] not take place - it [would] be difficult to carry out any type of reform whatsoever" (Hausner 1999, 30). As a result, the two-sides worked out a compromise that not only guaranteed the benefits to those who remained in the current system, but also insured those who opened a new private account against potential deficits.

What is remarkable about this process is that the opposition represented a clear minority of the population. Although the government had by 1996 a clear vision of what it wanted to do, and was supported in its efforts by more than half the population, the minority's concerns were both solicited and taken into account. There was no tyranny of the majority. Nor was there outright capture of the political process by minority special interests (e.g., Hellman 1998). In this regard, the "support of partisan actors across the political spectrum is particular to Poland, and the manner in which it was achieved is instructive for other democratic countries contemplating reform" (Orenstein 2000, 42). Therefore, if one applies Przeworski (1991) or Linz and Stepan's (1996) notions of what constitutes a functioning democratic system, then Poland must be counted among them.

---

are allowed to float no more than a 3% deficit annually. The fiscal strains of an unreformed pension system would make this all but impossible.

Chapter 4

The Case of Hungary

Like Poland, Hungary chose to introduce a mandatory but privately managed second pillar as part of its overall pension program. However, while the end result mimics that of its neighbor, the path taken and the details of the final legislation suggest some important differences. One unique feature was the inclusion of a guaranteed rate of return on these new private accounts; a guarantee backed by the central budget and general taxation. In doing so, the reformers re-introduced an element of inter-generational financing, as future taxpayers may now be required to compensate future pensioners for any relative losses incurred in their private accounts. Furthermore, the circular financing and investment requirements of these new private accounts effectively makes the nominally privatized pension system a PAYG system in disguise as all current contributions are still being used to provide benefits to current retirees. While the pension orthodoxy advocated by the World Bank and others allowed for some degree of variation in its application, this is by no means what they had in mind. The whole idea of pension privatization was to reduce, if not eliminate, this kind of cross-generational dependency. In accounting for this deviation, the Hungarian case reveals both the strength and limitations of opposition groups in general, and unions in particular. I begin, however, with the distributional consequences of the privatization period, and the creation of relative winners and losers.

Privatization in Hungary

In the ten years from 1988 to 1998, Hungary had three different and quite unique governments: a Communist regime that survived until 1990; a right of center government led by József Antall from 1990–1994; and a government made-up of reformed ex-communists and pro-market liberal democrats from 1994–1998.[1] As a result, the Hungarian experience with privatization is one complete with outright policy reversals and a great deal of uncertainty and change. Given these shifts in policy, it is not surprising that different relative winners and losers were created at different times by different programs.

---

[1] Antall died in office on December 13, 1993 and was replaced by the Minister of the Interior Péter Boross. Despite this, the entire period 1990–1994 is normally referred to as the Antall government as the first round of the 1994 election was held less than six months after his death. Boross's time in office is of no consequence here.

Before examining these periods, however, the legacy of the communist era must be briefly considered in terms of ownership and control. Building off reforms begun in 1968, managers and employees of Hungarian SOEs had been slowing gathering both control over the resources within their purview, and a considerable degree of autonomy from state ministries. Using their relative discretion under goulash communism, enterprise managers went on an international borrowing binge in the 1970s as the world's capital markets became inundated with petrodollars.[2] Unfortunately, like the rest of the borrowers, Hungary suffered severely as interest rose sharply in the 1980s. By 1988, Hungary had one of the world's highest per capita debt ratios and the highest such ratio in all of Europe (Fletcher 1995, 39). It was into this environment of heavily indebted, semi-autonomous firms that the process of privatization began in 1988.

The Period 1988–1990[3]

Designed with the extreme indebtedness of these firms in mind, the Communist regime introduced three main avenues for privatization: private placement, public offering, and so-called spontaneous methods. Through private placement and public offering, a heavily indebted firm placed a portion of its shares either in the hands of its creditors in exchange for debt relief (i.e., placement) or with new investors (i.e., offering) through the Budapest stock exchange (BSE) which reopening in 1990. The hope was that by placing a portion of their equity with either local banks, or directly with foreign investors, these firms would be able to raise the capital needed to stabilize operations in the face of reduced or discontinued state subsidies. Both programs, however, suffered from considerable public backlash following a number of share price fixing scandals and an ever-growing belief "that the Hungarian property was

---

2   Goulash communism was the term given to the relaxation of direct government intervention in the economy following the Soviet crackdowns in 1956. Essentially, an implicit deal was struck between the Hungarian leaders and their society: in exchange for not attempting another such revolt, a greater array of consumer goods would be allowed and the orthodoxness of the communist economic model would be lessened. Petrodollars refer to the huge influx of deposits to Western banks following the oil price hikes stemming from the 1973 Arab-Israeli war. Awash in funds, international lending rates fell dramatically, and as a result both developing and several communist countries took advantage of the opportunity and dramatically increased their borrowing. The crunch came a decade later as interests rose dramatically as a result of changes in the United States.

3   This period can also be considered one of pre-privatization as many of the transaction were not technically privatizing, but rather comprised the transfer of ownership to new or established state-owned entities, such as the state-owned banks or state-owned suppliers. Privatization in the "narrow sense of transferring property rights to new private actors" began in a more structure manner only in 1990 with the creation of the State Property Agency and is "better gauged by the quantity of foreign investment" (Frydman et al 1993, 133).

being sold out on the cheap to foreigners" (Akov 1998, 9).[4] From the government's perspective, however, sales to foreigners were crucial given the country's massive long-term debt obligations that stood in 1990 at more than $18 billion dollars (World Bank 2000). For this reason, the government had decided against the kind of give-away privatization schemes that Poland and the Czech Republic would later embark on whereby shares in SOEs were distributed to the public at-large either for free or for a nominal fee.[5] In the end, there was a widespread sentiment within the government that cash-based sales were the only way to go, and given the costs involved, that meant sales to foreigners.[6]

The dominant method of privatization during this period, however, was one whereby the managers of SOEs initiated and controlled "the privatization of their own firms," normally through conversion into joint-stock companies (Fletcher 1995, 30). These so-called spontaneous conversions often amounted to "employee or management buyouts at low prices, with [the] proceeds not accruing to the government," but rather to the enterprises themselves (Estrin 1990, 11). This too was fraught with scandal as many of the arrangements resulted in the "the effective asset stripping of the enterprise" (Lawrence 1993, 394). One common approach was to simply spin-off only the valuable portions of the SOE into a new enterprise, often in a joint-venture with a foreign partner, leaving the state to privatize or liquidate an entity with little value, no real productive assets, and *all* of the original enterprise's debts and liabilities.

In sum, there were two central problems with this early privatization period. First, there were was a growing belief among the public that the process was thoroughly tainted with scandal, and that the country's assets were being overtaken by foreigners. The only Hungarians who seemed to be benefiting were "the Communist party nomenclatura, who were lining their pockets as they receded from political power" (Fletcher 1995, 152). Second, there was a growing division between those SOEs that could attract buyers and foreign investors and those that could not. As a result, the period marks the beginnings of a widening income and asset gap between privatization's relative winners and losers. Moving from a fairly egalitarian society only a few years before under state socialism, income inequality was slowly becoming institutionalized by the runaway process of spontaneous privatization. A representation of this widening gap can be seen in Table 4.1, which provides a demographic assessment of this first period.

---

4   For an account of stock market manipulations, particularly the 1990 scandal involving IBUSZ, the largest Hungarian travel agency, see Fletcher 1995, 44–46.

5   For more on the voucher privatization in the Czech Republic, see Chapter 5, Frydman et al, 1993; Estrin 1994; Orenstein 1996; and Earle 1997. For more privatization in Poland, see Chapter 3, Frydman et al 1993; and Blaszczyk 1995.

6   An additional constraint was the limited availability of domestic savings. With over $6.7 billion dollars worth of property awaiting privatization, "it would have been unrealistic to expect Hungarians to participate" to a high degree as the nation's Gross Domestic Savings was only around $9 billion (Fletcher 1995, 147; World Bank 2000).

Table 4.1   The Relative Winners and Losers of the Transition, 1990

	Percentage of Households where at least one individual worked for or as	*Household Income Quintile (%)*				
		1st	*2nd*	*3rd*	*4th*	*5th*
Privatization	Fully privatized firm	7.7	11.6	18.0	27.3	35.4
	Partially state-owned firm	7.8	9.0	23.7	28.8	30.7
	Full state-owned firm	6.8	14.6	24.5	27.4	26.7
Foreign Ownership	Wholly foreign-owned firm	0.0	3.5	13.8	41.4	41.4
	Partly foreign-owned firm	6.0	8.0	22.9	27.9	35.5
	Wholly Hungarian-owned	8.4	13.7	22.1	27.0	28.8
Type of Firm	Joint stock company	3.5	5.8	23.0	28.0	39.7
	Partnership	6.5	9.2	21.7	27.1	35.4
	Private enterprise	10.9	14.9	14.9	25.7	33.7
Type of Job	Top manager	0.0	2.1	2.1	16.7	79.2
	Middle manager	0.0	3.3	6.6	21.3	68.9
	Lower manager	2.3	6.7	18.0	28.1	44.9
	Unskilled worker	15.7	20.3	27.6	24.4	12.0
	Performer of odd jobs	45.2	21.4	7.1	19.1	7.1
Pensioners	Old age pension	26.6	29.3	19.8	14.9	9.5
	Disability pension	23.2	27.3	22.9	17.6	9.0
	Widow's pension	48.3	24.5	12.6	7.0	7.7
Residence	Budapest	13.6	16.7	17.8	20.7	31.1
	Other major city	20.6	24.4	21.0	16.8	17.2
	Village	25.6	22.2	19.1	20.5	12.4
	Farm	31.8	36.4	18.2	13.6	0.0
Party Voted For in 1990 Parliamentary Election (column percentages)						
	MDF (winner)	31.1	34.7	30.3	30.3	30.1
	FkgP (coalition partner)	11.9	10.8	8.1	6.9	6.0
	KDNP (coalition partner)	7.4	4.2	3.1	4.4	4.2
	Fidesz	7.0	9.2	13.2	13.1	11.5
	MszP	2.9	7.8	8.1	6.4	12.9
	SZDSZ	14.4	14.8	21.4	22.6	23.3
	Does not know	21.4	14.0	10.6	9.1	5.7

Sample size: Individuals (7,125); Households (2,560); Quintiles (512).

Source: Hungarian Household Panel Survey, 1992.

The relative winners were largely those who worked for firms which attracted foreign investors and took advantage of the opportunity to reorganize themselves into a joint stock company or other type of legal entity; those who worked for a company so restructured where more then ten times as likely to be in the upper income quintile (Q5) as the bottom (Q1). The best method, however, for avoiding membership in the lowest income grouping, was to work for a foreign owned firm. Of those working for a multinational corporation (MNC), nearly 85% earned enough to place themselves in the upper 40% of households while not a single employee found himself among the bottom 30%. A strong geographical concentration is also clear as over 50% of those living in Budapest belonged to the nation's wealthiest households, while nearly 50% of those living in villages, and nearly 70% of those living on farms, belonged to the poorest. Also among those hardest hit were women as almost 50% of those collecting a widow's pension belonged to the lowest income households, while those collecting either an old age or disability pension faired considerably better.

The Period 1990–1994

While the principle of privatization was still widely supported in 1990, it significantly helped shape the debate leading up to the first post-communist election, which was ultimately won by the Hungarian Democratic Forum (MDF) on a pledge to limit past abuses and expand the ranks of those benefiting from privatization.[7] One group that Antall particularly hoped to reach out to was the new middle class he hoped his policies would create. In support of this objective, four main programs were undertaken: restitution; the privatization of small retail shops and services industries; an Employee Stock Option Program (ESOP); and the issuance of Existence or E-loans.[8] The result of extensive and difficult debate, including rulings by the Constitutional Court, the restitution program created compensation vouchers for those whose property had been confiscated after June 6, 1949 (the date of the communist coup)[9]. By imposing a modest per-capita limit on claims, the traditional power of large landowners was broken in favor of "what the government perceived as its prime constituency: the (now to be resurrected) postwar middle class" (Comisso

---

7   For more on the development of the party system, see Lawson 1999; Márkus 1999, 1996; Tóka 1998; Ágh and Ilonszki 1996; Ágh and Kurán 1995; and Cox and Furlong 1995.

8   Restitution, or reprivatization, involved the return of, or compensation for, assets seized during the communist era. The Hungarian experience differs remarkably from both the Czech Republic, which returned the physical property that had been confiscated to the original owners or their descendants, and Poland, which failed to enact any restitution program at all. The passage of this highly contentious legislation provides a useful insight to the political realities of time as the "end result was not intended by anyone," but satisfied everyone, including the Courts, enough that it could be enacted (Peter Mihályi 2001, personal communication). For an account of the program's development and passage, see Comisso 1995.

9   These vouchers were used to purchase set-aside shares that resulted from an "internal rule" adopted by the State Property Agency (SPA) that, in general, "no more than 51% of any enterprise" could be sold to foreigners (Peter Mihályi 2001, personal communication). The remaining 49% was set aside for programs like restitution and transfer to municipalities.

1995, 215). This class was also expected to benefit from the sale of the small and retail sectors; however, due to overvaluation by the State Property Agency (SPA), "nearly half the auctions [were] unsuccessful" as starting prices were "so high that nobody was interested in buying" (Frydman et al 1993, 136). Eventually, initial valuations/expectations were scaled back and by April 1992 over 10,000 shops and restaurants had been sold.

The two most well known privatization programs from this period, however, were the Employee Stock Ownership Program (ESOP) and the so-called Existence or E-loans. The ESOP was a management-employee buyout program under which a minority of employees (25%) could propose a purchase plan with shares discounted up to 50%. What separates this insider-program from earlier ones is that the SPA actively "attempted to screen out those ESOP buy-outs that were actually [just] management as opposed to management-employee" proposals (Filatotchev et al 1996, 71). This remarkably successful program resulted in the purchase of 148 firms by the end of 1994, with employees holding an average of 56% of the firm's shares, a stark contrast to their average shareholding of just under 3.5% in all other privatized firms (Filatotchev et al 1996, 70).[10] For the first time, employees could point to tangible benefits as a result of privatization.

Less successful, however, was the E-Loan program, which distributed preferential loans guaranteed by the National Bank; these loans could be used to purchase assets through the ESOP, buy flats or start a new business.[11] Soon after their introduction, many within the SPA came to see the program as a mistake as the loans were used almost exclusively by already established and successful medium sized firms in an effort to grow larger. According to one former privatization official, the whole process was little more than "an income transfer to the nouveau-riche" and was consequently lobbied against by the agency and eventually done away with in 1995 (Interviewee's identity withheld).

The publicly stated goal of Antall's government had been "the creation of a broad and powerful domestic class of owners [which would facilitate] an efficient economic system," however, officials acknowledged in private, that "(w)e have to learn to accept politically that the main force of the new Hungarian bourgeoisie will be the 'nomenklatura bourgeoisie'" (quoted in Greskovits 1998, 28-9).[12] The

---

10   While shareholders, and therefore entitled to dividends and a share of capital gains, studies suggest that these benefits made up an "insignificant" component of an employee's income suggesting that, while owners, the real "focus of [their] attention was on receiving hire wages and keeping their jobs" (Filatotchev et al 1996, 71).

11   The range of things with which E-loans could be used was expanded to flats (apartments) and start-ups after initially poor demand from the general public.

12   This private acknowledgment is contained in document prepared by the Working Group on Economic Strategy (WGES). This group was set up by the Minister of Privatization (Tamás Szabó) as an institutional weapon against the Minister of Finance (Mihály Kupa) in what had become a fairly intense rivalry between the two men. Although the larger WGES program envisioned by its members never materialized, its origin and demise reveal a great

creation of this new class, in part by the programs described above, can be seen in Table 4.2.

Table 4.2   The Relative Winners and Losers of the Transition, 1994

	Percentage of Households where at least one individual worked for or as	Household Income Quintile (%)				
		1st	2nd	3rd	4th	5th
Privatization	Fully privatized firm	9.9	10.8	21.5	24.8	33.0
	Partially state-owned firm	5.4	12.6	23.4	28.4	30.3
	Full state-owned firm	7.8	12.7	20.5	31.8	27.1
Foreign Ownership	Wholly foreign-owned firm	0.0	3.3	20.0	29.5	30.6
	Partly foreign-owned firm	8.3	9.3	22.4	24.9	35.1
	Wholly Hungarian-owned	9.7	13.7	21.7	27.0	27.9
Type of Firm	Joint stock company	5.6	12.0	22.5	29.5	30.6
	Partnership	8.6	10.8	22.0	27.1	31.5
	Private enterprise	15.2	14.3	21.7	23.5	25.4
Type of Job	Top manager	0.0	2.0	2.0	15.7	80.4
	Middle manager	2.5	0.0	9.1	27.3	61.2
	Lower manager	2.7	5.3	10.7	36.0	45.3
	Self-employed	11.8	8.2	18.5	15.9	45.6
	Unskilled	19.4	28.8	22.9	20.6	8.2
Pensioners	Old age pension	21.7	28.4	22.1	15.7	12.1
	Disability pension	26.9	31.1	17.9	13.6	10.5
	Widow's pension	48.6	21.5	13.2	10.4	6.3
Residence	Budapest	9.5	13.7	19.2	24.8	32.7
	Other major city	20.8	22.0	20.8	20.8	15.7
	Village	27.2	25.3	19.7	15.8	12.1
	Farm	45.8	29.2	20.8	4.2	0.0
Changes	In the same quintile as 1990	44.0	31.0	28.0	35.0	52.0

Sample size: Individuals (6,379); Households (2,263); Quintiles (453).

Source: Hungarian Household Panel, Individual Survey collapsed to household level, 1994.

As before, the surest method of avoiding membership in the lowest income quintile was to work for a wholly owned foreign firm as nearly 78% of their employees belonged to the upper 40% of household. New however, is the emergence of the self-employed middle class. Approximately 80% of households were at least one member was self-employed and owned their own business belonged to one of the upper three income quintiles. However, reflective of the worsening economic situation is the diminished effect of privatization in general as households working for fully privatized firms are no longer more likely to belong to the upper quintiles

---

about the inner workings of the MDF government. See Greskovits (1998) for a more detailed account and further references.

than those working for SOEs. In essence, as a result of the transition-induced recession, simply being employed in the private sector no longer carried the same assurances it did earlier. What mattered more, in terms of increasing total household income, was working for either a foreign owned firm or working for one's self.

The Period 1994–1998

Although the Antall government had achieved many of its goals while in office, it was already clear by May 1991 that things were not going to end well for the MDF. Beginning late that spring and continuing throughout the remainder of its term, polls showed that its support had dropped to around 11%, after having been elected with over 40% of the vote in 1990. This dramatic fall from grace was due to a combination of intense fragmentation, scandals, a worsening economic recession, and the perceived "neglect or at least the inadequate treatment of the economic issues," the net result of which was an overwhelming crisis of legitimacy (Márkus 1996, 18).[13] The price of this neglect came in the form of a crushing defeat in the 1994 election at the hands of the former communists, who promised to enact both a stabilization program and accelerate the privatization process.[14]

More than anything else, what defines this period is the fundamental change in philosophy toward the whole endeavor of privatizing state assets. To this point, privatization had been conceived, as it had across the region, as comprising restitution/ compensation, small and retail sector privatization, and the transformation of the large-scale industries with separate policies and procedures drawn up for each. By the second half of 1994, however, many in the SPA began to see a single, fundamental difference between the very large companies and all the rest. More specifically, they came to believe that the future of Hungary lay with 50 or so companies that were absolutely crucial to the development and well being of the economy. These firms it was decided had to be "skillfully privatized into good hands and" for as

---

13   What shook the public's confidence in the government more than anything else, however, was the 1991 taxi-drivers' strike over proposed increases in the price of gasoline. The first major protest of the post-communist era, which began on the anniversary of the 1956 invasion, was by all accounts miserably handled by the government, which declared the protest illegal and threatened police action. The MDF never truly recovered from the weekend-long crisis.

14   The re-election of the former communists only four years into the transition must be understood in the broader context of the developing party system. For more extensive accounts, see Cox and Furlong 1995. In brief, polls from 1991 to the summer of 1993 all showed the League of Young Democrats (Fidesz) well out in front. However, in the summer of 1993, with less than a year to go until the election, the party imploded. Its most popular figure (Gábor Fodor) left the party, its ideology on social issues was changed from being rather liberal to being extremely conservative and, as a result, almost all of its supporters went elsewhere. Most it seems found their way to the reformed ex-communists who, having done reasonably well in the 1992 local elections, went on to win the 1994 national election in a landslide.

much money as could possibly be obtained, while the rest were a "zero-sum game" in terms of revenue and needed to be privatized "peacefully and [could be used] to appease" certain players (Interviewee's identity withheld). To whom these latter firms were sold did not really matter, as they were unlikely to attract the interest of foreign investors, and domestic buyers were largely seen as interchangeable. However, since it was impossible to "judge the beauty contest" put on by revival domestic bidders, the decision was made to award the asset to the highest bidder as this was simply the "most defensible position" the government could take (Interviewee's identity withheld).

The other major privatization effort during this period was the sale of the state-owned banks. On the political agenda since as far back as 1987, bank privatization had been delayed for reasons ranging from the uncertainty over asset valuation, to the large number of recession-induced bankruptcies. In addition, the banks themselves were seen by some as having played an important and arguably beneficial role during the early years by providing easy loans to managers with whom they had established connections; (the public was naturally excluded from this easy money). Nonetheless, whatever its short-term benefits, officials knew that in the long run "state-owned banks involved in privatization is a bed of corruption," and that sooner or later they would have to be sold (Mihály Laki 2001, personal communication). Fearing the kind of corruption witnessed in Russia, the Minister of Finance and the Head of the National Bank, two formerly strong opponents of bank privatization, realized that it was only a matter of time before the mafia and corruption took hold of the Hungarian system. Through watching events unfold in Russia, these leaders had learned an important lesson: "if you let banks run politics, you ruin your democracy;" thus the decision was made to sell the banks as fast as possible even if it meant selling for "zero profit just to get the banks out of politics and party financing and corruption" (Peter Mihályi 2001, personal communication).

As a result of all of these programs, by mid-1996, when the process of reforming the pension system began in earnest, 70% of the economy had been transferred into private hands and the economy had recovered to almost 90% of its 1989 output (EBRD 1996, 11). Though focused on selling crucial remaining state assets into good hands (i.e., foreign investors), the Horn government also continued the further development of the middle class, albeit in a fairly laissez-faire manner. The distributional consequences of Horn's policies are presented in Table 4.3.[15]

Most noticeably different is that working for a foreign owned firm has lost some of the protection it had previously offered as a small percentage of its employees now belonged to the lowest income quintile. However, working for a firm that was at least partly foreign owned was still better in terms of income than working for one owned exclusively by Hungarians. Also of note is the limited participation of the middle class in voluntary pension funds (Pillar 3), which were created in 1993.

---

15   Privatization did not come to a close in 1997, however, following the Fidesz victory in the 1998 election, it was noticeably put on hold. Having campaigned against privatization and the unfairness of the transition, and with public support for privatization all but disappeared, it saw little reason to actively pursue the matter.

Table 4.3   The Relative Winners and Losers of the Transition, 1997

	Percentage of Households where at least one individual worked for or as ...	*Household Income Quintile (%)*				
		1st	*2nd*	*3rd*	*4th*	*5th*
Privatization	Fully privatized firm	18.1	13.2	16.1	20.4	32.2
	Partially state-owned firm	6.7	9.5	18.1	28.6	37.1
	Full state-owned firm	12.1	10.9	16.4	29.7	30.9
Foreign Ownership	Wholly foreign-owned firm	17.7	6.5	11.3	22.6	41.9
	Partly foreign-owned firm	8.4	9.2	13.7	25.2	43.5
	Wholly Hungarian-owned	16.2	12.5	18.1	23.8	29.4
Type of Firm	Joint stock company	9.1	11.9	14.8	28.6	35.7
	Partnership	18.1	11.2	18.5	19.3	32.9
	Private enterprise	18.5	13.5	14.3	21.9	31.9
Type of Job	Top manager	4.2	8.3	8.3	4.1	75.0
	Middle manager	3.6	1.8	0.0	20.0	74.6
	Lower manager	6.8	13.6	6.8	18.2	55.6
	Self-employed	16.2	8.1	9.1	26.3	40.4
	Unskilled	28.5	22.4	23.5	18.8	7.1
Pensioners	Old age pension	14.8	25.8	26.5	20.7	17.2
	Working & collecting pension	7.9	4.8	11.1	12.7	63.5
	Disability pension	35.6	20.3	23.3	15.3	5.5
	Widow's pension	42.5	31.1	10.0	7.5	8.8
	Had voluntary retirement acct.	4.1	10.2	14.3	23.5	48.0
Residence	Budapest	7.8	15.3	16.5	24.6	35.8
	Other major city	15.6	20.0	25.9	20.0	18.5
	Village	29.7	19.2	21.7	18.5	11.0
	Farm	25.0	50.0	25.0	0.0	0.0
Changes	In the same quintile as 1994	52.5	35.5	27.3	37.4	53.6
	In the same quintile as 1990	39.1	31.6	29.6	31.6	53.0

Sample size: Individuals (3,502); Households (1264); Quintiles 1,2,4, & 5 (253), 3 (252).

Source: Hungarian Household Panel, Individual Survey collapsed to household level, 1997.

While almost half of the wealthiest Hungarians maintained such a fund, less than 15% of the middle-income households were similarly preparing for their future.

The Income Consequences of Privatization

The cumulative effect of these programs had a direct and measurable impact on the distribution of wealth and resources in society. Certain groups clearly benefited from certain programs, while others appear to have been left relatively behind having gained little in the way of material or financial resources. Using the definitions of relative winners and losers presented in Chapter 2, a depiction of the resulting Hungarian income strata is presented in Table 4.4. One immediate observation is the remarkable stability that had set in by 1997. Between 1995 and 1997, almost 75% of the households consistently fell either below (52.6%) or above (21.1%) the

Table 4.4   **The Relative Winners and Losers of the Transition, 1995–1997**

Category	Definition	1996 Average Annual Income	Number of Households	Percent of Sample
Big Losers	Households with an income less than 50% of the mean in both years.	137,395 HUF	71	5.9%
Little Losers	Households with an income less than the mean but more than 50% of it in both years.	264,372	558	46.5
In Flux	Households whose relative position fluctuated from year to year.	347,592	319	26.6
Little Winners	Households with an income more than the mean but less that 150% of it in both years.	439,531	147	12.3
Big Winners	Households with an income in excess of 150% of the mean in both years.	918,506	104	8.7
	Average / Total	357,208	N=1,199	

Average household income in Hungarian Forints. In 1997, the average exchange rate was $1 = 187 HUF (World Bank, World Development Indicators).

Source: Hungarian Household Panel 1992–1997. Individual survey collapsed to the level of the household and adjusted for size and age composition.

mean. Of those whose position fluctuated, slightly more than half (57.3%) saw their situation deteriorate in the second year. Compared to Poland, the Hungarian reforms produced a great proportion of relative losers (52.4% compared to 40.7%) and a smaller proportion of those in flux (27% compared to 37%). The proportion of relative winners was roughly similar in both countries, with the Big Winners representing 8.7% in Hungary and 7.4% in Poland.

Actors and their Roles

Individuals

The relative winners and losers of privatization constitute the first set of actors, ones whose preferences in regard to pension reform alternatives varied, as indicated in Table 4.5.[16] Before addressing the data itself, one must consider the source and

---

16   Due to data limitations, it is not possible to use a two-year based definition as no time-series data of pension attitudes exists (i.e., the same person surveyed in consecutive years). As a consequence, a one-year snapshot (1996) is presented here. I would argue that since nearly 75% of households remained in the same category over the two-year period, a one-

funding behind it. This survey, and others like it, was conducted by TÁRKI, a private Hungarian research institute, "on the basis of an order received from the Pension Working Group of the Ministry of Finance and the Ministry of Public Welfare" (TÁRKI 1996, 2). Part of the funding for the Pension Working Group, and the surveys conducted by TÁRKI, was provided by the World Bank, which was promoting the idea of a mixed pillar solution. While the survey was not completely biased, the World Bank's preferred alternative was, by TÁRKI's own admission, put up against "two options [that were] let us admit, rather extreme" in nature (TÁRKI 1996, 7). Essentially, respondents were given the choice of either 1) doing absolutely nothing; 2) implementing World Bank's mixed pillar model with private accounts; or 3) completely ending the welfare state all together (see Table 4.5). They were never asked to independently chose between either 1) reforming the current PAYG system by increasing the retirement age and changing the contribution benefit link, or 2) introducing mandatory private accounts as called for by the World Bank.

With this as background, the numbers are actually quite revealing for the opposition they show. For despite being confronted with two extreme options that were never going to be considered, almost 50% of the transitions relative losers actually *preferred* one of these alternatives to the World Bank solution. Although we have no way of knowing what the support level would have been had they been offered more realistic alternatives, it seems reasonable to assume that support for the World Bank option would have fallen if they had been. That said, a sizeable segment of the wealthy (71%) supported the idea of including private accounts. While the question indicated that such accounts would be optional rather than mandatory, we can conclude that there was significantly more support for private provision of pension benefits among the transition's relative winners than among its losers.

Given the actual proposals that were considered and this data, however biased, I argue that there were essentially two alternative perspectives within the public at-large. The first centered around the government's proposed course of action which was to reform the existing system by adding mandatory private accounts, increasing the retirement age, and tightening contribution-benefit link. This option was primarily supported by the financial winners of the transition. Using the survey data above as an *optimistic* assessment of the public support for this approach across income groupings, roughly 70% of the biggest winners, 60% of the Little Winners, and ~50% of both loser groups make up the individuals supporting the government's (and the World Bank's) preferred solution. The second alternative was to reform the existing system without adding mandatory private accounts, and to do so in a manner that maintained a strong redistributive or insurance element within the system. This option was supported primarily by those left financially behind by the transition. Using the admittedly biased TÁRKI survey as a very *conservative* estimate of public opposition to the World Bank's advice, this group is comprised of about half of losers groups, 40% of the Little Winners and 30% of the biggest winners of the transition.

---

year snapshot does not seriously distort the image of the public's attitudes towards pension reform.

Table 4.5   Relative Winner and Loser Attitudes Toward Pension Reform

	Big Losers	Little Losers	Little Winners	Big Winners	Overall
Assuming reliable private accounts exist, would you prefer that:					
No changes be made to the current PAYG system.	28.0%	26.9	23.0	16.6	24.7
Compulsory contributions continue, but that above a certain amount, you be allowed to choose whether the additional payroll contribution goes to the PAYG pillar or your own private account.	52.3	54.1	62.2	71.0	58.2
There be no compulsory contributions and that you be allowed to contribute to your own retirement account if you choose. There would be no role for the state; upon reaching retirement age, you would have to either fend for yourself or rely on family.	19.6	19.0	14.7	12.4	17.1
Total (N)	168	542	352	145	1207
Currently two plans are under consideration in regard to pension benefits, which do you prefer?					
Plan 1: benefits will be based entirely on wages earned during employment.	27.8%	25.7	26.5	27.0	26.4
Plan 2: two-thirds of one's pension will be determined by wage earned and one third will be determined by the interest earned from separate payments made into a pension insurance company fund.	45.1	41.0	44.6	52.5	44.0
I prefer that no changes be made; the current system should be retained.	27.2	33.3	28.9	20.6	29.7
Total (N)	162	522	325	141	1150

Source: Omnibusz 1996, individual survey responses based on total household income.

Organizations

Trade Unions (the PIF and IRC Council Boards)   The trade unions were perhaps the most important non-governmental organizations involved in the process, a status secured through their formal position on both the Pension Insurance Fund (PIF) and Interest Reconciliation Council (IRC) boards. Created in 1993 when the pension system was formally separated from the general budget, the PIF board was made up of both union and employer representatives in equal proportion. Following the 1993 nation-wide election to select board members, the union half of the board was dominated by the post-communist trade representatives (MSZOSZ), and given the relatively weak and disorganized position of employer groups, "the post-Communist union federation effectively [controlled] both [the PIF and Health Care] boards" (Nelson 1998, 23). The power attached to this position was considerable as the PIF controlled of all the funds within the PAYG system, and this "control over large flows of money [permitted] financial maneuvering widely believed to have benefited the union as an institution, key leaders, and political parties" (Nelson 1998, 23). It is not surprising then that the MSZOSZ was "intensely hostile to the proposed reforms" which threatened to divert these funds to private pension accounts.[17]

The other major institutional source of union power was the tripartite labor council, the IRC, which was created in 1994 in an attempt to get the unions to accept marketization of the economy. The significance is that same union and employer groups were represented here as on the PIF, however, each board had its own unique set of interests and objectives. As a result, a latent fault-line was created within the MSZOSZ, and one that was ultimately used by reform proponents to co-opt union support from the IRC members over the strenuous objection of those on the PIF. Regardless of whether by fate or design, by giving the same union two different roles to play, it became possible to play one segment off against the other. I will return to this division, and how it was used against the opponents of radical reform later.

Public Consultation Groups   Chief among the public consultation groups was the Council of Elderly Affairs, a group which represented the clearest and most direct point of access for the old-aged as the group met directly with Prime Minister Horn and his senior deputies to discuss the proposed reform package (see Table 4.8 below). The Council was among the first private groups consulted following the drafting of the final proposal, and prior to its submission to parliament. Other important consultative actors were the Association of Large Families and the various women's groups, which sought recognition and inclusion of time, spent on maternity leave towards to the calculation of the number of years of service, a figure used to determine the amount of an individual pension award. These actors were ultimately successful in this effort. In general, however, "the impact of these actions was ... small: the voice of 'civil society' got little publicity in the media, and remained largely unknown to the general public" (Ferge 1999, 238).

---

17   It would be a mistake, however, to write-off all of the unions opposition as a narrow-minded attempt to keep its fingers in the till. Some of the opposition came from a steadfast ideological resistance to change on behalf the old guard that made up the bulk of union's left wing. In addition there were, and by many accounts continue to be, valid points of contention surrounding the pension reforms and their long-term sustainability. This word of caution was thoughtfully pointed out by Ivan Csaba of Central European University during our discussions in 2001.

One group, however, which did have a significant impact was the financial community, as the drafting committee put together by the Ministry of Finance was "packed with bankers and financial actors" whose time had been donated pro-bono by their employers (Interviewee's identity withheld). The justification for their direct involvement was that the technical nature of the reforms required an expertise that was beyond the scope of the Ministry's bureaucrats. In general, however, while there were channels for private actors to have their voices heard, outside those with direct formal links to either the Ministry of Finance or the Prime Minister's office, the general public had little direct impact on process.

Parties and Electoral Factors

Parliament and the Electoral Rules   The Hungarian parliament is a unicameral legislature consisting of 386 members who are elected using a two-ballot voting system.[18] With their first vote, voters cast a ballot for a candidate to represent their single-member district (SMD); there are 176 such SMD seats in the parliament.[19] Of greater interest here are the remaining 210 seats that are filled through a combination of a regional and national party-list system. As described below, the seat-division between these two levels necessarily varies from election to election, although there are always at least 58 national seats.

Hungary is comprised of 20 regional administrative districts that range in size and population.[20] Any party which fields candidates in more than one quarter of a region's SMDs has the right to establish a regional party list, so long as the total number of SMDs contested is at least two. On average each regional district (RD) sends seven representatives to parliament who are elected using a complicated quota system with remainder votes.[21] The only feature of concern here is the two-thirds requirement in allocating the remainders. As a result of this technical detail, "about

---

18   In order for the vote to be valid in either a single member district (SMD) or in a region, the turnout must be greater than 50%. In the event this fails to happen, a second round must be held in that district.

19   In order for a candidate to win an SMD seat, he must receive an absolute majority of the votes in the first round. Failing this, a run-off election is held between all candidates with at least 15% of the vote or the top three vote getters. Turnout plays a role in that all candidates can compete in this second round if the first round turnout was less than 50%. The winner of the second round is the one who receives the most votes, so long as the total turnout was at least 25% of those eligible. Second round run-off elections have been the norm since 1990.

20   Although not directly relevant to arguments presented here, it is nonetheless important that these districts not be misconstrued as states. In the words of one reviewer, "Hungary is a parliamentary republic without any trace of federalism" (Tóka 1998, 273).

21   See Appendix 8.3 in Tóka 1998 for a more detailed account the electoral mechanics. Essentially, the quota defines the number of votes required in order to be awarded one seat; one can think of it as the cost of a seat in terms of votes. For example if the quota was 10,000 and a party received 106,000 votes it would be entitled to ten seats and have a remainder of 6,000. If a party's remainder is at least two-thirds of the quota (e.g., 6,667) then it is entitled

one-fifth or more of the RD seats remain unallocated on the regional level and are added to the national pool of compensatory mandates," a move which, for reasons described below, effectively places them beyond the reach of regional parties (Tóka 1998, 272). A further hindrance to such parties is the requirement that to compete for what RD seats do remain at the regional level, a party must obtain at least 5% of the total national vote. Finally, as if to seal the fate of small parties everywhere, "the relatively small multi-member constituencies and the allocation rules significantly favour those parties that obtain at least 10–15 percent of the vote locally" (Tóka 1998, 272). In short, the electoral rules have effectively stacked the deck against small regional parties and shifted politics to the national level.

The final means of gaining membership in parliament is offered by the national lists and the compensatory mandates described above. However, once again the eligibility rules favor larger parties that compete nationwide for to register a national list, a party must have contested at least six of the twenty regions. No ballot is directly cast for these seats as the votes for qualifying parties are accumulated according to their as yet unused remainder votes, if any, following both the regional and SMD campaigns. Essentially, any votes for a qualifying party that have not yet been used towards the winning of an electoral mandate, are pooled and used to distribute the remaining seats.[22] Since the allocation of these compensatory mandates is a consequence of the RD and SMD remainders, the total number of national seats varies from election to election.[23]

The Party System and Social Cleavages   While the electoral rules described above clearly favor the development of larger national parties, "Hungary's relatively simple cleavage structure [also acts] as a gatekeeper against the entry of new parties" (Tóka 1998, 238–9). The polity can essentially be divided "into two camps, [one] a socially conservative, religious, somewhat nationalistic, and anti-communist camp; and [the other being] secular, morally permissive and generally less nationalist" (Tóka 1998, 239). In terms of salience, Kitschelt (1995) argues that there is a high degree of polarization around non-economic issues, and that in regard to economic policies, the level of polarization is unusually low. His research using factor analysis suggests that almost 48% of the variance in party position can be explained by their stance on non-economic issues such as abortion, education and the role of the church. Economic policies load highly on a second factor, although it can account for only 13.3% of variance in party position.[24] This second factor has been interpreted as the traditional left/right ideological cleavage and one that pits the socialists, majority

---

to one additional seat should any remain after one seat had been awarded for every full quota achieved among all the parties. In this example, it would not be entitled to an 11th seat.

22   Qualifying here means having competed in at least six regions and having won at least 5% of the total national vote.

23   The ratio of regional-to-national level seats in 1990 was 120/90; in 1994, it was 125/85.

24   A possible third factor can be identified around the issue of environmental protection, but it is seen as rather weak. See Kitschelt 1995.

winners of the 1994 election, against their coalition partners, the SZDSZ, and the other major pro-market party, Fidesz. In sum, Hungary is dominated by a "strong polarizing cultural dimension" which supports approximately seven different parties and is bisected "by a much less important and less polarizing economic left/right cleavage" (Tóka 1998, 256).

The significance of this is that the political space appears so constructed that there is little opportunity for a party or interest group to form based solely on the economic interests of retirees and pensioners. That pensioner parties are expected to struggle is of no great surprise as they generally do so everywhere in the world. However, the above research also suggests that because economic policy orientation is fairly weak, the interests of those both supporting and opposing radical reform of the pension system will most likely become entwined within larger existing institutions such as trade unions and the financial community. As a consequence, they must compete for attention and resources within a broader organization pursuing a variety of different interest simultaneously. I argue that the more diffuse and numerous these interests, the less of an impact any one segment will have, and that this will affect those incorporated into the trade unions to a much greater extent. The reason is that following the collapse of communism, trade unions underwent a prolonged identity crisis and never again managed to "speak with one voice" (Nelson 1998, 21). Caught between a solidaristic left-wing and a reformist element struggling to stem the tide of declining membership and influence, trade unions exhibited exactly the kind of diffusion of interests (i.e., employment, declining wages, working conditions, pensions ...) that weakened the relevant position of those primarily concerned with opposing radical reform of the pension system. I argue below that this forced incorporation into the trade unions, and the latent fault line described above between the representatives on the PIF and IRC boards, played an important role in allowing the proponents of radical reform to win the day. In short, the political environment appears such that those challenging the pension reformers had less of an opportunity to achieve political influence than they might otherwise have had in a broader political arena.

The Coalition Agreement   In the 1994 election, the reformed ex-communists, the MSzP, won with an absolute majority of the vote. Despite this, the decidedly left-of-center party chose to enter into a coalition with the right-of-center SZDSZ, "the most pro-market formation of all Hungarian parties at the time, but admittedly close to the MSzP on non-economic issues" (Tóka 1998, 261). While there may have been a certain logic to this partnership, and unlike the previous coalition government from 1990 1994, these two parties chose to enter into a written, contractual *Coalition Agreement*.[25] Beyond the standard specification of which party would receive which ministry, the agreement created a Coalition Coordination Council consisting of the Prime Minister, the Deputy Prime Minister, the chairman of each party, the leaders

---

25   For more on the decision to enter into coalition, see Körösenyi 1994.

of each parliamentary group, and one delegate each designated by the coalition partners. Of importance here is Section III, paragraph 3, which states that:

> It is the duty of the Coalition Coordination Council to settle affairs of the coalition partners that do not yield themselves for settlement under the Coalition Agreement, to prevent conflicts, and to clarify any other controversial issues. Either party may move to the convening of the Council. Each party shall have one vote in the Coalition Coordination Council and *decision making requires consensus* (Coalition Agreement of June 24, 1994, 8; emphasis added).

The importance of this is that in spite of holding an absolute majority in parliament, the socialists decided to enter into a very specific coalition agreement with the party with which it was most at odds on issues of economics. Furthermore, this agreement tied their hands somewhat by requiring a consensus of opinion in the Coordination Council whenever the two sides found themselves in disagreement, and given the gap between the extreme wings of both parties, such disagreements in regard to economic policy were a foregone conclusion. Therefore, I argue that the agreement played an important structural role in creating a centrist, compromise laden reform package in regard to the pension system. Essentially, it provided moderates in both parties with a basis to control their respective extremist elements.

Other Institutions

The Constitutional Court   The other principle governmental actor in Hungary is the Constitutional Court, whose eleven members are elected by a super-majority in parliament to a nine-year term.[26] What separates this Court from most others in the world is that under the constitution, "anyone can ask the Court to declare a law, decree or rule unconstitutional, even *before* it comes into effect" (Tóka 1998, 283, emphasis added). Essentially, the Court has the right to issue a ruling on any piece of legislation while it still being debated, or even drafted, by a parliamentary committee. It also has considerable discretion to broaden the scope of its findings beyond what is laid out in the original appeal. Following rulings on the compensation voucher program described earlier, and its voiding of significant aspects of the 1995 fiscal stabilization package, it was not difficult for actors to deduce the Court's position in regard to pension reform: any legislation that did not include a period of adjustment and due consideration of established rights under existing programs was never going to see the light of day.

---

26   During the period under study here, the court's members were all appointed by the previous MDF government.

Theoretical Expectations

The Hungarian government had two main reasons for proposing a reform package that included mandatory private accounts. First, acutely aware of the immediacy of the financial crisis and budgetary shortfalls facing the existing PAYG system, the Ministry of Finance became a vocal and forceful advocate of radical reform (Müller 1999). Basically, it sought to protect the central budget from the need to provide what promised to be ever growing subsidies or annual transfers to the pension system. Second, the enormity of the nation's debt burden gave the World Bank and the IMF considerable leverage with which to press for pension privatization (Müller 1999; Orenstein 2000). For example, the IMF promised to disregard any deficits that accumulated in the public PAYG pillar as a result of contributions being diverted to new, mandatory private accounts. Such an arrangement would have helped the Hungarian credit rating and consequently the ability to attract both foreign investment and borrow on the international capital market. It may also have helped Hungary renegotiate the terms of its debt burden. As a result, the onus of action here lies with those trying to block the advent of mandatory private accounts; for in the absence of any political pressure to do otherwise, the ruling coalition had both the intent and the votes to enact them into law.[27] Therefore, I begin with the likelihood that opposition groups would be able to organize and convey a credible electoral threat to politicians.

Reforming the System Without Mandatory Private Accounts

The alternative to the World Bank's proposed solution was to reform, but not fundamentally alter, the existing PAYG system. As seen in Table 4.6, the likelihood of successful collective action is deemed moderate, in that of the nine factors considered, only five are clearly increasing the probability within the aggregate of supporters. While the transition's relative winners are fairly likely to organize, the bulk of the public support for this approach resided within the transition's Big and Little Losers, two groups whose characteristics pose a higher barrier to organization. The first obstacle is their widespread geographic dispersion. This diffusion raises communication and organization costs, particularly among large groups such as the Little Losers who comprise almost half of the population. Further hindrances stem from the difficulty in mobilizing the group's available resources, and the lack of resource heterogeneity. This latter factor is often particularly critical for larger groups, as seen in the Perot example discussed in Chapter 2. The degree of heterogeneity is measured by conducting a statistical test for positive skewness in the distribution of household income among group members. If the distribution is positively and significantly skewed, then it is more likely that a sub-group, or in the extreme a single individual, will have the resources to provide for the collective effort. The income distribution among both the Big and Little Losers is negatively

---

27   The coalition nominally controlled 72% of the seats in parliament.

Table 4.6   The Likelihood of Collective Action in Support of Reforming and Maintaining the PAYG System

	Big Losers	Little Losers	Little Winners	Big Winners	Aggregate
Group Characteristics					
Geography	Diffuse (-)	Diffuse (-)	Dense (+)	Dense (+)	Diffuse (-)
Resource Quantity	High (+)	High (+)	High (+)	High (+)	High (+)
Resource Mobility	Low (-)	Low (-)	High (+)	High (+)	Moderate (0/+)
Resource Heterogeneity	No (-)	No (-)	Yes (+)	Yes (+)	Yes (+)
Interest Heterogeneity	Yes (+)	Yes (+)	Yes (+)	Yes (+)	Yes (+)
Electoral Appeal	Moderate	Very High	High	Very Low	High
Nature of the Objective					
Joint Supply (group size)	No (0/-) (small)	No (-) (large)	No (0/-) (small)	No (0/-) (small)	No (-) (large)
Exclusive Benefits	No (-)	No (-)	No (-)	No (-)	No (-)
Increasing Returns (group size)	Yes (-) (small)	Yes (+) (large)	Yes (-) (small)	Yes (-) (small)	Yes (+) (large)
Environment					
Other Actors	Yes (+)	Yes (+)	Yes (+)	Yes (+)	Yes (+)
Likelihood of Organizing	Low	Moderate	High	High	Moderate
Likelihood of Influence	Moderate	Very High	High	Very Low	High

skewed, indicating that it is very unlikely that any one member will have the quantity resources necessary to act differently from the rest of the group (Oliver et al 1985).

While individual characteristics may help or hinder certain income groupings, all groups are adversely affected by the nature of the objective itself. The first difficulty concerns jointness of supply, or whether or not individual consumption of the collective benefit is affected by the number of others who enjoy it as well. I argue that, barring extremely soft budget constraints, a PAYG pension scheme is a public good that cannot be provided in joint supply. In the presence of a hard budget constraint (i.e., where no deficits are allowed to accumulate), the total amount of funds available for pensions is limited by the contributions made. Therefore, one person's consumption of the public good necessarily prohibits someone else from consuming that part of the total benefit. Moreover, the aging population and declining birthrate in Hungary meant that over the near term, more and more people stood to become *legal* claimants on a smaller and smaller pool of resources. This lack of jointness lowers the probability of collective action, an effect that becomes stronger as group size increases (Oliver and Marwell 1988, 3).

A second factor working against them is the non-exclusionary nature of a public pension system. Although conditions can be applied, such as requiring at least 20 years of service or 20 years of paid contributions, those left behind by the transition were also the strongest supporters of a universal right to state pension upon reaching retirement age (Omnibuz 1996). As a result of this, however, each individual has a strong incentive to free ride on the contribution of others in attainment of the collective good. If such a universal right were to become law, then they would benefit regardless of whether or not they had contributed to its passage.

The one positive feature of the objective is that it temporarily offers increasing returns to organization; however, this effect is only beneficial for large groups seeking to change the existing system. For smaller groups and those seeking to maintain the status quo (i.e., to make no policy changes at all), no such advantage existed. The difference hinges on the effect demographic changes over time will have on the costs and benefits of a particular plan. In Hungary, the situation was one of a rapidly graying population with less and less young people to fund the retirement of the elderly. Under such circumstances, the status quo actually offered decreasing returns with the addition of each new old person. As the dependency ratio approaches 1:1, or surpasses it, more and more of each working person's wage must be withheld to fund a single retired person's pension. Thus, costs actually increase and benefits (may) decrease with the addition of the next retired person. This is exactly why the existing PAYG system was financially unviable and in need of reform. However, efforts to reform that system by increasing the retirement age did offer such returns. Because such a change effectively increases the number of young people paying into the system, the dependency ratio and the burden on each contributor falls with each one year increase in the retirement age. Likewise, the pool of elderly drawing on those contributions also falls, lessening the need to scale back benefits or lower annual cost-of-living adjustments. Among larger groups, this creates an incentive for a sub-group to undertake the challenge of organizing the masses. The logic being that, although the initial per-capita cost to organize maybe large, the potential pool of members increases with each one year increase in the retirement age, thereby reducing these per-capita costs. As a result, we should expect a higher prevalence of collective action among larger groups seeking reforms offering increasing returns than among those seeking reforms that do not.

If the group is small, however, then there are not enough potential members to eventually drive down the per-capita costs. Consequently, political entrepreneurs lose the incentive to act on behalf of the collective. So this incentive only applies to the Little Losers of the transition, and to opponents in the aggregate (i.e., all those who opposed mandatory private accounts). For the Big Losers, as well as the Little and Big Winners seeking this alternative, 2.8%, 4.6%, and 2.5% of the aggregate population respectively, the presence of increasing returns means that all three features of the objective lower the probability that they will successfully organize independent of other actors or each other.

While the likelihood of successful collective action is mixed, those opposing the introduction of mandatory private accounts did, in the aggregate, represent a credible electoral threat policy makers. Given the electoral rules described above, I use the threshold of 15% of the vote in a district as constituting a credible threat. Across income groups, the ability to convey this threat varies; however, all but the biggest winners were capable of delivering at least 15% of the vote in at least 9 of the 20 electoral districts. Those who gained the most financially from the transition were only able to do that in one district. Consequently, if those opposed to mandatory private accounts are able to organize and coordinate their pressure, then we would expect to see a favorable reaction among politicians.

Reforming the System by Including Mandatory Private Accounts

Table 4.7 provides a similar summary for those trying to adopt the World Bank's mixed pillar model. Once again, all five the group characteristics favor the relative winners of the transition over those left relatively behind financially. Among the Little Losers for example, only two factors, their large potential resource base and the heterogeneity of interest, increase the likelihood of collective action. The primary difference here lies in the nature of the objective sought. For those seeking to create mandatory private pension accounts, the issue of joint-supply is moot. Since each account is separate, and one can only claim the funds in one's own account, consumption by any one individual has no bearing on the next. Private pension accounts are private goods, not public or collective ones. The public benefit from such funds is more indirect in terms of the supply of savings generated for investment through the capital market. However, while the development of the Hungarian capital market clearly stood to be affected by the proposed changes, such benefits were at best the unintended by-products of efforts directed towards gaining greater control over one's own wealth and financial future.[28]

The irrelevance of joint-supply removes one potential obstacle to overcoming collective action. However, supporters of the World Bank program still had to confront the mixed incentives stemming from the non-exclusionary nature of the accounts and the increasing returns they offered. Although the funds in each account are private, and hence exclusionary, the theoretical issue here is whether or not someone who wanted mandatory accounts had an incentive to free ride on the

---

28   For more on the connection between the capital market and economic reform in Hungary, see Fletcher 1995. One could make the argument that the private accounts acted as a kind of selective incentive by which the greater public good, a well-supplied capital market, was achieved. However, as Fletcher and others have made clear, little or no discussion was given to the effect pension reform would have on the capital market.

Table 4.7   The Likelihood of Collective Action in Support of Mandatory Private Accounts

	Big Losers	*Little Losers*	*Little Winners*	*Big Winners*	*Aggregate*
Group Characteristics					
Geography	Dense (+)	Diffuse (-)	Dense (+)	Dense (+)	Dense (+)
Resource Quantity	High (+)	High (+)	High (+)	High (+)	High (+)
Resource Mobility	Moderate (0/+)	Low (-)	High (+)	High (+)	High (+)
Resource Heterogeneity	No (-)	No (-)	Yes (+)	Yes (+)	Yes (+)
Interest Heterogeneity	Yes (+)	Yes (+)	Yes (+)	Yes (+)	Yes (+)
Electoral Appeal	Low	Very High	Very High	Low	Very High
Nature of the Objective					
Joint Supply (group size)	Moot	Moot	Moot	Moot	Moot
Exclusive Benefits	No (-)	No (-)	No (-)	No (-)	No (-)
Increasing Returns (group size)	Yes (-) (small)	Yes (+) (large)	Yes (-) (small)	Yes (-) (small)	Yes (+) (large)
Environment					
Other Actors	Yes (+)	Yes (+)	Yes (+)	Yes (+)	Yes (+)
Likelihood of Organizing	Moderate	Moderate	High	High	Very High
Likelihood of Influence	Low	Very High	Very High	Low	Very High

contribution of others. Because the accounts would be mandatory of all new entrants to the workforce, and optional for all current employees, there was an incentive to free ride. The benefit of having the accounts could not be withheld from those who failed to actively contribute to the passage of the legislation. This universal feature makes collective action more difficult as each individual who wanted to see these accounts enacted could sit back and let the others do all the work. If the bill passes, everyone would be entitled to benefit from having a portion of their mandatory payroll contributions diverted to their own private account, regardless of any political effort on their part.

As with those seeking to block the World Bank program, those seeking its implementation were also faced with an objective that offered increasing returns, or alternatively, a diminishing marginal cost curve. The issues here are costs relating to the management of the private funds and their oversight. As the number of contributors rises, these costs are spread more diffusely lowering the per-capita charges to each account. Because the proposed second pillar was to be mandatory for all new entrants to the job market, and voluntary for those already in it, there existed a strong incentive for a sub-group to organize behind its creation. Regardless of short-term costs, in a few decades time 100% of the labor force would be contributing to the second pillar, thereby minimizing per-capital management fees and creating strong political pressure for effective oversight and regulation.

Combining these eight factors, (jointness being moot), the likelihood of these actors successfully overcoming the barriers to collective action is very high, particularly among the wealthier income groups. In the aggregate, seven of the eight factors are increasing the likelihood of organization. In terms of influence, the aggregate electoral threat is also very high, although across the income groups the credibility of that threat is bimodal. Only the Little Winners and Losers are capable of delivering a large portion of the vote everywhere. In fact, those left slightly behind by the transition, constitute between 36–72% of the vote in all but 2 districts, while the Little Winners represent at least 15% of the vote in 16 of the 19 districts for which data is available.[29] Putting the likelihood of organization and influence together, it seems reasonable that the proposed reforms would find a solid group of supporters actively seeking their adoption.

In sum, both supporters and opponents were likely to organize and find elements of electoral representation, although the likelihood seem to slightly favor the supporters of the World Bank's mixed pillar model. Given this, the existing institutions and written Coalition Agreement described above, it is not overly surprising that the final legislation resulted in a compromise-laden package that balanced the demands of both sides.

The Politics of Pension Reform in Hungary

The Proposal

Although some changes to the pension system were enacted during the early 1990s, such as the 1993 creation of the PIF, the real process of reform began in December 1994 with the formation of the Committee of the Reform of the Treasury

---

29   The 1996 Omnibuz survey aggregates Pest (coded district 13 in the dataset) into Budapest (coded 1). Budapest contains 343 observations (22.9%) while the surrounding region of Pest contains no observations. No explanation is provided why the capital's eastern half is not included separately.

(CRT).[30] Charged with addressing all aspects of government finance, a June 1995 subcommittee report proposed "a thorough restructuring of the existing public PAYG scheme, while maintaining it as the only mandatory pension tier" (Müller 1999, 72). Included along with the report were macroeconomic simulations based on available demographic data prepared by Mária Augusztinovics and the staff at the Institute of Economics of the Hungarian Academy of Sciences (HAS). These simulations showed that given the 1991 increase in the retirement age, it was possible to generate significant savings in the public sector scheme by reforming of the PAYG pillar (Mária Augusztinovics 2001, personal communication). However, despite being "received quite favorably" and formally accepted by the CRT, "this proposal was *never presented to the government*" (Ferge 1999, 236 emphasis in original).

Rather than accept a proposal of which he did not approve, the Minister of Finance, who also chaired the CRT, went ahead and "introduced (without any previous consultation with anybody involved in the reform operations) the idea of a funded privatized pillar, assigning to it a decisive role," although the exact extent of the system to be privatized was not given at the time (Ferge 1999, 236). Over the next few months, however, it became clear that the new Minister (Lajos Bakros) had in mind a 100% privatized system based on the Chilean model, and it was this initial proposal that became the focal point of discussion over the next two years.

The opposition to such a radical reform proposal was concentrated in the PIF and in the Ministry of Welfare (MOW), which had long favored extensive modification of the existing PAYG system over privatization. From 1994 to 1996, these two competing visions formed part of the larger confrontation within the government over economic policy and reflected the often personal rivalry between the Ministers of Finance and Welfare. The first break came in April 1995 when the Welfare Minister (Kovacs) resigned in response to the passage of the Bokros fiscal stabilization package (Danics 1998, 16). While the new Minister (Gyorgy Szabo) continued his department's opposition for a short time, by year's end he had suddenly begun to show a growing acceptance of a mandatory funded pillar. Following Bokros's departure from the Ministry of Finance (MOF) in February 1996, an initial compromise was reached whereby contributions would be split 50-50 between the PAYG first pillar and a new, but mandatory, second pillar that would be privately managed.

Although "accounts vary as to how this agreement came about," in the end the MOF gave up the idea of a fully privatized system and the MOW gave up its opposition to the introduction of mandatory private pension insurance (Müller 1999, 77).[31]

---

30   In 1991, parliament had passed resolution No. 60/1991 which foresaw the movement towards a three-tier pension system that was still publicly managed but supplemented by a voluntary third pillar. While some changes did take place between 1991 and 1994, little real progress was made. In fact, Maria Major, the head of Ministry of Welfare's pension reform team, said that as of 1996, "we were where we had been in 1990" (Danics 1998, 15).

31   Some accounts reference the influence of Prime Minister Horn in forcing his Ministers to reach a compromise (see Müller 1999, 77). Others suggest that it was the MOF, under the new leadership of Péter Medgyessy, that unilaterally made the 50-50 offer recognizing that a 100% Chilean model was not politically viable (Mária Augusztinovics 2001, personal

The one common element in all accounts, however, is the political pressure within the cabinet towards reaching a consensus, due in part to the Coalition Agreement and Section III, paragraph 3 described above. According to Maria Major, head of the MOW's pension reform team, the Welfare Minister's change of attitude was significantly aided by "meetings with interested members of the coalition" (Danics 1998, 16).

The result of subsequent negotiations, the ratio of contributions was further reduced to 2/3 PAYG and 1/3 funded in May 1996 when the full cabinet endorsed an inter-ministerial framework to draft the technical aspects of the reform package for submission to parliament.[32] The task of drafting changes to the existing PAYG pillar was handed to the MOW, while the MOF was to draft the new mandatory second pillar comprised of privately managed pension accounts. By the end of the 1996, the drafting was largely complete, and only then did the government begin to formally consult both private interest groups and entities such as the PIF, IRC and the Council of Elderly Affairs. A partial list of the groups with whom the government consulted is provided in Table 4.8; the prominence of the IRC, as designated veto player, is clearly apparent. The window for such public input was extremely short as the final legislation was submitted to parliament on May 28, 1997; however, the window for parliamentary debate was even shorter as the reforms were enacted under five separate laws passed on July 15th.[33] The new system took effect January 1, 1998 and was required for all new entrants into the labor market, while existing workers were entitled to choose whether they wished to remain in the old scheme or voluntarily opt to participate in the new mixed pillar system. Those who did not express a preference were left under the old arrangements. This distinction between new and established workers was a direct result of anticipating the Constitutional Court's

---

communication; see also Orenstein 2000, 37). Not inconsistent with either of these account is that the new Finance Minister threatened his resignation if Horn did not help compel acceptance from the MOW, and being unable to afford yet another ministerial resignation, the Prime Minister forced the MOW to accept the introduction of a mixed pillar (Peter Mihályi 2001, personal communication).

32   Although the final ratio set in the 1997 legislation was 75–25, many have argued that the "substantial compromise was to go down from 100% to 50%," that is to opt for the Argentine model rather than the Chilean one (Mária Augusztinovics 2001, personal communication). After that, whether the private funds received 33% or 25% of the contributions was of little substantive significance: mandatory, private pension insurance had come to Hungary.

33   The brevity of parliamentary debate is perhaps best understood in light of the fact that the coalition controlled 72% of the seats in parliament. Given this huge disparity, many of the potential veto players were actually outside of parliament per se in such bodies as the IRC and the various ministries (for more on veto players in the pension reform process, see Orenstein 2000). In addition, the left wing of the socialist party had made the IRC's consent a precondition for their support in parliament. Thus by the time parliamentary debate began, most (if not all) of the potential veto players had already been consulted; opposition parties were then given a brief period (40 hours of parliamentary debate) to have their say (see Ferge 1997, 1999). Although amendments were offered, no substantive changes were made.

preferences. While established workers had acquired rights under the old pension system, new workers, by definition, had not and could therefore be forced into the new arrangement (Nelson 1998, 27–28).

The Debate

The issue of reform ultimately amounted to a choice between either trying to fix the current arrangement, or to create a new multi-pillar system by adding mandatory private accounts. In the analysis that follows, I focus primarily on the aggregate population supporting one of these two approaches; however, this does not preclude the testing of the individual group hypotheses presented earlier.

Reforming the Existing System In the case of Hungary, the onus of action lay with those opposed to the creation of mandatory, private pension insurance following the conversion of the MOW in 1996. If they did nothing, the government's plan would simply have moved through parliament and become law; therefore, the more pressing need to organize rested with those generally left behind by the transition. While little organization or direct action is expected from the biggest losers, the increasing returns offered by the objective combined with their immense electoral potential made it extremely likely that someone would attempt to organize them. Given a general correspondence of interest, that task was quickly undertaken by the trade unions. Although declining in membership, the unions still possessed a nationwide geographical base that mimicked that of the transition's losers, and its existing institutional infrastructure offered one way to overcome communication barriers and other logistical obstacles.

For their part, the union dominated PIF "remained the only player obstinately refusing the idea of a mixed pension system" following the MOW's acceptance of private accounts (Danics 1998, 15). Believing that such accounts unfairly shifted a significant share of the risks towards lower income earners, the unions sought the continuation and reform of the existing pension insurance scheme for all citizens.

Table 4.8   Consultations Between the Government's Pension Working Group and other Political Actors

January 6, 1997	Coalition Partners
January 7th	Pension Insurance Fund (PIF)
January 8th	Parliamentary Representatives
January 14th	National Alliance of Pensioners
January 15th	Council of the Elderly
January 21st	Child and Youth Interest Reconciliation Council
January 22nd	Board of Directors of SZEF state and municipal employee's trade union
January 29th	Board of Directors of the MSZOSZ trade union
January 30th	Hungarian Socialist Party members of Parliament
February 4th	Interest Reconciliation Council
February 7th	Interest Reconciliation Council
February 13th	Conference organized by Sandor Nagy (former head of MSZOSZ and PIF)
February 17th	Hungarian Democratic People's party (MDNP)
February 19th	Hungarian Socialist Party of the Left Group
February 21st	Board of Directors of SZEF trade union
February 26th	MSZOSZ Council of Alliance leaders (including the President of the PIF)
February 28th	Interest Reconciliation Council
March (various dates)	
	Hungarian Socialist Party members of Parliament
	Alliance of Free Democrats (SZDSZ) members of Parliament
March 11th	Pension Insurance Fund
March 12th	Interest Reconciliation Council

Source: Orenstein 2000, 35.

In doing so, the unions became the channel through which the relative losers of the transition found their voice.

Hungarian unions, however, and the MSZOSZ in particular, suffered from too many internal cleavages to be a truly effective advocate. While the economic upheaval of the early 1990s had affected the entire economy, traditional blue-collar jobs in the heavy industries were among the hardest hit. Thus the core of the union's membership was primarily concerned with current wages, unemployment benefits and job creation, tasks that fell to the union representatives on the IRC. Although the MSZOSZ dominated both the PIF and IRC boards, the members on the latter proved, "according to varying interpretations, more flexible or opportunist" in their dealings with the government at the expense of those on the PIF (Nelson 1998, 23).

One source of this enhanced opportunism was that the left wing of the ruling Socialist party had made their support in parliament contingent on the IRC's consent, thereby making the IRC the effective veto-player and not the PIF. This status can be seen in the fact that government met with IRC representatives four times in less than five weeks to iron out a compromise; meanwhile it met with PIF only twice in the course of three months of pubic consultations during the Spring of 1997 (see Table 4.8). The IRC members made use of their veto-power by demanding and receiving a number of concession, ones which reveal the division of interest between the IRC and the PIF as most were aimed at union member's immediate pocketbooks. For example, the decision was made to postpone the reform of disability pensions that had been widely used to ease unemployment strains in the past; in addition, a two-year delay was agreed in the introduction of a revised indexation formula, which promised to adversely affect the value of existing pensions (Nelson 1998, 23).[34] The most significant demand of all, however, was a guarantee to participants under the new system that they would not receive a pension lower than what they would have received under the old system, so long as they had contributed to the new second pillar for at least fifteen years.[35] Although the value of this guarantee was understood to be dependant upon whatever changes future government's might make to the benefits provided under the existing PAYG pillar, the guarantee is generally credited for the greater than expected number of people who voluntarily switched to the new mixed system as it ostensibly eliminated all the risk.

Although the combination of the guarantee and the temporary concessions satisfied many of the opponents, some, including most of the union's PIF members, remained steadfast in their opposition to even a partial privatization of the pension system. The union's leaders, however, were satisfied that their demands had been incorporated, for while they were not directly and loudly for privatization, they were no longer extremely vocal in their opposition either (Mária Augusztinovics 2001, personal communication). While the above concessions certainly played a part in their turnaround, the most important factor had less to do with "the pension reform itself than to [the union's] political concerns" (Nelson 1998, 24). With union membership in steady decline, the MSZOSZ feared it would lose its remaining influence if the nationwide elections to the IRC and PIF boards were allowed to go forward as planned in 1998. To avoid this, a deal was worked out by the IRC members whereby the government agreed to ask each of the "sides" in the Pension and Health Fund Boards (that is, labor and management) to reach agreement among themselves regarding how to allocate their seats. That formula was ratified in legislation passed in summer 1997 [and the election plans were abandoned]. The unions then reached an agreement [among themselves] allocating 7 of 15 labor seats to MSZOSZ and dividing the balance among other major labor federations. MSZOSZ therefore maintained control over the Pension and Health Insurance Boards, in exchange for dropping opposition to the modified pension reform (Nelson 1998, 24).

---

34   This temporary concession became even more temporary after the Fidesz victory in the 1998 election. It voted to immediately switch to the Swiss indexation formula rather than wait until 2000. Swiss indexation adjusts pensions according to the movement of both wages and prices. If inflation falls, as was expected, pensions will not be increased as much as they would be under existing arrangements.

35   The level of the guarantee appears somewhat open to interpretation. Palacios and Rocha state that the "guarantee is equivalent to around 93 percent of the pension which would have been received if the worker had remained in the pure PAYG scheme;" however, they go on to note that "in addition, there is type of relative rate of return guarantee" which is somewhat difficult to evaluate in monetary terms as a great deal of discretion appears to exist on behalf of regulators (1997, 29).

Although widely criticized by many, including the union's PIF members as well as the government's coalition partners, the deal went ahead, or so it appeared (Augusztinovics 2001, personal communication; Nelson 1998, fn 10). A year after the pension reforms had gone into effect, the Constitutional Court struck down this arrangement; however, before new board elections could be called, the newly elected Fidesz government did away with both boards altogether making the matter moot.[36]

I argue that what ultimately hindered the opponents of pension privatization was that the unions, as well as the public opposition itself, were not completely of one mind or opinion. Aided by internal fault lines within the unions, the proponents of radical reform were able to win over at least their tacit support and approval in exchange for a number of general concessions on relatively minor points. The 20% of the Little Losers who wanted to do away with payroll contributions altogether, along with those who sought a continuation of the status quo, were ultimately unable to effectively organize a separate opposition. In a sense betrayed by the union leadership, the PIF members and the steadfast opponents to pension privatization were simply out maneuvered and unable to effectively organize a separate opposition.

Radical Reform (Adding New, Mandatory Private Accounts)   Both the Little and Big Winners of the transition were highly likely to successfully organize themselves (Table 4.7). The evidence suggests that they were able to both organize and influence the process. The avenue of access for that influence was through the ruling Socialist party and their coalition partners, the Association of Free Democrats. Although much of the Socialist's support had fallen from the absolute majority enjoyed in 1994, the party could still count on around 30% of each income group's vote in a hypothetical next-Sunday election, while its coalition partner could roughly expect a further 10% of the Little Losers and 15% of transitions biggest winners to vote for them.[37] Thus, in pushing for the implementation of private pension insurance, the government was reflecting the interests of its core supporters.

These interests, and resulting pressure, can be seen at both the commercial and individual level. At the commercial level, they appear most visibly in the relationship between the financial community and the Ministry of Finance in what amounted to a coalition between the bureaucracy and the large financial firms. The latter's primary concern regarding the new second pillar was the question of access to, and management of, the new funds. As the drafters and consultants of the actual legislation, the bankers and insurers were able to secure a significant role for themselves. Even though the legislation required second pillar funds to be invested primarily in government bonds, these actors were allowed to play the profitable role

---

36   It is now widely surmised throughout Budapest that the government fully anticipated the Court's action when it made the agreement in 1997. Whether this is a case of post-hoc cynicism or an accurate reflection of what went on is difficult to say.

37   The socialist majority had been steadily declining throughout its period in office. Although it would go on to lose the 1998 election, its biggest supporters remained those with incomes above the mean.

of middle-man. Their other area of concern centered on the private, voluntary mutual benefit (VMB) funds, which had been in existence since 1993.[38] As a result of direct pressure from the Hungarian Federation of Mutual Funds, with the support of the government's Supervisory Authority, the financial community was able to extract an important concession that "the corporate constitution of the new, mandatory pension funds [would mirror] that the existing VMB funds" (Müller 1999, 82). By ensuring themselves a place in both the second and third pillars, the industry had covered itself against potential losses fearing that some "clients would be less inclined to engage in voluntary retirement provision, once the [mandatory second pillar was] created" (Müller 1999, 82). No matter what an individual decided to do, banks and insurance companies were guaranteed a piece of action.

The concerns of transition's relative winners were twofold. First, they were concerned with the oversight and administrative costs of the new private pillar. Second, they had concerns over the tax implication of changes to the VMB funds. While their direct involvement is difficult to pinpoint due to the correspondence of interest with the government's own proposal, their concerns were clearly and directly conveyed the MOF through a series of Ministry-ordered surveys conducted by TÁRKI, as well as through more private means. These surveys showed, perhaps not surprisingly, that the two most important factors in choosing a fund were that "it manage the funds safely even if it pays a lower interest rate," and that the money "should be handled by competent experts and the highest possible profits should be achieved" (TÁRKI 1996, 37). Although the perceived importance of expertise clearly rose with the level of household income, the sentiment was so widespread (and reasonable) that these concerns were effectively built-in to the pending legislation.

Professionalism was also a factor concerning the voluntary third pillar, and was likewise incorporated into the VMB funds. Under the new package of laws, the existing VMB statue was amended so that all funds were required to apply for a license, and after receiving it, had six months to recruit two thousand members if they wished to continue operating. This high threshold gave a clear advantage to larger firms, such as banks and insurance companies, that had pre-existing client lists along with internal marketing and sales departments with which to recruit the required members (Nelson 1998, fn 12).[39] As a result of the membership requirement, the field is currently made-up of thirty-five companies, five of which have around 80% of the total membership and control approximately 70% of the estimated $420 million invested.

---

38   These so-called third pillar funds numbered more than 250 by 1997 and pooled the contributions of around 600,000 employees, a figure which represented more than 15% of the labor force (Nelson 1998, 26).

39   Evidence of the membership requirement's affect can be seen as only "about fifty [of the 250 existing funds] applied for licenses when the reforms went into effect in January 1998, and only a handful [of those] had recruited 2000 members as of March 1998" (Nelson 1998, fn 12).

The advantage of this concentration for contributors is that the wider membership base reduces per-capita costs and introduces economies of scale while still maintaining a level of competition. As for expertise and experience, four of the top five funds are run by Dutch (Nationale-Nederlanden and Aegon), German (Allianz) and Swiss (Credit Suisse) financial giants; the fifth, and the largest fund overall, is managed by the country's largest, privately held bank (OTP) which is traded on the Budapest stock exchange. While these characteristics alone do not necessarily entail good corporate governance, the five, particular the four West European firms, are generally regarded as solid, well-managed, professional financial institutions.

While the professionalism of the private funds was clearly important, the more pressing matter for individual Big and Little Winners was the significant 50% tax deduction on contributions made to the voluntary funds. In light of this considerable deduction, which has since been reduced to 30% by the Fidesz government which came to power in 1998, many have taken full advantage by contributing the maximum allowable under the law (Mária Augusztinovics 2001, personal communication). While on the surface this tax deduction would appear to benefit everyone, in practice it was only of use to the wealthiest households as the poorest households either paid no tax, and hence had no use for such deductions, or simply could not afford to do without all of their take-home wages.[40] The bottom line is that in a desire to ensure sufficient support for the proposed legislation, the Socialist government did not attempt to tamper which such privileges.[41] With these assurances and measures in place, a large segment of society was lined-up in support of the government's efforts to partially privatize the pension system.

Conclusion

By 1997, the Hungarian pension system had reached its limits; without fundamental reform, the system was on the brink of bankruptcy. While something had to be done, there existed an open and intense split between those who sought to reform the existing PAYG system, and those who sought to implement a new, private

---

40   While the 1997 legislation stated the new second pillar could only accept contributions from employers, the VMB funds could do so from both employers and employees alike. In practice, employers today provide roughly three-fourths of all the contributions to these voluntary funds, the advantage being that they do not have to pay social security taxes on that part of the employee's wage. From the employee's perspective then such contributions have become an important fringe benefit to working for a successful company; for employers, the third pillar has become a useful tool to both attract and retain highly skilled labor. Thus in many ways membership in the VMB funds is more a function of "the internal labor market of the company" than self-interested behavior on the part of employees (Robert Gál 2001, personal communication).

41   A similar restraint was shown in regard to certain "specialized groups," such as the railway system, which had "been permitted to accumulate massive arrears to the pension system over many years" (Nelson 1998, 25). The government managed to avoid "potential opposition from these groups ... by postponing any attempt to alter their privileges" (Ibid).

arrangement modeled on the Chilean and Argentine experience. The above analysis shows the political process in Hungary responded to the demands of both groups.

For those trying to block the advent of mandatory private accounts, the success or failure of their political efforts rested in large part on the correspondence of interest between those left financially behind by the transition and the country's trade unions. This coalition proved a mixed success. Aided by the highly credible electoral threat posed by the former, and the access granted by the formal standing of the latter on the IRC and PIF boards, the partnership was in a position to demand and extract concessions. The results of this pressure can be seen in the legislative and lobbying record, which point to several small victories as well as the inclusion of a guaranteed rate of return on the new accounts. That same record, however, suggests that the unions may not have been the best vehicles for public opposition. Caught trying to defend both low skilled wage earners and retirees at the same time, the unions were extremely fragmented and easily divided. Ultimately, the government was able to play the union's larger political and survival goals against the narrow issue of pension reform. However, while able to employ a divided-and-conquer strategy, the government was forced to offer concessions, phase-in periods and a publicly guaranteed rate of return in order to successfully placate the opposition.

While there remained some who "felt marginalized by what they viewed as a steam-roller process ... most major stakeholders felt they had been consulted and had an impact on the outcome" (Nelson 1998, 29; see also Ferge 1997). Although this consultation was limited to those groups who managed to overcome their own collective action problems, the political process did respond, at least in part, to the policy demands of those who successfully organized. Although ultimately unsuccessful in their efforts to formally block the advent of mandatory private pension provision, opponents did not walk away empty-handed.

For those seeking to implement the World Bank model, the situation was somewhat easier. Because the government, for largely its own fiscal reasons, sought to implement a private pillar, there was little need for its supporters to mount an aggressive campaign. Although they made their concerns about tax-benefits and the professionalism of the funds known, it is difficult to evaluate the extent of their collective efforts. Consequently, a comparison with the Czech experience (Chapter 5) may help to clarify their role as "the political leverage of the ... advocates of a mandatory [individually fully funded] scheme was clearly insufficient to induce a revision" in the Czech Republic (Müller 1999, 145). What we can draw from the Hungarian experience is that this group was able to effectively overcome the barriers to collective action. We can see the evidence of their organization in lobbying efforts behind various regulations, safeguards and tax incentives. However, more importantly perhaps, was the role their sizeable electoral weight played in brining about the initial compromise between the MOF and MOW. For while the written Coalition Agreement forced the partners to negotiate, it is not clear that the pro-privatization forces would have had the leverage to pressure the Minister of Welfare without the public support and lobbying pressure exerted by financial community behind them.

In sum, the Hungarian experience suggests a functioning democracy in the sense describe by Przeworski (1991) as well as Linz and Stepan (1999). The process of privatization created both relative winners and losers of resources, and consequently changed both their preferences over policy and their ability to defend those preferences politically. Aided by some factors and hindered by others, both groups were faced with a collective action challenge if they sought to influence the reform process. Although motivated towards different objectives, these domestic political actors took what was a standard set of policy proscriptions from the World Bank and fashioned themselves a unique set of reforms. In doing so, they demonstrate the extent to which domestic politics can shape international policy pressure as the final result converted what was to be a mixed-pillar system into a PAYG system in disguise. While this does not appear to the original intent of any actor, it was the political result of a deliberative process involving actors with divergent preferences over policy outcomes. In that sense, the democratic process worked.

Chapter 5

The Case of the Czech Republic

While the Czech experience is comparable to that of Poland and Hungary's in many respects, its initial starting point and debt situation, its 1993 velvet divorce from the (now) Slovak Republic, and the continual presence of Vaćlav Klaus from 1989–1998 provide three significant points of departure. The first reflects a slightly different historical and economic legacy. Although both Hungary (1956) and Czechoslovakia (1968) rebelled against Soviet control, and were crushed for their efforts, their subsequent reactions were radically different.[1] A decade after the Soviet invasion, the Hungarian communists, under the leadership of Janos Kádár, struck an implicit deal with the general population: in exchange for not attempting another such revolt, citizens would be granted a greater array of western consumer goods and reduced centralized control over the economy. As part of what eventually became known as Goulash communism, Hungary began a period of economic reforms in the 1970s that created the beginnings of a private sector.[2] In contrast, Czechoslovakia reverted back to a bastion of centralized planning and communist control, so much so that when the privatization process began in 1990, essentially 100% of the economy rested in state hands. One significant political consequence of this reassertion was that it effectively prevented the emergence of powerful managers and other firm insiders, groups who were among some of the early big winners in both Poland and Hungary. As a result, with no firm-level opposition to overcome, the Czech government was able to proceed with its privatization program much more quickly than either of its neighbors (Frydman et al 1993, 52).

Likewise, this orthodox version of state planning and centralization meant that the Czechs never borrowed heavily in western capital markets during the 1970s, and as such, avoided the crippling debt-ratios that plagued both Poland and Hungary following the surge in interest rates in the early 1980s.[3] Consequently,

---

1   Poland for its part can be seen as having posited a similar challenge to Soviet control in the 1980s beginning with the uprising in Gdansk, the creation of Solidarity, and ultimately the declaration of martial law by the Polish government.

2   Goulash is a Hungarian stew of mixed vegetables, potatoes, beef, and a lot of paprika! The term was meant to convey both the mixed provision of goods by the public and private sectors, as well as the notion of being full and satiated - something goulash definitely accomplishes.

3   Like many developing countries in the 1970s, Poland and Hungary took advantage of the incredibly low interest rates offered by western banks to borrow large sums of money while the more orthodox communist states, primarily East Germany and Czechoslovakia, remained ideologically opposed to such endeavors. Following a change in U.S. monetary

fiscal authorities in the Czech Republic were comparatively less encumbered than most other countries in the region when it came to government spending.[4] More importantly, the relative lack of external debt meant that when the time for pension reform came, the World Bank and other advocates of the Latin American models found little in the way of leverage with which to pressure the Czechs.

A second critical difference is the peaceful division of Czechoslovakia on January 1, 1993. Always richer and more developed than rural Slovakia, the partition served to unify and accelerate the reform process on the Czech side of the border as most of the struggling state-owned enterprises (SOEs), along with most rural cooperatives, were located in Slovakia. This uneven distribution of industrial capacity and income meant that the "new Slovak industry was ... much more subject to the post-communist shock, [while] the Czech industry could more easily adapt to new conditions" (Frydman et al 1997, 49). In essence, the velvet divorce freed the Czech Republic from the more unproductive and uncompetitive elements of the Czechoslovakian economy, thus greatly simplifying the privatization of its remaining firms and leaving its economy in relatively sound financial shape.

The final point of departure is the continual presence and leadership of Vaclav Klaus. Finance Minister from 1989 to 1992 and Prime Minister from 1992 to 1998, Klaus, along with Dusan Triska, designed and executed the Czech privatization program from start to finish. This long-term continuity presents a marked divergence from the experiences of Poland and Hungary, each of which went through multiple governments and periods of outright policy reversal as they attempted to privatized their SOEs from 1989 to 1997. In designing procedures for the liquidation of state assets, both Klaus and Triska were acutely aware of the political consequences such programs would have. In commenting on the task ahead, Triska, the former Deputy Finance Minister and Director of Privatization within the Ministry of Finance, said that

> The most bitter pill that our nation will have to swallow is to see who will be the winners and who will be the losers in the process of transformation and privatization. The winners will certainly be the old winners and the losers will be those who were also the losers under the previous regime (Triska 1991, 27).

Hoping to avoid such a continuity, the pair designed programs that gave no special rights or privileges to enterprise insiders; instead, they sought to create a large and diffuse class of business owners "firmly committed to the new regime" (Frydman et

---

policy, world wide interest rates sky-rocketed in the 1980s leaving borrower nations in severe financial difficulty. For more on the resulting debt crisis around the world, see Devlin 1989; Sachs 1989.

4   The East German case must be considered separately in this regard. While another of the hard-line followers of state planning, the German Democratic Republic (GDR) never borrowed large sums of money from the west either. However, its transition is inseparable from the unification with the Federal Republic, which has pumped billions of marks (euros) into the former GDR over the past decade.

al 1997, 88). Klaus quickly sought to attach that commitment to his own career and political party, the Civic Democratic Party (ODS). In the end, the Czech experience resulted in a larger and more diffuse group of winners than had been created in either Poland or Hungary, where firm insiders were often able to extract a disproportionate share of the benefits.

While these differences help set the tone for the Czech experience, the underlying challenge and debate in regard to social welfare reform was identical to what took place in Poland and Hungary. Although unemployment pressures were not as severe as in either of its neighbors during the early 1990s (1993–1996 average: 3.3%), unfavorable demographic trends forced the nation to consider ways to reform its pension system. By 1995, the nation's pension ranks had swelled to the point where the burden of providing for three pensions could only be distributed among five workers (system dependency ratio: 0.591) (Czech Statistical Yearbook, various years). It has been estimated that the country's low fertility rate could further dwindle this support base to four workers (system dependency ratio: 0.771) by 2030 (Kral 2001; Lasagabaster et al 2002; own calculations).

It is unclear at exactly what point a pension system becomes politically and financially unviable, however, it is clear that under any definition the Czech PAYG system was approaching it by the end of the 1990s. Some type of reform was essential; however, the particular characteristics of that reform effort would prove to be the result of a political battles of wills fought out in the Czech Parliament. My central argument is that both the combatants and their respective capabilities can be traced in part back to the political consequences of privatization.

Privatization and the creation of Winners and Losers

With unemployment fairly low throughout the early years of the transition, it was the privatization of state assets that had the largest affect on household welfare and income as it created an entirely new income hierarchy. This remarkable transformation can be classified into three distinct periods: restitution (1990–1991), the small and retail sector (1991–1993), and the privatization of large SOEs (1993–1997).[5] When taken in combination, these three programs transferred approximately two-thirds of all state assets into private hands by the end 1993 such that eighty percent of the adult population was a shareholder in some enterprise of the domestic economy (Coffee 1996, 114).[6]

5 For a detailed review of Czech privatization programs, see Earle et al 1994; Kotrba 1994; Matesova and Seda 1994; Coffee 1996; Akov 1997; and in particular, Frydman et al 1993.

6 This does not imply that the programs were without criticisms, particularly in the area of corporate governance. For more on issues of corporate governance in Eastern Europe resulting from privatization, see Frydman et al 1996.

Restitution

Unlike the Hungarian restitution program, which provided financial compensation for assets seized during the communist era, the Czechs simply returned the physical property itself. Poland by comparison, failed to agree politically on any particular method and hence did not undergo a period of restitution. Despite a fair amount of confusion, controversy and numerous District Court rulings to settle particular claims, the program was widely seen as both "a successful political strategy and economic policy" (Earle et al 1994, 58). Politically it created a large body of support for the new government, an important consideration "during the painful periods of macroeconomic stabilization between 1990 and 1991" (Earle et al 1994, 58–9). Economically, by providing potential entrepreneurs with assets and collateral, restitution helped jump-start the development of new and often innovative firms, ones which tended to outpace both their privatized and state-owned competitors in terms of sales, profits and salaries (Frydman et al 1997, 80 and Table 3.15).

These economic benefits can be seen in Table 5.1, which reveals a noticeable bias towards higher incomes among the self-employed. Of those households where someone was registered for private business, almost 30% were among the wealthiest 20% of households, while only 13.3% belonged to the poorest quintile. However, the effects of restitution were not completely one-sided. When asked to estimate the insurance replacement value for all household assets, even the poorest households (quintile 1) reveal the acquisition of valuable assets; of all the households with assets worth over 1 million Krowns (Kčs) [~$33,900 in 1991], 28.5% were among the poorest 40% in terms of monthly income. With the bottom quintile earning an average of only 1,623 Kčs per month (~$55), it is extremely unlikely that these assets were purchased directly. Although no direct link to restitution is possible with this data, it seems reasonable that at least some portion of these households gained their assets through the program.[7] This same uniformity of assets, but not income, can be seen in the ~20% of each quintile that owned their own homes, which is precisely the percentage to expect if there were no relationship between income and home ownership.

Small Industry and Retail Sectors

Begun in 1991, the Czech experience with small and retail sector privatization differs radically from Poland or Hungary's in that no specific privileges were set aside for firm insiders.[8] Instead, the government sought to implement a program guided by

---

7   Due to the very decentralized nature of the restitution process, there is very little data available. Claimants filed directly with the current tenant or holder and no central record was kept concerning the transactions. In the words of one former government official, "statistical data about restitution processes in the Czech Republic does not exist" (Klvačová 1996, 4).

8   This does not mean, however, that insiders were at a disadvantage. Although official data regarding the new owners is unavailable, a random survey conducted by the

Table 5.1   The Relative Winners and Losers Following Restitution

		Household Income Quintile (%)				
	Percentage of Households where ...	*1ˢᵗ*	*2ⁿᵈ*	*3ʳᵈ*	*4ᵗʰ*	*5ᵗʰ*
Privatization	Someone is registered for : Private business	13.3	18.7	17.2	21.2	29.6
Occupation of the primary earner	Administrative/Management	14.0	14.0	16.3	18.6	37.2
	Sales Worker	17.1	19.5	24.4	31.7	7.3
	Service Worker	31.7	12.9	15.8	18.8	20.8
	Industrial Production	17.7	21.2	20.7	20.7	19.8
The family owns	The family home	21.7	17.9	18.6	21.7	20.2
	A car	13.9	18.4	21.6	23.6	22.6
	A cottage	13.8	10.1	21.2	30.7	24.3
Insurance estimate of all household assets	Less than 200,000 Kčs	25.9	23.6	20.4	15.4	14.7
	200,000 – 499,00 Kčs	20.0	18.5	21.2	21.4	18.9
	500,000 – 1 million Kčs	13.3	21.4	20.4	22.8	22.1
	Over 1 million Kčs	16.4	12.1	12.1	22.4	37.1

Sample size: N= 1,299; Quintiles 1, 2, 4, & 5 (260), Quintile 3 (259).
Source: Economic Expectations and Attitudes 4, December 1991.

speed, equity and fairness, and the enforcement of the new owner's right to control the firm (Matesova and Seda 1994, 5). Rarely used to privatize entire companies, the legislation (Law 427/1990) was most often invoked to separate a particularly desirable asset from the larger firm, although items deemed "technologically necessary" to the parent company were exempt (Kotrba 1994 4; Earle et al 1994, 62). Like restitution, this program too proved relatively successful despite widespread reports of corruption, fraud and collusion among bidders to drive the auctions into a second round where assets could be had for a fraction of their original starting price (Akov 1997, 26). By the end of 1993, 22,345 items had been sold with an average starting price of $33,700 and an average selling price of $48,300 (Earle et al 1994, Table I.B.6; 70; Akov 1997, 25–6). Although a profit was generally made in each auction, the proceeds did not flow to the enterprise, but rather into a central fund administered by the Fund for National Property. In this regard, "firms were pure losers in the small privatization" period (Kotrba 1994, 4). First, they were required to absorb any debt liabilities attached to the asset in question, and were then denied compensation for whatever had been purchased. Finally, they were left

---

Privatization Project of Central European University found that 53% of the new owners of retail trade, catering and service-related establishments had worked in some capacity for the former enterprise that had owned the asset. Given that insiders generally possessed better information about the asset's true value, "it may not be surprising that they [won] about half the auctions" (Earle 1994, 70).

to continue operating as best they could after having been stripped of almost every non-technologically necessary piece of equipment in their possession.

As far as individuals are concerned, the trend begun under restitution continued as the greatest benefits again went to the private sector entrepreneur. As seen in Table 5.2, almost 60% of all self-employed business owners belonged to the top income quintile, while those who still worked for a SOE had only a 16.6% chance of earning as large an income. Having gained so much in recent years, it is not surprising that the wealthiest household were also the most ardent supporters for the quick continuation of privatization, even if it meant assets could fall into "unproper hands" (Economic Expectations and Attitudes 7, Question 27). Also in-line with expectations is the fact that an employee had a 16% better chance of being in the upper income quintile if he worked for a firm involved with foreign investors than if he worked for a purely domestic company.

Large Scale Privatization

It was partly with this kind of widening income distribution in mind that the Czech reformers designed their unique approach to large scale privatization, one which in stark contrast to its neighbors did not heavily rely on direct cash sales.[9] Although several different techniques were employed, the process was ultimately dominated by the use of vouchers due to the "discretion given" Prime Minister Václav Klaus (Frydman et al 1997, 89). Driven by an overwhelming desire to break with the past, Klaus sought to create a large and diffuse class of business owners by using vouchers to essentially give-away state property.

Under the program, any Czech citizen over the age of 18 who resided in the country could, for a nominal fee, purchase a voucher book worth 1000 points; these points were then used to bid on the shares of large SOEs, which had been reorganized into joint-stock companies. The winning bidders became shareholders in the new private enterprise. Over three-quarters of the adult population participated in the program, but an unanticipated wrinkle quickly emerged. Recognizing that the program would result in extremely diffuse ownership spread among hundreds of thousands of small shareholders, young entrepreneurs and large financial institutions created a series of mutual funds which offered to purchase individual voucher points in exchange for shares in their new funds. Often promising outlandish short-term returns, these investment privatization funds (IPFs) "managed to obtain 71.5% of all the voucher points available in the first round" and 64% in the second (Frydman

---

9   Due in part to immense foreign debt obligations, Hungary, and to a lesser extent Poland, followed a comparatively simple strategy of competitive bidding and cash payments. This entailed a considerable degree of foreign involvement as locals did not have the financial resources to compete for the most attractive firms and enterprises. For a more detailed look at the Polish and Hungarian privatization programs, see Chapters 3 and 4 respectively; see also Frydman et al 1993.

Table 5.2   The Relative Winners and Losers Following Small Privatization, 1993

	Percentage of Households where ...	*Household Income Quintile (%)*				
		1st	*2nd*	*3rd*	*4th*	*5th*
Position and Firm-type	Owner of a private firm with one's own employees.	5.4	10.8	21.6	16.2	46.0
	Owner of a private firm w/o one's own employees.	14.3	8.6	11.4	8.5	57.1
	Employee in a private firm not created by privatization.	8.5	14.6	19.2	23.1	34.6
	Employee of a privatized former SOE.	5.5	20.0	25.5	23.6	25.5
	Employee of an SOE not yet privatized.	8.9	21.7	23.6	29.3	16.6
	Employee of another state organization.	10.7	14.4	23.1	32.8	19.0
The Pace of Privatization	Should proceed quickly even if assets end up in improper hands.	14.0	14.0	16.3	18.6	37.2
	A major part of the firm's capital comes from abroad.	5.6	15.7	18.0	21.4	39.3
Foreign Investment	A small part of the firm's capital comes from abroad.	0.0	13.3	13.3	46.7	26.7
	Firm's capital comes solely from domestic sources.	9.6	17.7	23.4	25.9	23.4
Pensioners	Still active in the labor force.	6.7	15.6	26.7	26.7	24.4
	No longer active.	54.2	26.7	11.6	3.6	4.0
The Family Owns	The family home	16.8	20.1	18.8	21.0	22.4
	A cottage	10.5	11.0	19.7	23.3	35.5
	A trade shop or business	13.9	3.1	15.4	13.9	53.9
Insurance Est. of all Household Assets	Less than 200,000 Kčs	38.7	21.7	18.4	12.9	8.3
	200,000 – 499,00 Kčs	20.5	23.5	21.8	18.6	15.4
	500,000 – 1 million Kčs	9.5	19.1	22.6	23.0	25.8
	Over 1 million Kčs	12.0	13.0	15.3	25.9	33.7

Sample size: N= 1,095; Quintiles (219)

Source: Economic Expectations and Attitudes 7, November 1993.

et al 1997, 91).[10] Beyond the quantity of points accumulated was the even greater concentration of points held in these funds. Although over 400 IPFs were created, by 1994 the top seven controlled almost 45% of all the voucher points, and five of these were controlled by state-owned banks.[11] Thus, a rather perverse situation emerged whereby nominally privatized companies were owned by IPFs, which in turn were owned by state-owned banks.[12] Despite concerns over corporate governance, and whether these firms were actually private, the voucher program did succeed in transferring the bulk of the remaining state assets to new owners in very short amount of time. As with the previous periods, there were relative winners and losers. The biggest winners were again the private sector entrepreneurs (Table 5.3); 85.5% of the new owners of firms (with employees) belonged to the top 40% of households in terms of monthly income. By comparison, almost half (47.3%) of the employees still working for a SOE belonged to the bottom most income quintiles, suggesting that these employees had been left behind by the transition.

It is also interesting to note that, in the wake of the free give-away, a fundamental reversal had taken place among the wealthy in regard to the pace of privatization. Following the cash-based auctions of the small privatization period in 1993, over 30% supported the idea that privatization should be completed as quickly as possible, even if it meant assets would end up in improper hands. Following mass-based voucher privatization, 37.3% now strongly disagreed with that sentiment. Forced to compete with everyone else in the essentially free giveaway of state assets, support for the concept evaporated. Nevertheless, the relative proportion of those who felt that they personally had gained from the voucher experience was largely uniform across income quintiles.

---

10   The slippage (from 71.5% to 64%) has been credited in part to publicity about individuals who managed to do very well on their own in the first round. Feeling more confident, many more people opted to bid alone in the second round (Coffee 1996, 136).

11   For more on the investment privatization funds, see Myant 2003, particularly Chapters 7 and 8.

12   I am indebted to Professor Jan Hanousek of the Center for Economic Research and Graduate Education (CERGE) of Charles University, Prague for insightful guidance and expert advice on the often murky terrain of Czech privatization, investment funds and the role of state-owned banks. For more on IPFs and state banks, see Róna-Tas 1997.

Table 5.3   The Relative Winners and Losers Following Voucher (Large) Privatization, 1996

	Percentage of Households where ...	*Household Income Quintile (%)*				
		1st	*2nd*	*3rd*	*4th*	*5th*
Position and Firm-type	Owner of a private firm with one's own employees.	4.4	2.9	7.3	20.3	65.2
	Owner of a private firm w/o one's own employees.	18.4	5.3	10.5	23.7	42.1
	Employee in a new private firm (not a former SOE).	19.9	12.0	18.3	23.0	26.7
	Employee of a privatized former SOE.	18.7	18.7	22.1	21.8	26.7
	Employee of an SOE not yet privatized.	21.4	25.9	21.4	16.1	15.2
	Employee of another state organization.	16.8	13.3	25.0	23.8	21.1
The Pace of Privatization	Should proceed quickly even if assets end up in improper hands.	22.2	23.4	18.3	19.1	17.0
	Definitely disagrees with this statement.	12.8	6.9	16.7	26.5	37.3
Participated In Voucher Auctions?	First Round	16.9	19.7	20.1	20.1	21.5
	Second Round	17.8	19.9	20.3	20.8	21.3
Profited from this Participation?	Yes, profited from vouchers.	17.7	18.5	19.0	19.8	25.0
	No, did not profit from them.	22.3	22.4	20.6	21.7	19.9
Proportion of Vouchers Placed in an Investment Privatization Fund (IPF)	1st Round: None	11.0	17.2	16.6	25.4	30.4
	About half	16.1	18.8	25.0	21.4	18.8
	All	20.5	21.7	21.7	19.2	16.8
	2nd Round: None	11.4	17.0	15.4	25.5	30.8
	About half	19.8	17.8	21.9	26.0	14.6
	All	22.9	24.0	23.0	16.4	13.8

Sample size: N= 1,429; Quintiles 1, 2, 4, & 5 (286), Quintile 3 (285).
Source: Economic Expectations and Attitudes 9, January 1996.

To this point, I have relied on the use of household income quintiles to assess the relative winners and losers because of their intuitive and implicit test for variation. However, the size invariance of quintiles prevents testing the theoretical predictions of the model. Therefore, the relative winners and losers of the transition are placed into categories on the basis of their household income as a percentage of the mean household. Using the four-fold classification described in Chapter 2, the new Czech income strata is presented in Table 5.4

Table 5.4   The Relative Winners and Losers of the Transition, 1996

Category	Definition	1996 Average Monthly Income	Number of Households	Percent of Sample
Big Losers	Households with an income less than 50% of the mean.	2,965.81 Kčs.	124	8.7%
Little Losers	Households with an income less than the mean but more than 50% of it.	5,812.60	815	57.0
Little Winners	Households with an income more than the mean but less that 150% of it.	9,172.67	316	22.1
Big Winners	Households with an income in excess of 150% of the mean.	17,602.22	174	12.2
	Average / Total	7,744.14	N=1,429	

The average monthly household income is in Czech Krowns. In 1996, the average exchange rate was $1= 27.15 Kčs.

Source: Economic Expectations and Attitudes 9, January 1996.

Actors and Their Roles

Individuals

The relative winners and losers of privatization constitute the first set of actors, ones whose preferences in regard to pension reform alternatives varied considerably, as indicated in Table 5.5. The poorest Czech households were roughly evenly split between those who sought to reform the existing system, and those who sought to replace it with a universal flat-rate pension. Only 5.7% of the transition's biggest losers were in favor of creating a system of privately funded accounts. Among the wealthiest households, a clear majority favored reforming the current system, but in a manner that tightened the contribution/benefit link. Although the wealthy were the strongest supporters of implementing mandatory private accounts, a majority of all income classes preferred reforming the existing system as an alternative. This alone suggests that those wishing to create mandatory private accounts faced an up-hill struggle and were a clear minority, amounting to only 6.8% of the total population.

Table 5.5   Relative Winner and Loser Attitudes Toward Pension Reform

	Big Losers	Little Losers	Little Winners	Big Winners	Overall
Type of Pension System Preferred:	(Column Percentages)				
Pensions are paid by the state from the state budget to all people at a flat-rate. In addition, everyone can purchase his/her own private, supplemental insurance.	44.4	45.7	28.8	27.3	40.1
Pensions are paid from a pension fund. Everyone contributes to this fund according to his/her income, and pensions are calculated according to these payments.	50.0	50.6	60.5	56.3	53.1
The state only cares for the needy. Others pay their own private insurance and pensions are calculated according to these payments.	5.7	3.6	10.7	16.5	6.8
Total (N)	124	798	243	176	1,341

Do you favor lowering the retirement age to 53–55 years for women and to 60 years for men?					
Yes	84.7	80.6	64.9	65.5	76.2
No	15.3	19.4	35.1	34.5	23.8
Total (N)	124	798	242	174	1,334

Source: Economic Expectations and Attitudes 10, January 1997.

Social Cleavages

Following the peaceful division of Czechoslovakia in 1993, the most salient remaining cleavage was the socioeconomic divide (Mansfeldová 1998, 204).[13] The result of the growing income and asset gap described above, this cleavage proved the most polarizing force in the political arena, and one that pitted the transition's relative winners against its relative losers. One focal point of this confrontation proved to be the extent to which the communist past needed to be undone, an issue which put on the political left on the defensive.[14] However, unable to prevent a certain degree of retrenchment and reversal, this mounting pressure actually led "trade unions [to] become more active" as more and more communist-era policies were either scaled back or abandoned (Mansfeldová 1998, 204). In pension reform, the unions felt they finally had a issue they could successfully defend. Helped by the polarizing

---

13   For more on the breakup of Czechoslovakia, see Wolchik 1994.

14   The extent to which anti-communism influenced Czech events is perhaps best exemplified by 1991 Lustration Law. The act, extended in both 1996 and 2000, barred former communist officials and police agents from holding public office.

nature of the underlying social cleavage in society, the trade unions became one of the principle defenders of the existing system, largely through their position on the Tripartite Council and their ties to the Czech Social Democratic Party.

The Tripartite Commission

In an attempt to counter balance the influence of unions, the government set up the Council of Economic and Social Accord (RHSD) in 1990.[15] "Since no single business association" existed in the wake of the communist collapse, the government "decided to create one" (Orenstein and Desai 1997, 47). The resulting Council was empowered to review and discuss all social legislation prior to its submission to parliament. If a consensus is reached, then it "is considered 'binding' on all parties. Although such an agreement has no legal status, it is considered a gentleman's agreement. If no consensus is reached, the government is required to report the positions of the other social partners when it presents the legislation or program to parliament" (Orenstein and Desai 1997, 48). In practice, the business or employer side of the Council has proven to be particularly weak and ineffective. Previous research reveals

> that most [business associations] have failed to set their own agendas or pursue them with any vigor and instead provide free consultation services to state institutions. Thus far, Czech business associations have responded more to political incentives for institutional survival than to any economic incentives they might have for collective action (Orenstein and Desai 1997, 44).

This weakness left the unions as the more dominant actor on the Council, where the Czech-Moravian Chamber of Trade Unions (ČMKOS) acts as an umbrella organization. Not formally affiliated with any political party, the Chamber has steadfastly attempted to maintain its independence (Mansfeldová 1998, 204). Of all the non-governmental actors, the ČMKOS was the strongest advocate of maintaining the status quo and an extremely vocal critic of creating mandatory private accounts, believing that such a move "would destroy social solidarity" (Müller 1999, 141). At one level, it saw the proposed increase in the retirement age as a direct affront to its members. In trying to prevent such action, the ČMKOS organized a petition that was ultimately signed by over 630,000 people. It also sought to protect its members' contributions by demanding that their payroll deductions, which were creating a surplus in the PAYG system at the time, be formally separated from the state budget (Müller 1999, 137). As in other countries, cash-strapped budget officials had been known to use this annual surplus to cover other non-pension related spending priorities. Realizing that Klaus was committed to some type of reform, and generally unwilling to accommodate their status quo oriented demands,

---

15   The Council was renamed to the Council for Dialogue of Social Partners in 1995. Hereafter, the tripartite organization is simply referred to as "the Council."

the Chamber eventually pressed for and won a series of concessions that included a universal flat-rate pension paid for by general taxation (Müller 1999, 137).

Political Parties

The ODS   The party of Prime Minister Vaćlav Klaus, the ODS led the government coalition from 1992-1997 with the ODA and the KDU-ČSL.[16] For its part, the ODS remained fairly "ambiguous" on matters relating to pension reform, reflecting Klaus's often inconsistent behavior and rhetoric: extremely liberal in regard to the European Union and in the press, but not so when it came to social matters and actual polices (Ondřej Schneider 2001, personal communication).[17] Part of this indecision came from being located between coalition partners holding diametrically opposed views. On the right, lay the ODA, which strongly favored creating new private accounts; on the left lay the KDU-ČSL, which favored a "more traditional social welfare policy" (Müller 1999, 138.) The bulk of this ambiguity, however, was the result of simple strategic behavior in the face of overwhelming public opinion. Having seen the polls, Klaus, ever the political realist, was unwilling to risk actively supporting the idea of private accounts in the face of significant public opposition (Stark and Bruszt 1998, 168). He was, however, convinced of the necessity to increase the retirement age, regardless of the public outcry. Confronted with the stark reality by demography experts from Charles University and a series of economic advisors, Klaus believed that any attempt to reform the current system without such an increase would only prove disastrous.

The ODA   The Civic Democratic Alliance (ODA) was a junior coalition partner and the most vocal advocate for creating mandatory private pension accounts. Despite its cabinet-level influence, however, the ODA was never able to move its more cautious senior partner to support the idea. It therefore sought to champion the cause on its own, a choice which contributed to its electoral demise in 1998 (Ondřej Schneider 2001, personal communication). However, while this decision added to the party's woes, much of the damage had already been done. Ultimately, it was the party's consistent advocacy of pro-market reforms that doomed its electoral chances in 1998, particularly in the wake of a severe fiscal and financial crisis during the period 1997–1998.[18]

---

16   A fourth party, the Christian Democratic Party (KDS) merged with Klaus's ODS in the spring of 1996. For simplicity, I subsume them here under the ODS.

17   For more on Klaus's chameleon-like qualities, see Orenstein 1996, 1998.

18   Following its electoral defeat in 1998, the party completely collapsed; its remaining members now reside within the Quad Coalition. They currently occupy only a handful of Senate seats and have no members in parliament. In sum, their adamant support for pro-market policies cost them to the point that they are no longer an independent player on the political scene. Today, they only exist to a degree within the Quad Coalition, but do not have any real influence in it (Ondřej Schneider 2001, personal communication).

The KDU-ČSL   The other coalition party at the time was the Christian Democratic Union-Czechoslovak People's Party (KDU-ČSL), a center-right party that sought both decentralization and a strong social policy. The group saw itself as the opposition force within Klaus's cabinet, and openly clashed with the ODA on issues relating to reforming the pension system. Opposed to mandatory private accounts, the party sought to reform the existing system. In the end, the party abstained from voting on the final legislation feeling it did not go far enough to protect social welfare, although this did not prevent the legislation (Act 155/1996) from passing by a narrow margin (Müller 1999, 137).

The ČSSD   The Czech Social Democratic Party (ČSSD) was the primary opposition party. Overtime, its vote share increased as it became more and more moderate. In regard to pension reform, the party opposed the idea of radical reform and sought instead to reform the existing PAYG system. Eventual winner of the 1998 election, the party has since been "dogmatic" in its insistence that mandatory private accounts will "never" become part of the Czech pension system (Ondřej Schneider 2001, personal communication).

The Left Block   This coalition of the Left Bloc (Levý bloc) and the Communist successor party, the Communist Party of Bohemia and Moravia (KSČM), has been largely kept out political decision making as all other parties have refused to work with it in government. The voice of the extreme left, the coalition strongly opposed the introduction of mandatory private accounts. It was also highly critical of the privatization process, the devaluation of the Czech Krown and the culture of a market-based society more generally.

The LSU   A left of center party, the Liberal Socialist Union (LSU) struggled throughout its existence and was wiped off the political map in the 1996 election. Although holding 16 seats following the 1992 election, the LSU was "unable to frame [its] own strategy in a publicly convincing fashion and thus ... dissintegrated in the 1992–1996 legislative term" (Kitschelt et al 1996, 214). Given the focus here on the 1995 Pension Reform Act (Law 155/1995), the party is of no real relevance for current purposes.

The SPR-RSČ   The Assembly for the Republic -Czechoslovak Republican Party (SPR-RSČ) is an extreme right-wing party with a questionable commitment to democracy. As a result, every parliamentary party has refused to cooperate with it, effectively rendering it a non-entity for current purposes.

The DŽJ   The one remaining avenue, particularly for retirees, was offered by the Pensioners for a Secure Life (DŽJ), a left-wing social movement/political party. However, as with pensioner parties everywhere, the DŽJ struggled to gather enough votes to break the 5% threshold and was ultimately more of "a pressure group rather than a party" (Müller 1999, 142). Although the group still exists, it did not have any seats in parliament while the legislation under consideration here was being drawn up or voted on.

The Electoral Rules

The Czech Republic is a bicameral system using proportional representation to elect the more dominant lower house, while majority rule is used to directly elect members to the Senate. The focus here is on the lower house which requires a 5% threshold for individual parties, and a 7-11% threshold for coalitions. Since 1990, this system has supported between four and six parties, however, as discussed above, two parties (the communists and the far-right) are essentially *persona non grata* as all others have refused to work with either of them. Despite the fact that so few parties have ever actually broken the 5% threshold, Klaus's government moved to close the door to the future development of new, smaller parties. Following reforms in 1995, all parties were required to deposit 200,000 Kčs (~$7500 in 1995) for every constituency they wished to contest (Mansfeldová 1998, 227); there are eight such districts in total. While this amount may not seem terribly high, the deposit is only returned to parties that succeed in gaining at least 5% of the vote. Consequently, smaller parties only tend to run where they know they can win. The more significant electoral feature, however, is the inclusion of preference voting whereby party officials determine which candidates will appear on their party list, but voters themselves are allowed to determine the final order of those names. The existence of this kind of preference voting is generally expected to weaken party cohesion as individual candidates are forced to compete *within* their own party in an attempt to distinguish themselves to voters. As a result, one would expect to see less partyline voting within parliament as more and more members break with the party leadership in an attempt to appease their local constituents.

Theoretical Expectations

Mandatory Private Accounts

I begin with the rejection of the World Bank's advice and the refusal to implement mandatory private pension accounts. A summary of the hypotheses for both the relative winners and losers of the transition, as well as the aggregate population is provided in Table 5.6. While the overall likelihood of collective action is quite high in the aggregate, looking across the income categories, it appears as if the wealthy had to do the bulk of the heavy lifting. Of the five group characteristic measures, only one (the heterogeneity of interest) is favorable among the biggest losers of the transition. In contrast, among the biggest winners all five are increasing the likelihood of successful collective action. With over 40% of its members residing in Prague, this small group was very likely to both recognize its shared interest and successfully communicate and coordinate a lobbying effort. That effort was further

Table 5.6   The Likelihood of Collective Action in Support of Mandatory Private Accounts

	Big Losers	*Little Losers*	*Little Winners*	*Big Winners*	*Aggregate*
Group Characteristics					
Geography	Diffuse (-)	Diffuse (-)	Diffuse (-)	Dense (+)	Dense (+)
Resource Quantity	Low (-)	High (+)	High (+)	High (+)	High (+)
Resource Mobility	Low (-)	Low (-)	Moderate (0/+)	High (+)	High (+)
Resource Heterogeneity	No (-)	No (-)	No (-)	Yes (+)	Yes (+)
Interest Heterogeneity	Yes (+)	Yes (+)	Yes (+)	Yes (+)	Yes (+)
Electoral Appeal	Very Low	Very Low	Very Low	Very Low	Very Low
Nature of the Objective					
Joint Supply (group size)	Moot	Moot	Moot	Moot	Moot
Exclusive Benefits	No (-)	No (-)	No (-)	No (-)	No (-)
Increasing Returns (group size)	Yes (-) (small)	Yes (-) (small)	Yes (-) (small)	Yes (-) (small)	Yes (-) (small)
Environment					
Other Actors	Yes (+)	Yes (+)	Yes (+)	Yes (+)	Yes (+)
Likelihood of Organizing	Low	Moderate	Moderate	Very High	Very High
Likelihood of Influence	Very Low	Very Low	Very Low	Very Low	Very Low

enhanced by the large and highly mobile set of financial resources each member possessed.

Independent of other groups, the biggest winners were also aided by a fair degree of both resource and interest heterogeneity. The former is measured by conducting a one-tailed test on the skewness of the income distribution across members. If it is significantly and positively skewed, then it is more likely that at least one member will be able, if not willing, to bear a disproportionate share of the costs. With household incomes ranging from 16,000 to 93,000 Kčs, there is considerable variation among members around the mean of 28,000. Because of the survey data used, it is impossible to conduct a similar test for interest heterogeneity (there is no variation in a categorical response, and respondents were not asked to state how strongly or intensely they desired each possible outcome). However, the qualitative evidence and the figures in Table 5.5 suggest that all groups had at least some variation in the intensity of interest.

In terms of the objective sought, the outlook is mixed with one factor making collective action more likely and one making it less. In the case of private accounts, jointness of supply is not relevant because individual pension accounts are private goods, not public or collective ones. The public benefit from such funds is more indirect in terms of the supply of savings generated for investment through the capital market. However, while the capital market clearly stood to be affected by the proposed changes, such benefits comprised only a small part of the debate and were only raised as a selling point by liberal economists, bankers and investment funds (Ondřej Schneider 2001, personal communication). There is no evidence their arguments held any sway with the general public.

The two remaining characteristics concern the incentive to free ride, and whether there are increasing returns to organization. The presence or absence of an incentive to free ride depends on the excludability of the objective sought. Although these are private accounts, the theoretical issue is whether or not someone who preferred their creation could free ride on someone else's effort to bring them about. Because the program would be mandatory, there is such an incentive. Whatever the cost involved in producing the collective/individual benefit, everyone is better off letting some else pay for it because they cannot be excluded if the effort is successful. On the positive side, mandatory private accounts do offer increasing returns. At issue here are the costs relating to the management of private funds and their oversight. As the number of contributors rises, these costs are spread more diffusely lowering the per-capita charges to each account. Because the proposed accounts were to be mandatory, there existed a strong incentive for a sub-group to organize behind its creation: if past into law, 100% of the labor force would eventually be contributing, thereby minimizing costs and creating strong political pressure for effective oversight and regulation. Finally, individuals seeking this objective were not alone in their efforts. The ODA was very active as a junior coalition partner in trying to mobilize support. That these efforts ultimately proved unsuccessful is beside the point. The party's organization and infrastructure made the coordination of members and their resources more efficient and easier to manage. Taken together, these eight factors (jointness being moot) suggest that, in the aggregate, the likelihood of successful collective action is very high, but that success appears to rest on the wealthier supporters becoming involved. The problem, however, is that even if the group did succeed in organizing, it offered no real electoral reward or threat to any political party. Both individually and as a collective, the advocates of mandatory private accounts had a very low electoral appeal. Of the eight electoral districts, the aggregate of supporters only broke the 5% threshold in seven and never constituted more than 8.9% of vote anywhere. So while organization seems likely, political influence does not.

Adding a Universal Flat Rate

The figures in Table 5.7 represent individuals seeking the quintessential public good, one characterized by jointness of supply and the non-excludability of benefits. While these factors provide mixed incentives, in the aggregate, collective action again seems likely. However, unlike those seeking mandatory private accounts, this group was not dependent on just the wealthy for its success, for the Little Losers were almost as likely to organize as the transition's biggest winners. The only group characteristic clearly working against them is their diffuse geographic distribution as members can be found all over the country. Although this kind of diffusion normally hinders the mobility of available resources, particularly among large latent groups, the Little Losers had an important institutional ally to help overcome these logistical hurdles, namely the trade unions. As described above, the unions were the most vocal advocates of a legal right for all citizens to a state pension regardless of past contributions. With union offices and lines of communication already established around the country, the Little Losers, who also constituted the bulk of the remaining union membership, were able to lower the transaction costs involved in mobilizing their own resources. The presence of both statistically significant resource heterogeneity, and interest heterogeneity also aided the Little Losers in their efforts.

The biggest challenge comes from the nature of the objective itself, as its universal nature provides a strong incentive to free ride on the contributions of others. Because all citizens would be legally entitled to benefits regardless of whether they had either contributed to the legislation's passage or had ever paid taxes (i.e., non-excludable), there is a strong incentive, particularly among poorer members, to free ride. However, because the government was to guarantee a set level of benefit regardless of the how many people collected it, the objective does appear to offer a benefit in joint supply. The critical assumption here is a soft-budget constraint. In other words, as the population ages, and more and more people begin to collect this flat-rate, the government must be willing to either raise taxes or borrow the funds needed to cover the expense. If one assumes a hard-budget constraint, where deficits are not allowed, then the level of pension benefit must fall with each new retiree. Clearly this was not what the proponents had in mind. While questions of indexation (i.e., adjustments for inflation and the cost of living) must be considered, in the short-run, the government's ability to raise taxes and go into debt translates into a benefit that is not affected by the number of people who enjoy it. Under such circumstances, large groups are more likely to recognize and act on their collective interest (Oliver 1993; Oliver and Marwell 1988).

Table 5.7 **The Likelihood of Collective Action in Support of Introducing a Universal, Flat-Rate Pension**

	Big Losers	Little Losers	Little Winners	Big Winners	Aggregate
Group Characteristics					
Geography	Dense (+)	Diffuse (-)	Diffuse (+)	Dense (+)	Diffuse (-)
Resource Quantity	Low (-)	High (+)	High (+)	High (+)	High (+)
Resource Mobility	Low (-)	Moderate (0/+)	Moderate (0/+)	High (+)	Moderate (0/+)
Resource Heterogeneity	No (-)	Yes (+)	No (-)	Yes (+)	Yes (+)
Interest Heterogeneity	Yes (+)	Yes (+)	Yes (+)	Yes (+)	Yes (+)
Electoral Appeal	Moderate	High	High	Low	High
Nature of the Objective					
Joint Supply (group size)	Yes (0/+) (small)	Yes (+) (large)	Yes (+) (large)	Yes (0/+) (small)	Yes (+) (large)
Exclusive Benefits	No (-)	No (-)	No (-)	No (-)	No (-)
Increasing Returns (group size)	No (0/-) (small)	No (-) (large)	No (-) (large)	No (0/-) (small)	No (-) (large)
Environment					
Other Actors	Yes (+)	Yes (+)	Yes (+)	Yes (+)	Yes (+)
Likelihood of Organizing	Low to Moderate	High	Moderate	High	Moderate to High
Likelihood of Influence	Moderate	High	High	Low	High

A final factors working against all groups seeking a flat-rate is the lack of increasing returns. The issue here is ultimately a function of demographic trends, which in Eastern Europe means considering the effect of adding an additional old person to the costs and benefits of a particular plan. The key centers on their opposition to further increases in the retirement age, a move that would have offered increasing returns by effectively increasing the tax-base. While this would have helped, over 63% of those who sought a universal flat-rate strongly agreed with the notion of *lowering* the retirement age, a move that actually offers *decreasing* returns as the population ages. In contrast, only 43% of those who sought a reformed

PAYG system, and the 28% of those who sought radical reform, were so strongly in favor of such a move.

The big difference between the those seeking a universal flat-rate and mandatory private accounts can be summed up in two words: electoral appeal. Whereas the latter never managed to constitute even 9% of any district, the former comprised between 34–46% of every electoral district. While not the largest fish in the political sea, they clearly represented a credible electoral threat to policy makers. Therefore, given the likelihood of successful collective action, one would expect to see a universal flat-rate pillar added to the Czech pension system.

Reforming the PAYG System

The third and final alternative was to reform the current system. Both in the aggregate and across income groups, the likelihood of successful collective action was moderate to fairly high (see Table 5.8). While several factors contributed to this, the large quantity of resources overall, and the statistically significant resource heterogeneity within both the Little Losers and the Big Winners appear to be particularly helpful. The difficultly or challenge here lies with the objective itself, as it offers neither jointness of supply nor exclusive benefits. The lack of jointness is the result of tightening the contribution benefit link, and the desire to avoid or minimize future deficits. Essentially, barring extremely soft budget constraint, a PAYG pension scheme cannot be provided in joint supply. If the total amount of funds available for pensions is limited by the contributions made, then one person's consumption of the public good necessarily prohibits someone else from consuming that part of the total benefit. Moreover, the aging population and declining birthrate meant that over the near term, more and more people stood to become *legal* claimants on a smaller and smaller pool of resources. The lack of jointness decreases the likelihood of collective action, particularly among larger groups. This hindrance is faced by each income classification and the aggregate population overall.

The one positive aspect is that a reformed PAYG system offers increasing returns to organization, at least in the short-run. Because raising the retirement age increases the number of young people paying into the system, the per-capita costs (payroll withholdings) can be reduced with every one year increase in the retirement age. This creates an incentive for young political entrepreneurs to attempt organizing the masses; the higher the age limit, the greater the number of people paying into the system and the less each young person must contribute.[19]

---

19   In the long run, the viability of such a solution will be determined by the fertility rates of future generations. In the political short-run, however, the young gained an incentive to organize behind alternatives that increased the retirement age. Likewise, the elderly had an incentive to have the retirement age increased as the best defense against a declining replacement rate or benefits was a larger pool of contributors, and a smaller pool of recipients. It is unclear how those at the margin came down on the issue. One the one hand, they would be required to work longer, however, in doing so they would also be making the system more viable for themselves when they retired.

Table 5.8   The Likelihood of Collective Action in Support of Reforming and Maintaining the PAYG System

	Big Losers	*Little Losers*	*Little Winners*	*Big Winners*	*Aggregate*
Group Characteristics					
Geography	Dense (+)	Diffuse (-)	Diffuse (-)	Dense (+)	Diffuse (-)
Resource Quantity	Low (-)	High (+)	High (+)	High (+)	High (+)
Resource Mobility	Low (-)	Moderate (0/+)	Moderate (0/+)	High (+)	Moderate (0/+)
Resource Heterogeneity	No (-)	Yes (+)	No (-)	Yes (+)	Yes (+)
Interest Heterogeneity	Yes (+)	Yes (+)	Yes (+)	Yes (+)	Yes (+)
Electoral Appeal	Low	High	High	Low	High
Nature of the Objective					
Joint Supply (group size)	No (0/-) (small)	No (-) (large)	No (-) (large)	No (0/-) (small)	No (-) (large)
Exclusive Benefits	No (-)	No (-)	No (-)	No (-)	No (-)
Increasing Returns (group size)	Yes (-) (small)	Yes (+) (large)	Yes (+) (large)	Yes (-) (small)	Yes (+) (large)
Environment					
Other Actors	Yes (+)	Yes (+)	Yes (+)	Yes (+)	Yes (+)
Likelihood of Organizing	Moderate	Moderate to High	Moderate	High	Moderate to High
Likelihood of Influence	Low	High	High	Low	High

In terms of the potential for electoral influence, only the Little Losers and the Little Winners were capable of conveying a credible electoral threat. The Little Losers by themselves constituted between 23–38% of the vote in every district, while their slightly richer cousins added a further 6–15%. In the aggregate, supporters of reforming the current system made up between 49–60% of the vote. Therefore, with a group this likely to overcome the obstacles to collective action, we should expect to see a reformed PAYG pension system based around a tightened contribution-benefit link.

The Politics of Pension Reform

Although the demographic handwriting had been on the wall for several years, it was not until 1995 that serious effort was expended to deal with the issue. The delay, however, should not be misunderstood as the issue had been logically placed on the back burner as the future continuity of Czechoslovakia itself had yet to be decided. Ultimately, a peaceful separation (i.e., the velvet divorce) took place on January 1, 1993. Given the significant income disparity between the Czech and Slovak portions of the country, it made little sense to attempt a sweeping reform of the pension system until after the issue of continued union or breakup had been resolved. Once this issue had been settled, the three policy alternatives were quickly taken under consideration.

New, Mandatory Private Accounts

The first alternative was to follow the Latin American experience being advocated by the World Bank. Several factors combined, however, to limit the Bank's influence. First, as noted at the start of the chapter, the Czechs were not burdened with large foreign debt obligations and consequently the representatives of the Washington Consensus never "had any leverage" with which to pressure policy makers (Ondřej Schneider 2001, personal communication; see also Müller 1999). Second, by nonetheless pushing the neo-liberal agenda with such determinacy in the face of widespread public opposition, the World Bank actual made matters worse for those domestic actors trying to include mandatory private accounts (Ondřej Schneider 2001, personal communication). The harder the World Bank pushed, the more resistant the public seemed to become. Finally, given the historical and cultural legacy of social protection in Europe over the past century, a 100% Chilean style system was widely seen as political, socially and culturally unviable. The effect of this legacy can been seen in the electoral arena as demonstrated by a 1996 median-voter based study which concluded that "radical changes in the present design of social welfare in the Czech Republic ... [are] politically infeasible" (quoted in Müller 1999, 138). This same resistance can also be seen in Table 5.6 above as only 6.8% of the population was in favor of a Chilean style solution. One additional reason for the public opposition was that the privatization era was full of scandals and the apparent squandering of money. In short, the market mechanism did not appear all that it was purported to be. That, when combined with the fact the current system had never been in default or late in making payments (unlike Russia for example,) created a perception that the system was not actually broken, and therefore did not require radical repair. Arguments about the future or long-term viability often carry little weight in the political present. Despite the apparent electoral suicide risked by political parties advocating such a move, the ODA did attempt to champion the cause; however, as the 1998 electoral results suggest, it paid a price for doing so.

Beyond the small proportion of the public supporting its efforts, the party was also backed by the financial community, which included both academics, bankers and investment professionals (Müller 1999, 140). The logic behind their argument was that the proposed reforms were inadequate to the task at hand. In this regard, they seem to have a valid point because "without substantial [additional] changes, the Czech pension system by 2020 will have accumulated a debt of 1.5 trillion Czech Crowns, or $50 billion (roughly 40% of that year's projected GDP)" (Jelinek and Schneider 1997, 77). In short, simply increasing the retirement age and tightening the contribution-benefit link were insufficient to ensure the viability of the pension system for the next generation.

However, as likely as these actors were to overcome their collective action problems, the only available receptive point of entry to political process was a junior coalition partner (the ODA) hovering around the electoral threshold. The best these proponents were able to press for was the continuation and extension of the voluntary, but privately managed supplemental insurance accounts introduced in 1994.[20] Originally intended as a company sponsored savings plan by both the unions and business groups, Klaus elected to create a more individual-based system that provided little or no tax incentive for employers to match employee contributions (Müller 1999, 133–4). The only incentive that was successfully elicited was a government-funded subsidy to encourage participation. However, wanting to prevent the accounts from becoming a fringe benefit paid by employers, the subsidy only applied to individual contributions and was limited to a maximum of 150 Kčs (~$4) per month.[21] Although widely used by older workers, the funds have proved less enticing to younger generations, due in part to the checkered past experienced by some of the funds (Lasagabaster et al 2002, 3). Although most are run by large financial institutions, and are relatively stable, a number have collapsed over the years thereby adding fuel to the fire of those seeking to block their mandatory extension to the entire labor force.[22]

A Universal Flat-rate Pension

This alternative was largely preferred by the relative losers of the transition (see Table 5.6). While little collective action is expected from the transitions biggest losers, the Little Losers represented the quintessential large latent group as they amounted to just over half the population and could be found everywhere. However, as noted above, though very likely to organize, they would have benefited greatly from outside assistance in overcoming their widespread geographical distribution.

---

20   It is estimated that by 2000, around 2.3 million people, or roughly half of the labor force was actively contributing to their own supplemental accounts (Lasagabaster et al 2002, 2).

21   Interestingly, this has encouraged many retirees to continue contributing to their accounts. They pay in enough to earn the maximum subsidy and then collect it all back at the end of the year (Ondřej Schneider 2001, personal communication).

22   One additional source of resistance to marketization came with the 1997 financial crisis. The more the public learned of the failures and risks inherent in a market economy, the greater the reluctance to turn the provision of social welfare over to private management.

In what amounted to a correspondence of interests and geographic scope, their cause was taken up by the Czech labor unions.

Claiming to represent its members as well as the poorer members of society, the ČMKOS forcefully made its views known. They were so forceful in fact that Prime Minister Klaus walked away from the discussion table for six months in 1994–1995 (Orenstein and Desai 1997, 49). Feeling frustrated by the lack of results through formal channels, in March 1995 the union organized the largest anti-government protest rally since the collapse of communism six years before (Müller 1999, 137). While it would be a mistake to read too much into the demonstration of 60,000 people and a handful of periodic work stoppages, the cumulative pressure exerted by the unions on behalf of their membership and those left behind by the transition did result in a number of concession, including the incorporation of a new, universal flat-rate pillar.[23] While not replacing the central earnings-related reform of the PAYG system, a universal minimum monthly pension of 1,060 Kčs (~$40) was added. Part of the political support for this inclusion came from both a junior coalition partner, the KDU-ČSL, and from the opposition ČSSD. Where these groups failed, however, was in their efforts to prevent an increase in the retirement age, one of the key components of reform legislation. In this regard, the realities of the demographic trend won out, although not without high political drama as discussed below.

Reforming the PAYG System

The choice of reforming but not dismantling the current system, largely centered around increasing the retirement age and tightening the contribution-benefit link. The former was designed to simply keep more people in the contribution phase of the PAYG arrangement. Making changes in benefits and contribution rates also offered a means of salvaging the existing system, one which led the Czech Republic on the first day of its existence (1/1/93) to re-instituted an employee's contribution of 6% of gross wages.[24]

The tightening of the link between contributions and benefits was supported by an absolute majority of each of the four income groups above (see Table 5.6). Pleas for the continuation of solidaristic principles not withstanding, it was simply too popular a proposal to argue against. However, more controversial was the proposal to further increase the retirement age to 62 for men and from 57–61 for women by 2007 (Müller 1999, 136).[25] As seen in Table 5.6, over 80% of the transition's losers were in favor of undoing the increases that had already been introduced, a move

---

23   It is important not to conflate actual union membership with the union's ability to speak for the poorer members of society, particularly in the Czech Republic. As a result of being tainted by the communist past, formal union membership had been dropping precipitously since the collapse of Communism.

24   The employee contribution had been dropped in 1952 in the name socialist progress.

25   The variation for women was a function of the number of children and the time spent on maternity leave.

favored in fact by all income groupings. How did the government manage to ignore such overwhelming public opposition? With only economists, financial advisors and "demographic experts from Charles University" warning of the impending difficulties raised by an aging population, the answer appears to be that Klaus simply chose to ignore the opposition refusing "to compromise on core elements of [his] social policy" (Müller 1999, 139).[26] In the end, although this particular aspect was resoundingly opposed by all facets of the general public, its was ultimately deemed necessary in order to counterbalance the ever increasing unfavorable demographic trends.

Finally, along with the increased retirement age, a new method of calculating earnings was introduced which reflected the demands of junior coalition partners, the Christian-Democratic, as well as the main opposition party, the Social Democrats. Under the new legislation, the earnings portion of the calculation was no longer based on the best five income years during the last decade worked, but rather as the average over the last thirty years (Schneider 1996, 26). This clearly benefited those who had been hardest hit by the transition.

Conclusion

Although not on the verge of immediate collapse, the Czech pension system was in need of reform by the mid-1990s. The 1995 Pension Insurance Act modified that system by slowing increasing the retirement age and introducing a new benefit formula that was more tightly linked to contributions. While there are many factors that combined to bring this about, the above analysis suggests that this result is due not simply to lack of fiscal deficits and the absence of World Bank influence. While these factors appear to account for the ruling ODS's position, particularly the rather noticeable absence of the Ministry of Finance in the debate, the final legislation reflects pressure brought to bear by various domestic groups. The clearest example is the inclusion of a new, universal flat-rate pension paid by the state regardless of past contributions, an aspect that was only included following considerable pressure by the unions, a junior coalition partner (the KDU-ČSL), and the major opposition party (the ČSSD).

---

26   The increase in the retirement age almost brought down Klaus's minority government in December 1996. Despite the risks, the ODS was adamant claiming that the increase contained within the 1995 Act was "a real accomplishment;" In response to efforts to repeal it, one ODS official proclaimed to the media "We will not budge an inch" (Mortkowitz 1996). Another member of parliament is reported to have confirmed that "several [ODS] ministers were ready to step down in the case of parliamentary defeat" in the face of a proposed ČSSD pension bill that would have reversed the age increase (Mortkowitz 1996). Today, the opposition to this issue has largely faded, even among the unions, as "the overall perception of reform alternatives has shifted" (Müller 1999, 141). Essentially, the realities of the demographic trends have set in and the shock of the increase has worn off.

The Czech experience also suggests that the winners of privatization have not come to dominate the political arena. Although they were more likely to overcome the barriers to collective action, they still had to operate within a democratic environment. With so little electoral credibility behind them, there was little they could do to bring about mandatory private accounts. Likewise, that the losers of the privatization period could find at least some recourse within the political process also suggests that the democratic process is functioning in the Czech Republic. Although major transitions like privatization and the advent of democracy contain significant path dependent elements, the winners from one transition are not necessarily likely to be winners of the next. Just as the beneficiaries of the communist era were displaced, at least in part, by the redistribution of assets brought about by privatization, the winners of that process were forced to accommodate the needs to those left behind in regard to reforming the pension system.

As a result, the Czech experience suggests treating the country as a consolidated democracy.   Again, Przeworski's (1991) argument is essentially that what distinguishes democracies is that the losers do not wreck the playing field when they lose; rather, they agree to continue playing believing that they might win the next political contest. The Czech case, like that of Poland and Hungary, shows that only six to seven years into their transition, the losers were able to do just that. Those left financially behind were able to block unwanted reforms; they were able to extract concessions and they were able to push the inclusion of measures not originally conceived of, or wanted, by the central government. As a result, the country becomes more readily comparable for political scientists who wish to include it alongside the democracies of the Pacific, Americas, and Western Europe. Although winners and losers were created by the earlier process of privatization, the former do not necessarily always win, nor do the latter always necessarily continue to lose. The political process has proven itself susceptible to influence and interest representation by both, and that contestation means that it is simply a democracy with no special need to identify it as transitional or East European.

Chapter 6

Conclusion

This research set out to answer two fundamental and related questions. First, how do international pressures for reform interact with domestic politics to produce policy outcomes? Second, what does this interaction tell us about the status of the democratic process in each country? I have addressed both of these questions in the context of efforts to reform the pension systems in Poland, Hungary and the Czech Republic. Thanks in part to the uniformity of the policy advice and pressure exerted by the international community, the case of pension reform provides a natural research design with which to evaluate these questions. Since we can hold the international half of the equation constant, it is possible to evaluate how different domestic environments interacted with it. In doing so, we can also assess the status of the democratic process in terms of its openness to domestic interest representation.

The Interaction of Domestic and International Politics

The existing literature (e.g., Müller 1999, Müller et al 1999, Orenstein 2000) argues that the international community, particularly the World Bank, played a critical role in setting the reform agenda as well as helping individual countries design and implement a mixed pillar pension system. The argument is that, as one of the major post-war economic organizations, the World Bank has a powerful ability to influence and set agendas "through the formulation and diffusion of reform ideas" (Orenstein 2000, 11–12). At one level, the evidence in support of this assertion is overwhelming. Throughout its history, the World Bank has played a major role not only in formulating development strategies, but also in providing the funding to help implement them. In this regard, pension reform proved to be no different. With its neo-liberal assumptions about the marketplace, and the role of the state in it, the World Bank quickly became a strong advocate of both the Chilean, and to a lesser extent, Argentine models of reform which focused on a tightened-contribution benefit link and fully-funded, privately managed individual accounts. By the end of the 1990s, at least seven different countries in Central and Eastern Europe had considered ways to implement this model, strongly suggesting that the World Bank's advice had become a focal point for reformers (Cain 2001).

At another level, however, the impact of the World Bank and the Washington Consensus is less straightforward. In some instances, states do submit to the policy pressure exerted on them by international actors, as Thailand and Malaysia did in the wake of the Asian financial crisis for example. In other instances, however, countries forcibly resist such pressure because they either fundamentally question the soundness of the policy demands, or they fear a domestic backlash should they implement what are often painful and unwanted reforms. The ongoing struggles of Argentina, which recently defaulted on payments due the World Bank rather than impose renewed austerity measures, immediately comes to mind. This same mixed pattern of acceptance and rejection can be seen in the cases examined here, suggesting that the degree of international influence is variable and contingent on certain domestic factors.

In regard to pension reform, Müller (1999) provides us with two of these factors. She argues that the extent of international influence varies according to the "the financial situation of the existing public PAYG schemes and the degree of external debt" (Müller 1999, 53). Put simply, the greater the fiscal crisis facing the existing pension system, and the larger the international debt burden, the more susceptible a country becomes to the World Bank's influence. For Müller and others, this helps explain the timing of reforms. It also confirms what former Speaker of the House Tip O'Neill observed when he referred to Social Security as the third rail of American politics: Politicians will only touch it when they absolutely have to. However, there is more to the timing issue. For example, why, if the Polish pension system was in trouble as early as 1990, was the World Bank's policy advice largely ignored until 1996? Likewise, Hungarian officials knew their pension system was facing a financial abyss for years, and both countries had sizeable international debt burdens. Why did both countries wait over five years to begin undertaking reforms? Why did the external pressure from the World Bank not resonate with the deteriorating financial situation earlier? The evidence presented here highlights the importance of domestic institutions and politics. For example, it was not until the Polish Constitutional Tribunal put a stop to the practice of making *ad hoc* changes to pension benefits that the idea of radical reform finally made it onto the political agenda. Even then, interpersonal rivalries stalled the process for over a year and a half, despite continued pressure from the World Bank, the continued deterioration of the pension system, and the continued presence of significant foreign debt obligations.

So while the World Bank played an critical role in making these states aware of the Chilean experience, and in providing both funding and experts to advice them, it was only when domestic actors for their own reasons were willing to accept the idea of partial pension privatization that the idea was finally placed on the active political agenda. Nonetheless, Cain (1999) correctly points to the roughly simultaneous (~1994–1999) consideration of the mixed pillar model by seven different countries in the region as evidence that domestic politics alone cannot account for the timing of reforms either. There is clearly an interaction. While the sample size here precludes a more rigorous quantitative analysis, the experiences of Poland, Hungary and the Czech Republic do suggest a number of qualitative inferences.

First, Tip O'Neill was right. Politicians will avoid confronting the issue for as long as possible. In Poland, fifteen separate modifications were made to the existing system between 1990 and 1995, none of which fundamentally addressed the fiscal crisis facing the system (Cain 1999, 6). It was not until the Constitutional Tribunal eventually found a number of these measures unconstitutional that political leaders were forced to confront the issue in a more substantive manner. The most blatant example of avoidance, however, can be seen in the Czech Republic which has still not dealt with the underlying problems brought on by a rapidly aging society. Though currently viable, without further reforms, the pension system will face fiscal deficits totaling almost 40% of GDP in 2020 (Jelinek and Schneider 1997, 77). The bigger problem for Czech reformers, however, is that no current politician expects to be in office 2020. Moreover, current Czech leaders are acutely aware that both the Polish and Hungarian governments were voted out of office at the next election after having introduced mandatory private accounts. They are also aware that the one Czech party that did actively support the idea (the ODA), was voted into oblivion in part for its efforts to bring about such accounts.[1] So while Müller is right suggesting that a fiscal crisis is important, these cases also suggest the need for strong political leadership. In the absence of either, many political elites seem unwilling to risk the electoral backlash that has so far been associated with the World Bank's mixed pillar model.

The second general conclusion is that international influence rises as the public confidence in the system falls. Note that this does not directly follow from there being a fiscal crisis in the pension system. Most pension systems around the world face some degree of crisis as the post-war generation begins to retire. What matters more is a belief that the current system no longer functions, is inherently unfair, or that the amount received is inadequate for the new costs of living in a market economy. In other words, the third rail must no longer carry any voltage. When that happens, political elites will begin to search more rigorously for solutions.[2] We can see this not only in renewed dealings with the World Bank, but also in the study-visits Polish reformers took to Sweden to learn about notional defined

---

1   While lobbying for pension privatization certainly contributed the fall of the ODA, one should not infer that this issue was the primary factor. The ODA had long been a vocal and active advocate for pro-market reforms in all areas. In the wake of a severe fiscal and currency crisis throughout 1997–1998, the public had little interest in hearing further about the supposed benefits of a liberal, market economy.

2   A similar argument can be found the in U.S. in regard to the prominence of social security reform in the 2000 and 2002 elections. Tanner (2002) goes as far as to claim, "the 2002 congressional elections may finally have turned off the juice [electricity] to the third rail and opened the way to Social Security reform," by which he refers to Republic plans to allow a partial diversion of mandatory social security contributions to individual accounts invested in the stock market. That said, it was not until 2005 that President Bush, after having won reelection, began campaigning for such a policy change. The evidence to date, however, suggests that many in his own party remain unconvinced that they can pass such a measure and survive reelection themselves. Under the U.S. Constitution, Bush cannot run again, a fact which largely explains why he waited until after winning reelection in 2004 to begin pressing for the introduction of private or, as Republicans prefer to call them, individual accounts. Thus, it remains to be seen just how much juice the third rail still carries in the U.S.

contributions. Initially, the idea of even partially privatizing the pension system was met with extreme skepticism by almost every political leader in the region. It was only after the continued deterioration of the pension system led to a widespread loss of confidence among the public that they began to seriously consider the idea. I therefore agree with Cain (1999) that major reforms were only undertaken when there was an "apparent convergence of elite and popular opinion" (Cain 1999, 7).[3]

Beyond the issue of just how and when radical reform found its way onto the political agenda is the question of choosing which paradigm to follow, as well as the World Bank's influence in drafting the actual details of the legislation itself.[4] In regards to the former, Müller argues that the World Bank was able to not only set the agenda, but to do so in a manner which helped its preferred outcome emerged as the paradigm of choice (Müller 1999, 54 and fn 41). This degree of influence stemmed from a combination of "expert-based knowledge transfer, and" attractive loan packages which helped to ease the decision making of local policymakers (Müller 1999, 54). She goes on to argue that trade unions and other "secondary internal actors ... may influence the details of the local pension reform outcome, but not the basic paradigm choice" itself (Müller 1999, 54).

While I agree with her assessment that decision makers in the region generally had more room to maneuver than their counterparts in Western Europe, the Hungarian experience raises a potential counter-example regarding the ability of domestic actors and interest groups to shape the paradigm. I say potential in that it rests on how one chooses to characterize the current Hungarian system. On paper, it is a mixed pillar model along the lines laid out by the World Bank. In practice, it is a PAYG system in disguise that is still based on inter-generational transfers. By requiring that current contributions to the individual accounts be invested in government bonds (in order to pay current benefits under the public pillar), and that future taxpayers guarantee the rate of return on these private accounts, it is somewhat ambiguous just what paradigm was finally adopted. This end result was clearly not the original intent of the reformers who proposed the mixed pillar model. Somewhere along the line, significant and fundamental changes were incorporated as a result of pressure applied by secondary domestic actors and interests groups, changes that go well beyond the mere details suggested by Müller.

In Poland too, the choice of the mixed pillar paradigm seems offer a challenge to this argument. While the international community clearly played a significant role in the paradigm choice, there was no significant opposition to overcome. As Gourevitch pointed out, "when policy and interests of the strongest coincide, it is not clear that

---

3   Cain argues that this is only an apparent convergence in the sense the policy makers hoped to reduce expenditures while the public hoped to retain, if not increase, the benefits they were receiving. The common theme, however, was that the existing system was no longer viable and needed to be changed.

4   I interpret Müller's use of the word paradigm to mean the choice between radical reform of the pension system (including adoption of mandatory private accounts), and simply reforming the existing PAYG system.

the state has produced the result" (Gourevitch 1978, 906). Likewise in this case, the general correspondence of interest makes assertions of who chose what difficult to sustain. Most secondary actors and trade unions, along with a substantial majority of the population, supported the mixed pillar model. By 1996, the public had, by-and-large, lost its confidence in the ability of the existing system to provide benefits as scheduled, or in a quantity sufficient to provide adequate income to retirees. When offered an alternative paradigm by Labor Minister Leszek Miller in 1995, the public overwhelming indicated its preference for more radical reform (Hausner 1999, 15). Therefore, one could equally claim that domestic actors would have chosen such a reform package independent of the World Bank's pressure and advice.

In addition, there is substantial evidence suggesting that certain domestic actors, primarily farmers and segments of the legal community, were sufficiently powerful politically to choose a *different* paradigm for themselves altogether. Although the majority of the public is covered by the new reforms, almost 30% of the labor force managed to have itself exempted. Likewise in the Czech Republic, where the World Bank had little leverage or input, the paradigm choice again conforms to preferences of both a parliamentary majority and the majority of the general public. Never having experienced a suspension of benefits or other major problems with the existing system, most actors saw little need to radically overhaul the system.

I argue that the paradigm choice was a function of both domestic and international pressures. The fact that seven different countries adopted the new pension orthodoxy, and an eighth (the Czech Republic) considered it, is strong evidence that the World Bank played a critical role in placing a particular reform alternative on the political agenda. There is also a strong correlation between the presence of a severe fiscal crisis in the pension system and large external debt obligations with adopting a more radical set of reforms. While this could be attributed to greater leverage on behalf of the World Bank, it also correlates with stronger public demands for more decisive reforms. It is where these interests correspond that mixed pillar models have been adopted. Ultimately the choice of which paradigm to follow is domestic political decision. However, the international community can significantly impact this choice in two ways.

First, it can expand the set of policy options under consideration by providing expert information and guidance. Throughout their history, the World Bank and International Monetary Fund (IMF) have had, at times, profound influence over the process of reform in a variety of countries (see for example Stiglitz 2002; and Williamson 1990, 1993). With fairly specific ideas about how best to reform pension systems, the World Bank became a forceful advocate for its mixed-pillar model, a synthesis of the previous experience with mandatory, private retirement accounts in both Chile and Argentina. These institutions used their international standing, resources, and other means of influence to press for the inclusion of their particular policy preference on the agenda of countries needing to undergo pension reform. The strongest evidence for this agenda expansion lies in the fact that when first confronted with the Latin American models in the early 1990s, almost every politician in Central and Eastern Europe rejected them as too far removed from the European and communist-era traditions of social welfare protection. Nevertheless, roughly five years later, many of these same politicians were enacting modified versions of these models into law. What changed their view was their continued interaction with World Bank officials, and the funding the Bank provided for conferences, study visits and other activities. Whatever path dependent or cultural and historical legacies the existing systems may have had, the fact remains that the World Bank was able to introduce an alien policy option into the mix, and endow it with sufficient credibility that seven countries in the region eventually adopted some form of it.[5] Under any definition, this was an act of political power and influence.

Second, international actors can change the costs and benefits associated with each alternative. The principle vehicles for this are the loan programs the World Bank can offer to bridge funding gaps, and, working with the IMF, deals whereby deficits in the public pillar resulting from diverted contributions would not be held against the country in future negotiations. Just such an offer was made to Hungarian reformers, one which promised to lower the costs associated with the mixed pillar model; that the IMF later reneged on this understanding is beside the point. This kind of leverage alters the decision calculus made by local elites. So while the international community did not dictate policy outcomes anywhere, it certainly helped influence and structure the terms of debate, as well as the costs and benefits associated with each alternative.

In terms of drafting the legislative details themselves, there is again an interaction between domestic and international actors. In countries where radical reform was accepted as necessary, the World Bank was invited to participate largely on account of its technical expertise as well its willingness to provide much needed financial resources. In Poland for example, it funded and provided the director for the Office of the Plenipotentiary. It also provided technical experts and funding for the Hungarian reform efforts, which included surveys designed to show widespread public support for adopting private accounts.[6] In the Czech Republic, where both political leaders and the general public were opposed to such reforms, no such advice or support was solicited and was in fact largely rejected when offered.

---

5   On path dependency, see North 1990; on its relation to pension reform in Eastern Europe, see Inglot forthcoming.

6   As discussed in Chapter 4, the surveys in question were performed by a private research agency under contract to the Ministry of Finance, which was well known to favor the adoption of a mixed pillar solution. The surveys were paid for by the Ministry with the assistance of funds provided by the World Bank. Although this appears to be a rather blatant attempt to provide a client with what they wanted to hear, it does not appear to have been terribly successful. Almost 50% of those with the lowest household incomes preferred one of two extreme and unrealistic alternatives (see Table 5.6).

The Status of Democracy in Central and Eastern Europe

The second goal of this research is to assess the status of the democratic process in each country. To address this, I focus on the politics of interest representation and the ability of like-minded individuals to influence the political process; in particular, I focus on those adversely affected by the transition to a market economy. The focus on the economic losers is driven by Przeworski's (1991) notion that what distinguishes democratic political systems is that those who lose in one round of decision making choose to continue working within the same framework in the belief that might win the next political contest. I have argued here that the transition to market economy, particularly the redistribution of assets through privatization, created relative winners and losers throughout Central and Eastern Europe. In addition, I have shown through survey data that these groups formulated divergent preferences over how to reform the pension system based on their financial standing. In sum, the case of pension reform strongly supports the argument that Poland, Hungary, and the Czech Republic are functioning, consolidated democracies whose transition periods came to an end as early as 1996–1997.

Although Schedler (1998) and Collier and Levitsky (1997) point to considerable confusion and divergence in the literature over just what constitutes a consolidated democracy, I follow the more functionalist view taken by Linz and Stepan (1996) outlined in Chapter 2.[7] They argue, "that a consolidated democracy requires, among other things, the crafting of agreements about the institutions for generating public policies" (Linz and Stepan 1996, 269). Their criteria for a consolidated democracy are further elaborated in Table 6.1.

While I would agree with their assessment that the Poland of the early 1990s struggled with many of these criteria, the Poland reflected here, as well as Hungary and the Czech Republic, score remarkably well. The battle over pension reform was fought out among groups with divergent preferences over competing policy alternatives. Each group attempted, with varying degrees of success, to collectively organize in defense of its interests. While not above direct protests and demonstrations, such as strikes and marches, they also chose to work through existing institutions with established routines, such as the tripartite councils. Finally, their overall intent was to shape and direct the path of reform in a manner consistent with their interests. I would argue that the most open and competitive process took place in Poland. This was due mainly in part to the conscious decision of political leaders that reform could only be successful if it was supported by a "broad-based social consensus" (Hausner 1999, 30).

---

7   For more on the consolidation of democracy, see Chapter 2. See also Anderson et al 2001; Dawisha and Parrott 1997; Gunther et al 1996; Linz and Stepan 1996; Mainwaring et al 1992; Schedler 1998; Schmitter and Karl 1991; Zielonka 2001; Zielonka and Pravda 2001. The cases of Central and Eastern Europe are specifically addressed in the Anderson, Dawisha, Linz and Stepan, Zielonka, and Zielonka and Pravda volumes.

Table 6.1   Politics in a Consolidated Democracy

Value or Attitude	*Political Society in a Consolidated Democracy*
Basis of Action	Interests
Actors	Groups
Attitude towards "internal differences"	Accepted as normal
Attitude towards "internal conflict within democratic comunity"	Effort to organize, aggregate and represent
Attitude towards "compromise"	Positive
Attitude towards routinized institutions	Positive
Attitude towards "antipolitics"	Negative
Attitude towards state	Strive to direct it

Source: Linz and Stepan 1996, Table 16.1.

As such, the Office of the Government Plenipotentiary drew together not only international experts and consultants from the World Bank, but also a diverse group of domestic actors ranging from the trade unions to the existing bureaucratic institution that managed the PAYG system. While differences of opinion existed, the designing and implementation of the new mixed pillar system was characterized by negotiation and compromise stretching across two different governments. For example, initially diametrically opposed in how to use the proceeds from privatization, Solidarity and the left-of center government negotiated a compromise solution that included aspects of each party's position. For its part, Solidarity ensured that those left financially behind by the transition would directly gain a share of the proceeds from privatization which they could use as "seed money" for their new, mandatory private accounts. The union also won the right of older workers to obtain extra shares under a so-called "generation preference" provision to avoid leaving them "in a relatively worse situation" than younger workers (Hausner 1999, 27). For its part, the government ensured itself of the resources necessary to bridge the gap in the public pillar as younger workers began diverting a portion of their monthly contributions to their own private accounts.

Not far behind, the experiences of Hungary and the Czech Republic also point to the ability and willingness of those adversely effected by previous policy decisions to work through existing procedures in order to have their voices heard. As noted above, opposition groups in Hungary were able to effectively mitigate the introduction of mandatory private accounts. Through concerted, organized effort, they were able to extract a guaranteed rate-of the return on these new accounts, effectively removing any risk workers may have had in opting to join the new system. In the Czech Republic, the transition's losers were able to extract, over the Prime Minister's objection, a publicly funded, universal flat-rate pillar to compensate for the tightened contribution-benefit link, which promised to adversely affect poorer workers. The Czech case also clarifies how and why proponents of the new pension orthodoxy were so unsuccessful in their efforts. Though able to effectively overcome the barriers to collective action, the group suffered from a severe electoral concentration that significantly limited its ability to carry influence with political leaders. With most of the public still confident in the existing system's ability to provide for retirees, and satisfied with proposed amendments, there was little demand for more radical reforms such as introducing mandatory private retirement accounts.

Before concluding, a word of caution and perspective is in order. For while I would argue that these countries function like consolidated democracies, "consolidation does not necessarily entail a high quality democracy" (Linz and Stepan 1996, 30). A variety of criticisms and concerns have been leveled at the quality or depth of democracy in each of these countries, and throughout the region as well (see for example Ost 1993). In regard to Poland, Król argues that "the lack of public debate [about major political issues] creates a formidable obstacle to the development of democracy, as major issues are not discussed or well understood" (Król 1999, 71). In regard to Hungary, Ferge argues that civil organizations "did not have the necessary material and symbolic resources [to inform and mobilize the public against pension privatization]: these remained concentrated in the Ministry of Finance and were used in a biased way. Also, the time the government allowed to consult citizens was too short to start a successful information campaign" (Ferge 1997, 141). In regard to the Czech Republic, Kavan and Palouš argue that:

> There is little doubt that the full transformation of Czech society into a democratic one depends on the creation of a democratic culture, and this will be a long-term process involving generational change.... The crucial weaknesses of Czech democracy are the weakness of 'politics from below'; an underdeveloped legal and political culture; the vacuum that has been created between individuals motivated by self-interest and institutions of public power; the lack of interest in a proper dialogue; and the difficulties of public communication and understanding" (Kavan and Palouš 1999, 90–91).

While there is merit in each of these arguments, they could likewise be leveled at the United States or Western Europe. For example President Bush's recent efforts to generate a debate on, and support for, Social Security reform suggests that the American public remains largely uninformed about what Social Security actually is, how it is financed, and what its problems are. Electoral turnout hovers around 50% in many elections on both sides of the Atlantic. Armies of mobilized civil organizations remain largely a feature of idealized visions of democracy; in their place, politics is widely now seen as dominated by special interests and, more so in the U.S. than Europe, the role of money in politics. In Europe, recent efforts by the member states of the European Union (EU) to enact a Constitution have so far met with resistance as both French and Dutch voters have rejected the proposal in national referendums.[8] In the French case, it has been argued that

---

8   The No-votes on the Constitutional referendums can be seen as largely a protest vote against the sitting governments rather than a specific commentary on the proposed Constitution itself. It has also been suggested that voters are reacting "to the enlargement

Regrettably, [the highly competitive, well educated and well-informed French who operate in the global sphere and account the for the overall performance of the French economy] take no part in the public debate, where politicians and journalists talk primarily to one another. In turn, these professionals hardly share their knowledge with a much larger group of people who rely on the mass media for distraction rather than information, and who feel increasingly anxious about their future (Ockrent 2005, 1).

In other words, these types of shortcomings are part and parcel of life in a democratic regime. No country lives up to the ideal of democracy. While some countries may at times come closer to it than others, the critical issues are 1) whether or not the country has crossed some minimal threshold to even be considered a democratic regime, 2) how long it manages to maintain its position on that side of the threshold, and 3) over time, how much closer towards the ideal-type it manages to progress. In this light, 'the consolidation of democracy is an ongoing, evolutionary process throughout the world and is hardly ever static, even in well established pluralist democracies like the UK or USA, Switzerland or Holland" (K. Crawford 1996, 84). I have argued and tried to demonstrate empirically that Poland, Hungary, and the Czech Republic crossed that initial threshold by the mid-to-late 1990s. How long they will maintain this position is a question necessarily regulated to the realm of speculation, however, both the theoretical (e.g., Przeworski 1991; Przeworski et al 1996; Linz and Stepan 1996) and empirical evidence presented here suggests that their democracies are likely to endure. More recent events are also encouraging, suggesting that some of Kavan and Palouš' concerns may be mitigating. For example, in the Spring of 2005, public pressure forced the resignation of Czech Prime Minister Stanislav Gross following the revelation of just how exactly he was able to afford a luxury flat (apartment), complete with indoor swimming pool, in one Prague's nicer neighborhoods in 1992. It turns out he had some very good friends in the business community who were more than happy to provide the money needed.[9] His resignation on April 25, 2005 suggests that there are now standards or expectations about what constitutes acceptable behavior under the new democratic regime, and more importantly, that political elites can and will be held accountable for violations.

Conclusion

Sartori (1970) demonstrates the advantages of concept differentiation, that is defining concepts in terms of more specific attributes that place them in narrower categories.

---

of the Union to Eastern European countries – a process that was finalized a year ago but was never submitted to them [i.e., the voters] and hardly explained" (Ockrent 2005, 1). While this may reflect the so-called democratic deficit within the European Union, it also reflects the quality of democracy in the member states themselves in terms of how elites interact and explain their actions to the public.

9   A similar housing scandal in the U.K. led to the resignation of Peter Mandelson, the country's Trade Minister, in 1998.

One of the most commonly used attributes to describe and subdivide the countries of Central Europe and the former Soviet Union is the use of the word transitional. While a great deal of mileage has been garnered from this, it leaves open one important question. How do we know when the transition period has ended?

This research provides an empirical test to help answer this question in terms of achieving a minimal level of consolidation. Across all of Central Europe and the former Soviet Union, the events of 1989-1990 unleashed a broad series of transitions covering almost every aspect of social, political and economic life. At its core lay the twin and intertwined goals of creating a more open political and economic system. In short, to establish a democratic polity and a market based economy. Central to the creation of the latter was the privatization and redistribution of state-owned-assets. This process, carried out in a variety of different manners, created relative winners and losers of resources and fundamentally changed income patterns. Also closely interwoven with this transition were significant changes within the labor market, including the advent of unemployment and the increased used of early retirement. This, when combined with an aging population and a decreased fertility rate, meant that every one of the twenty-five countries in Central and Eastern Europe, including the former republics of the Soviet Union, has had or needs to address the issue of pension reform.

In this regard, the politics of interest representation associated with reforming the welfare state offers a critical and comparable test case with which to assess whether the transition to democracy is at least minimally complete. It also offers a significantly larger sample with which to further investigate the interaction between domestic and international actors. Because the policy advice from the international community remains the same for all twenty-five countries, it is possible to gain a better understanding of the domestic conditions which affect the extent of its influence. Moreover, a comparable measurement of how far these countries have transitioned politically would also be possible. The experiences of Poland, Hungary and the Czech Republic in regard to pension reform suggest that these three countries have completed the first step in this process, and are consequently now more readily comparable for scholars and researchers alike. There is no need for an asterisk, footnote, dummy variable or other such qualifier when including them alongside the more advanced or generally accepted democracies. In terms of how they construct, formulate and implement major public policy decisions, they are not qualitatively different from the democracies of the Pacific, Western Europe or North America.

Appendix 1

A Pension System Primer

Major Traditions in Welfare Provision

Bismarckian Welfare Tradition

First created by the Prussian elite in the 1880s, welfare systems of this type are designed to maintain income levels into retirement. This continuity is achieved by tightly linking individual benefits to the mandatory, individual contributions paid over the course of one's working career. The intended consequence is that wealthier workers will receive higher benefits, while poorer workers will receive comparatively lower benefits. Bismarck and the other Prussian elites hoped that by not upsetting the existing distribution of wealth, the existing distribution of political power would also remain in tact. Seen in this light, the introduction of pension and welfare benefits was part of an effort to coopt or appease the rising socialist movement that threatened their hold on political power. In short, the hope was that workers would be satisfied with the addition of retirement and other benefits in lieu of actual political rights, influence, and control. To further instill the idea that they were being accepted by the existing political order, organized labor unions were invited to jointly administer the pension system in conjunction with employers and the government through a conservative, corporatist arrangement.

Beveridgean Welfare Tradition

Originating in William Beveridge's 1942 report to the British Parliament, this system of welfare provision relies on general tax revenue, as opposed to a dedicated tax such as the payroll tax, to provide benefits. With the goal of preventing extreme poverty among the elderly, a flat (or fixed) rate benefit is provided as an income floor below which no retiree is allowed to fall. Like the Bismarckian tradition, which was a response to the rise of organized labor and socialism in the late 1800s, Beveridge's proposal was a response to the events of the day, namely the Great Depression and the economic turmoil of the 1930s. Following the worldwide economic collapse, which wiped out the savings and earnings of millions, the idea was to create a social safety net for all before another such crisis came along. By nature of its universal character, the system helps redistribute income across society, as even those who did work extensively during the adult-lives are eligible for benefits later in life.

Three Worlds of Welfare Capitalism

Esping-Andersen (1990) describes three basic welfare types that have emerged over the last century. First, there are the liberal welfare states characterized by "means-tested assistance, modest [i.e., limited] universal transfers, or modest social-insurance [where] benefits cater mainly to a clientele of low-income, usually working class, state-dependents" (Esping-Andersen 1990, 26). In these systems, there is often a stigma attached to the collection of welfare benefits, which are normally quite small. This stigma is either actively or passively encouraged by the state in an effort to promote reliance on work and the market. Essentially, individuals are supposed to fend for themselves through the marketplace (i.e., supply and demand) and only come to rely on the state for welfare assistance for brief periods of transition before returning to the labor force. Long-term reliance on welfare is stigmatized and discouraged. He classifies the United States, Canada and Australia as the classic examples of the liberal model.

Second, there are those modeled after the Bismarckian tradition, which he calls the corporatist welfare states. Unlike the liberal model, which holds the market in highest esteem, the goal here is the "preservation of status differentials, " which are maintained by minimizing the amount of redistribution entailed in the provision of benefits (Esping-Andersen 1990, 27). Where the conservative traditions wield their strongest influence is in regard to notions about family, and more specifically, a women's role in it verse the workforce. In most cases, no benefits are provided to non-working spouses nor are there provisions for day-care or other measures which might ease a women's entrance into the workforce (Esping-Andersen 1990, 27). Germany, Austria, France and Italy are the primary examples of this world of welfare. Overtime, the extent to which these systems are biased against women entering the workforce has generally softened, although they do not approach the level seen in the social democratic states described below.

Esping-Andersen's final classification contains the social democratic welfare states. These countries are primarily geared toward promoting "an equality of the highest standards, not an equality of minimal standards as was pursued elsewhere" (Esping-Andersen 1990, 27). One the one hand, this entails universal coverage, in that rights (entitlements) are available to all, but also that benefits are related to earnings. Consequently, there is little in the way of private provision in terms of welfare benefits as the universal state system "crowds out the market" (Esping-Andersen 1990, 28). Unlike the conservative traditions outlined above, this model of welfare preemptively subsidizes the family in terms of child and day care, consequently making it easier for women for enter and remain in the workforce. Doing so is often critical, as the tax base necessary to provide such extensive welfare benefits requires near full employment (i.e., all those seeking a job are able to find one). As he makes clear, these states are both "genuinely committed to a full-employment guarantee, and entirely dependent on its attainment" (Esping-Andersen 1990, 28). The Scandinavian countries are the primary examples of this type of welfare system.

Glossary

Actuarial Fairness

Actuarial fairness implies that the individual cost of insurance reflects the risk associated with each individual. In health care systems for example, this entails that smokers pay higher premiums than non-smokers, or that professional stuntman, who are almost certain to get injured at least once in their careers, are almost uninsurable. In pension systems, it means that individual retirement benefits are closely related to individual contributions, and that consequently, that the system will minimize the degree of income redistribution.

Annuity

An annuity is series of payments made under a contract over a period of at least one year; such contracts are bought and paid for in full at the start of the period. In short, in exchange for a lump sum payment up-front, individuals are guaranteed that benefits will be paid out over a longer period of time, typically for life. These benefit payments may be either fixed, in which case the same amount is received each period (monthly, biannual, annually ...), or variable in which case the amount is subject to change. This variation can be the result of either an inflation adjustment or that the benefit is a function of variable investment returns made with the underlying assets. For present purposes, the issue of an annuity enters in regard to how an individual will receive the assets in their mandatory, private retirement account (below). One option is that the individual receive the total value of the account as a lump sum upon reaching retirement age. More likely however, is that the individual will be required by law to use the accumulated assets to purchase an annuity from a private company, in which case the principle will remain within the capital market.

Annuities typically include a right of survivorship that provides either a lump sum death benefit, or transfers the payments to a designated beneficiary for the remainder of the period. Because annuities are typically contracted to provide benefits for life, there is an issue of adverse selection. Clearly, providers wish to enroll those who are likely to live the shortest, while evidence from the U.S. suggests that those seeking to purchase an annuity are more likely to live longer lives (World Bank 1994, 329). Because the private annuity market tends to attract wealthier buyers, who also happen to live longer, many argue that the government should require all retirees (assuming all have mandatory private accounts) to purchase an annuity. If they become mandatory, then the purchase price of an annuity will fall, as it will reflect the risks associated with providing an annuity to someone with an average life-expectancy, rather than the higher life-expectancy associated with wealthier individuals (World Bank 1994, 329).

Argentine System

In 1993, concerned with an aging population, resulting fiscal challenges, and a desire to showcase its neo-liberal credentials, the Argentine government gave workers the option of joining a mixed pillar pension system. The country's universal PAYG pillar (below) was maintained for all, while those who wished, could also divert a portion of their contributions into a private account, which would be managed by a private investment company. Like the Chilean example (below) upon which the Argentines modeled this innovation, the investment practices related to these accounts are closely monitored and regulated by the state.

Under the new system, the public PAYG pillar is financed by employer contributions that were initially set at 16% of wages and slowly reduced to 7% by 2001. This defined benefit (below) component replaces roughly 28% of the average wage. For their second pillar, workers were offered a choice. They could select a defined benefit PAYG option administered by the state that would replace approximately an additional 30% of the average wage, assuming 35 years of contributions. Alternatively, they could opt for a defined contribution (below) scheme in which 11% (after administrative cost deductions) of their wages would be deposited into a private account. The estimation was that this option would replace approximately an additional 35% of wages. In comparison then, both options offered roughly the same level of retirement benefits: ~28% + either ~30% (PAYG) or ~35% (private account).

Finally, all current workers were awarded a defined compensatory benefit to reflect past contributions to the old system. For those opting for a new private account as their second pillar, one can think of these funds as providing an initial starting balance based on their past contributions to the old system. In total, it was expected that the first, second, and compensatory benefit would replace about 80% of the average wage. Unfortunately, the Argentine economy was severely affected by both the Mexican peso crisis in 1995 and the Russian decision to default on debt obligations in 1997. The subsequent recession has placed significant financial strains on the economy, the labor market, and by extension the pension system. Due to rising unemployment, many Argentines are now reaching retirement age without having qualified for full benefits.

Chilean System

In 1981, Chile passed legislation to phase out its PAYG pension system and replace it with a system of mandatory, private retirement accounts. This was the first ever complete privatization of a state-run pension system, whereby the defined benefit PAYG system was converted into a defined contribution scheme. Workers are now required to contribute 10% of their wages (limited to the first $22,000 of income) into a personal account, which is then managed by one of eight private pension fund companies. The investment practices of these companies are closely regulated, and individuals may change companies once every five months if they become dissatisfied for any reason. The government has guaranteed the assets of each pension fund as well a rate of return. This asset guarantee has been called upon once, in 1984, when a life insurance company went bankrupt. Workers are also charged an additional 3% of their salary that goes toward the administrative costs and commissions (fees) charged to each account, as well as the financing of disability and survivor's pensions. The switch was required for all new entrants to the workforce and optional for those currently in it, although financial incentives were offered to encourage people to voluntarily make the switch to the private system. The self-employed are exempt from the program, while the military and the police were allowed to maintain their rather generous defined benefit PAYG systems. Politically, the feasibility of this dramatic change rested on the dictatorial power held by General Augusto Pinochet. Consequently, many more-democratic states have questioned the relevancy and applicability of the Chilean example to their situation.

The new Chilean system actually has three pillars, although the focus has always been on the new, mandatory private accounts that make up the second pillar. The first pillar compromises a means-tested pension for those who never contributed to the old system or failed to do so for at least 20 years. This benefit, however, is incredibly small as it amounts to only about 10% of the average monthly salary. The second pillar is the new, defined contribution system where workers contribute 10% of their earnings to a private account. Finally, there is a third pillar that offers tax incentives for those wishing to fund a voluntary, private retirement account. Individuals may either open a new account, in which case the returns are tax exempt although the principal contributions are not tax deductible, or they may combine their additional deposits with their mandatory second pillar contributions into one account. In the latter case, both the additional deposit and the investment returns are tax exempt. In either case, the pension benefit collected in retirement is treated as ordinary income and taxed accordingly.

Defined Benefit

Defined Benefit (DB) schemes are the traditional basis for PAYG pension systems. Each individual's benefit at retirement is a function of a politically determined formula that combines some measure of the person's income and their length of time in the workforce. The former is often an average calculated from the best five, ten or thirty income-earning years. The idea behind the longer periods is that most people, unlike professional athletes for example, typically earn less when they are young and more when they are older. The critical feature, however, is that the benefit to be provided in the future is defined in the present. While the definition may change over time as the formula is amended, the provision of a benefit is guaranteed by the state and/or the firm. In practice, such guarantees not inviolable, as discussed below in regard to under-funded (or unfunded) defined benefit plans.

Defined Contribution

In defined contribution (DC) systems, individuals are required to set aside a portion of each paycheck into their own private account. These contributions may or may not be matched by their employer. The key feature is that the money stays with the individual. Future retirement benefits are a function of the actual deposits paid in and the accumulated interest and earnings on those funds over time; one's actual benefit is, therefore, undefined or variable depending on investment returns and other factors. Because of the individual nature of the accounts, DC systems come closest in terms of actuarial fairness.

Fully Funded

A fully funded system is one where tangible, accumulated assets balance all liabilities. Mandatory savings plans, for example, are fully funded, whereas defined benefit PAYG systems are not. In the former, benefits are financed from the returns generated over time on the accumulated assets in each person's account. In the latter, benefits are financed through a claim on present and future tax collections; there are no actual assets available to finance either present or future benefits. The provision of benefits rests on a political promise to raise the revenue needed, a promise that can theoretically be withdrawn or amended at any time.

Many, but not all, private pension plans in Europe and the United States are required by law to be fully funded. Those that are chartered as such are required to set aside assets to sufficient to meet all present and future liabilities even if the firm or employer were to go out of business. Plans that are not required to be fully-funded are typically labeled under-funded (or simply unfunded), as benefits can only be met in part by existing assets. One of the dangers inherent in an unfunded pension system was brought to light in the spring of 2005 when the U.S. air carrier United Airlines was allowed to abandon its future pension liabilities as part of the firm's court-approved bankruptcy restructuring plan. In its place, United workers will now draw a pension from the U.S. Government's Pension Benefit Guarantee Corporation; however, their benefits are likely to be half or less than what they would have received under the firm's under-funded, defined benefit plan.

Today, much of the talk is about the unfunded liabilities facing particular national pension systems. These liabilities result from the way in which PAYG systems are financed and the political bargain on which they are predicated. The critical feature of this bargain is the idea that once an individual has paid into the system via the mandatory contributions, he or she becomes legally entitled to future benefits. It is this notion of an entitlement that one has in some sense actually paid for, as opposed to one that is just handed out by the government, that makes changing PAYG pension systems so difficult politically. However, these benefits (future liabilities) are not backed (covered) by any present asset. Instead, there is an implicit promise that the government will have the coercive resources necessary in the future to extract the taxes necessary to fund these benefits. The concern today is that as the large numbers of baby-boomers begin to retire, the revenue raised from future payroll taxes will be insufficient to meet called-for defined benefits. For example, over the next 75 years, the U.S. government has promised (as of March 2005) $3.7 trillion more in benefits than it plans to collect in payroll taxes. While this number may seem astronomical, it is necessary to keep in mind the considerable number of educated guesses that must be made in calculating such a figure. For example, among the variables that must be included are: the future rate of economic and population growth; the fertility rate of future generations (i.e., the fertility rate of women not yet born themselves); changes in life expectancy and medical science; immigration; the age and productivity of future immigrants.... Depending on the estimates used, the extent of the unfunded liability can be either smaller, or as most critics suggest, much, much larger.

Indexation

Indexing in regard to pensions means adjusting annual benefits for inflation. These annual cost of living adjustments can be based either on changes in prices, wages, or some combination. Over long periods of time, wages typically grow faster than prices due to increases in productivity. Thus indexing can become heightened politically when and if a proposal emerges to change a wage-indexed pension system to one that is price-indexed. If the change is made, then future benefits will not rise as quickly as would have been anticipated under the previous arrangement. This effectively lowers the real value of future retirement benefits; however, it also lowers their cost as well, which is the primary reason politician in a variety of countries are presently considering making such a change.

Individual Retirement Account (IRA)

IRA's are a type of voluntary, supplemental pension account available in the United States. Individuals may set aside up to $4,000 per tax year (rising to $5,000 in 2008) in a private account; these accounts are typically invested in mutual funds, which can be accessed upon reaching a certain age, or in some cases before. There are penalties associated with most types of early withdrawal, although this varies depending on whether one has opened a traditional or a Roth IRA. In the former, taxpayers can take an immediate income tax deduction for the current tax year on contributions made to their account, and the assets are allowed to grow tax-deferred until withdrawal. Upon reaching retirement age, the individual is tax liable for all capital gains. A 10% penalty applies on most, but not all, withdrawals taken before age 59 ½. Under a Roth IRA, there is no immediate tax deduction for contributions made to the account, however, the investment gains are free from federal taxation, and the funds may be withdraw at any time without penalty or tax assessment. The catch is that individuals may only open a Roth if their adjusted gross income is less than $95,000 for those filing as single, or $150,000 for married couples filing jointly.

Means-Tested Benefits

Means-tested benefits are only provided to those whose total income falls below a specified level. This essentially allows the targeting of government provided welfare benefits to the poorest elements of society.

Mixed Pillar / World Bank Model (Partial Privatization)

Outlined in considerable detail by the World Bank (1994), the model is based on three interrelated pillars. The first pillar compromises a mandatory, public pillar (i.e., administered by the government) that is financed by taxation on a PAYG basis. This pillar is primarily responsible for the degree of income redistribution within the system. The second pillar contains mandatory, fully-funded, private retirement accounts. These accounts may be funded either by individuals or by occupational pension plans. This defined contribution component is primarily responsible for the degree of actuarial fairness within the system. Finally, the third pillar consists of voluntary, privately managed retirement accounts that may or may not have tax-advantages. This pillar is primarily responsible for allowing individuals to personalize their retirement needs by providing a supplemental benefit over and above what is provided by pillars one and two.

The World Bank argues that by combining these three elements, in proportions not specified, it will be possible to do "what is best for the old population and what is best for the economy as a whole" (World Bank 1994, 48). It was this model that World Bank advocated strenuously to Central and Eastern Europe during the 1990s.

New Pension Orthodoxy

The new pension orthodoxy refers to the rigid adherence of bringing neo-liberal, market-based principles to the provision of old-age retirement benefits. In short, it is the strict advocacy of adding mandatory, private accounts to an existing PAYG system, or replacing that system with such accounts altogether.

Notional Defined Contribution (NDC)

A hybrid PAYG system that attempts to combine the traditional elements of defined benefit (DB) with the idea of individual accounts and the actuarial fairness contained in defined contribution (DC) schemes (above). In practice, the system operates like any other PAYG system in that current contributions are used to pay current benefits. What changes is how these contributions are accounted for and how future benefits are linked to them. In essence, they are individual accounts funded on a PAYG basis.

The first step involves creating hypothetical, or notional, individual accounts for all taxpayers into which their normal, monthly payroll deductions will be nominally deposited. Each account then accrues interest according to a formula determined by politicians that is typically indexed to changes in either wages, prices, or some combination of the two over time. At retirement, each individual's benefits are a function of the accrued balance in his or her fictional account. The account is fictional in that no assets where set aside in the individual's name; each individual's contributions were immediately used to provide benefits to existing retirees. Consequently, the private account exists on paper only as an accounting technique. Since the account contain no real assets, an individual cannot claim the balance as either a lump sum or use it to purchase an annuity from a private bank or insurance company. Instead, the government uses the balance in each notional account to calculate an annuity it will provide to the individual on a continuing PAYG basis, that is from the regular tax payments of existing and future workers.

The principle difference for beneficiaries is that their individual benefit is now based on their actual history of contributions over the course of their career, as opposed to an average of their best five, ten or thirty income-earning years as is typically the case in defined benefit PAYG systems. In this way, the switch to NDC introduces a greater degree of actuarial fairness, limiting the degree of income redistribution. Adopted in Sweden in 1994, Italy (1995), Latvia (1996), Kyrgyz Republic (1997), Poland (1999), and Mongolia (2000) have each since followed suit as part of reforms to their PAYG systems.

Old-Age Dependency Ratio

This is the ratio of elderly to those of working age. The ratio is defined slightly differently in numerical terms by different sources. For example, the World Bank uses the ratio of those over the age of 60 to those age 20–59. In other cases, the working population includes those 18 and over. The ratio provides a measure of the demographic balance in society.

Pay-As-You-Go (PAYG) Financing

This is a method of financing current retirement benefits from current taxpayers, normally through a dedicated tax paid by either employers, employees, or a combination of both. The system is based on an intergenerational agreement and reliant on favorable demographic ratios for its long-term viability. Most pension systems are, or were, financed at least in part through this method. As noted above in regard to fully funded systems, what makes changing or reforming PAYG systems so difficult politically is that unlike many other forms of government assistance, individuals feel a strong sense of entitlement to their PAYG benefits because they have, from their perspective, been paying for them in advance their entire lives. While in practice, their contributions were used immediately to pay current retirement benefits, people often feel as if they are due their money back when they retire. Consequently, any effort to change the existing system is certain to meet with vocal and fierce resistance.

Pre-funding (of benefits within a PAYG system)

Not found in any of the countries examined here, the issue has relevance for PAYG systems that are currently viable financially, that is able to meet current benefit obligations from current contributions, but face a point in the future where the system will become financially insolvent (i.e., unable to meet its benefit obligations). The best current example is Social Security in the United States.

Following recommendations of the 1981 Greenspan Commission, the payroll tax collected from both employers and employees was slowly raised to 7.65% from a rate of 6.7% in 1983. The net result of the tax increase was an annual social security surplus as contributions far exceeded the benefit levels of the 1980s and 1990s. Under the law, all government trust funds, such as Social Security or the Federal Highway trust fund, must use any annual surplus to purchase government bonds; (the government then uses this revenue to help minimize its current fiscal year budget deficit.) By 2003, the Social Security trust fund had amassed over $1.46 trillion in such bonds that will be used to supplement the provision of future benefits when the baby boomers begin to retire in 2008.

In essence, what the Greenspan commission recommended was to change social security from a purely PAYG arrangement to one that contained an element of pre-funding. Starting in 2009, retirement benefits will be financed from two sources. First, and primarily, benefits will be provided by current workers as is normal for a PAYG system. However, they will also be supported from a second source, namely the revenue from the sale of the government bonds purchased over the last 16 years due to the higher payroll tax imposed in 1983. In other words, from 1983, and continuing until 2009, current workers have been not only supporting current retirees as per the PAYG mechanism, they have also been setting aside government bonds to pre-fund their own retirement benefits. It is expected that the accumulated bonds will last until 2017, at which time Social Security will revert back to being a purely PAYG system.

Rate of Return

A rate of return is the appreciation of a capital asset as a percentage of the asset's original cost. The term has several applications in regard to pension or retirement systems. Primarily, the issue relates to the rate of return to be expected within the new, mandatory accounts that comprise the second pillar of the mixed pillar model. These defined contribution accounts will be invested in various mutual funds with the hope that they will appreciate in value over many decades. This appreciation drives the rate of return.

One of the principle arguments for such private accounts is that they can take advantage of the generally high rates of return offered by the capital market over many years and decades of investment. However, this focus on the historical rate of return hides the volatility inherent in the market, both individually and over time. At the individual level, each investor yields his or her own unique rate of return based on the allocation of an individual portfolio. Some individuals will achieve returns that exceed the average rate while others will not; more importantly, some investors can and will lose money, even in a year when everyone else has made money on their investments. Examining the average rate of return across the market will hide this fact. A similar problem occurs with looking at average returns over time. While long-run investments in the U.S. capital market have, for example, consistently yielded positive returns, the same cannot be said on a year-in and year-out basis. To know that one's investments have yielded an average of 9% per year over the past 20 years will offer little consolation if over the last two years, the value of one's portfolio has dropped by 30%. This becomes especially true the closer one becomes to retirement age. Sudden shifts in the annual rate of return can have profound effects on employment decisions as well as the quality of life one can expect in retirement. For example, the bursting of the tech bubble in 2000–2001 severely eroded many of the gains made during the 1990s. Anyone heavily invested in technology stocks at the time, and in their early 60s, may very well have lost a significant portion of his or her retirement savings, with very little time remaining to gain it back before entering retirement.

The other aspect of a return relates to PAYG pension systems. To make sense of the rate of return offered by this type of system, it is necessary to first clarify the definitions of savings and investment. Savings is defined as income not otherwise used for consumption; it is in effect, a residual. Investment is the purchase of a capital asset (i.e., a stock, bond, deposit certificate...), with the hope that it will appreciate over time. Seen in this light, it should be clear that PAYG pension systems are neither savings nor investment. First, nothing is saved. In a balanced system, all current contributions are used to fund current benefits; there is no residual. Even in the current case of the U.S., where contributions exceed benefits, there are no savings. As explained above in regard to pre-funding, the excess contributions are required by law to be used for the purchase of government Treasury securities. The government then uses this added revenue to finance its current consumption through the general budget (e.g., defense spending, education, parks and recreation...). Nothing is left over (except the bonds themselves which are essentially promises or claims on future government revenue).

Second, in a balance system, no assets are purchased with the contributions collected; instead they are immediately transferred to retirees, who in most cases use the money to fund their own consumption needs. Pure PAYG systems are transfer mechanisms; they are not a means of savings, nor are they a form of investment. The only exception to this is in the case of pre-funding, where government bonds are purchased with excess contributions. These assets do offer a rate of return; however, as a percentage of all contributions received, the amount left over for such purchases is very small.

In what sense then is there a rate of return in a PAYG system? The short answer is that there is none, at least not in the financial or economic sense. Again, such systems are an immediate transfer mechanism, not a form of savings or investment. There is, however, a political rate of return (see Cordes and Steuerle 1999). PAYG systems are normally defined benefit systems (above), meaning each individual has an expectation about what they will receive in annual retirement benefits, even if they will not begin receiving these benefits for decades to come. Consequently, each person can think about a return in terms of the total financial value of all benefits to be received in retirement as a percentage of the total value (adjusted for inflation) of the transfers paid into the system over the course of a working career. There are, however, a couple of caveats to this type of thinking. First, this return is largely a function of political decisions, not the appreciation of some underlying capital asset. Politicians can cut present and/or future benefits at any time, albeit perhaps at a severe political price to themselves. They can also, as Chile did in 1981, cancel the program altogether in favor of some new system where acquired rights and entitlements under the old arrangement may or may not be retained. In other words, the rate of return rests on the maintenance of a political promise over time. Second, this type of return is also dependent on life expectancy. If a worker dies one month before becoming eligible for benefits, his or her return is net negative: a career's worth of payroll taxes were paid in, but no benefits will ever be received (his or her dependents may or may not be able to claim survivor benefits depending on the situation). In this sense, PAYG systems are discriminatory against those who die young, and overly generous to those who live significantly longer lives. With a retirement age somewhere in the 60s, someone living to age 100 will likely receive far more in benefits than they ever paid in payroll taxes. Thanks to advances in modern medicine, it is now entirely possible to have paid in for 35 years, and collect benefits for over 40.

Replacement Rate

The replacement rate is the percentage of a worker's wage that is replaced by a pension upon retirement. The particular wage figure used in the calculation is typically an average of earnings during the individual's base period as specified in the relevant law or contract, often the five or ten highest income-earning years of employment. A variety of base periods exist, including an average of all life-time earnings. Clearly, it is in the individual's best interest to weight more heavily, or ideally exclusively, the highest income-earnings years. The wage and income figures from previous years must be converted to present-day values prior to averaging in order to account for inflation over time.

Solvency

Solvency generally means having sufficient assets to meet liabilities. In regard to pension systems, a solvent system is one that has the financial assets to provide all the benefits due retirees over a 75 year period (technically, this is known as sustainable solvency in the parlance of American actuaries). As such, a solvent system is fully funded, as described above. PAYG systems are considered solvent if they are capable of meeting current obligations from current payroll tax receipts; if the system requires outside transfers, from general tax revenue for example, to meet these obligations, then it is commonly referred to as insolvent, or facing a solvency crisis.

System Dependency Ration

This is the ratio of the number of retirees receiving a pension divided by the number of workers funding those pensions through payroll taxes in the same period. As life expectancy continues to rise, and fertility rates continue to fall, this ratio is rapidly approaching 1:1, and in many countries is expected to exceed 1.0 some time later this century. The ratio highlights the limits of financing pensions through intergenerational transfers, such as is the case with PAYG pension systems. For example, in 1950, the Hungarian ratio was 0.124, meaning that the cost of providing a single pension could be spread among eight workers (1/8=0.125). By 2000, the ratio had climbed to 0.809, meaning that the burden of providing a single pension could no longer be born by eight workers, but had instead to be met by contributions coming from only 1.2 workers. Estimates suggest that by 2050, the burden of each pensioner's benefits will have to met by a single worker.

Similar trajectories have taken place, and are projected to continue, across advanced industrial societies, including Britain and United States. For example, when the U.S. Social Security system began paying benefits in 1940, the burden of providing a single pension could be spread out among almost 42 contributors; in 2005, that same burden is being met by only three. As an estimated thirty million baby boomers begin to retire over the next twenty-five years, the depth of contributors in the U.S. will fall to the point where only 2 workers (in 2030) will be able to fund each pension, as opposed to the initial 42 in 1940. It is this kind of demographic trend that is driving attempts to reform pension systems throughout the industrialized world.

Universal Flat-Rate Pillar

This is a pension provided by the state to all retirees regardless of past employment or tax history. The benefit amount is fixed, or flat, for all recipients. This component is often labeled the zero pillar within the mixed pillar system (described above). Its intent is to provide an income floor for all retirees, regardless of circumstance.

Voluntary Supplemental Insurance

This type of insurance comes in a variety of forms. Generally speaking, it refers to individual contributions to a private retirement account. These funds may or may not be matched by an employer or the government, and there may or may not be tax benefits associated with the contributions made to such accounts. In the mixed pillar model, these types of accounts typically comprise the third pillar and are designed to allow individuals the opportunity to tailor their individual retirement needs.

Appendix 2

Coding Scheme For the Model of Collective Action

Group Characteristics

Geography

In Poland, groups having a *Dense* distribution of members are defined as having 40% or more of the group residing in 5 or less of the 46 regions, else the group is deemed *Diffuse*.

In Hungary, groups having a *Dense* distribution of members are defined has having 40% or more of the group residing in 3 or less of the 20 regions, else the group is deemed *Diffuse*.

In the Czech Republic, groups having a *Dense* distribution of members are defined has having 40% or more of the group residing in 2 or less of the 8 regions, else the group is deemed *Diffuse*.

Resource Quantity

In all three countries, groups with a *High* degree of resources are defined as either 1) possessing sufficient members to constitute 15% of the total population, or 2) to be the relative Big Winners of the privatization period, a group whose high level of household income entails a significant degree of disposable income.

Only the Little Winners of the privatization period are deemed to have *Moderate* degree of resources, however, only if the total size of the group is less than 15% of the total population; if the group is larger than this, than it is deemed to have a high degree of resources. Their relative household income entails a degree of disposable household income.

In all three countries, the relative losers of the privatization period are defined to have *Low* levels of resources unless they are a large group representing at least 15% of the total population, in which case they are defined as having a high level of resources, albeit fairly latent in nature. These groups possess little to no disposable income or other financial resources.

Resource Mobility

In all three countries, groups with a *High* degree of resource mobility are either 1) groups with a dense geographic membership (as defined above), 2) the relative Big Winners of the privatization period courteous of their high degree of disposable income, or 3) the Little Winners of the privatization period so long as they are densely concentrated (as defined above).

Groups with a *Moderate* degree of resource mobility are either 1) a relative winner of the privatization period (big or little) but are saddled with a diffuse membership, or 2) a relative loser of the privatization period (big or little) but having the benefit of a dense membership.

Groups with a *Low* degree of resource mobility are groups of relative losers of the privatization period (big or little), which are saddled with a diffuse membership.

Resource Heterogeneity

In all three countries, groups that possess a positively skewed distribution of adjusted household income that is statistically significant at 0.05 level. In Stata (the statistical software package), the built-in function (sktest) was used.

Interest Heterogeneity

All groups in all three countries are deemed to have a positive degree of interest heterogeneity based on a reading of the literature in each country, as well as the correlation between attitudes and income. The fact that most poorer respondents supported reforms to the existing arrangement while wealthier households supported more radical reform is at least suggestive of a continuum of support within each income grouping. I would argue that the poorer the respondent, the more strongly she is likelihood to oppose being forced to rely on mandatory private accounts with a very stringent contribution-benefit link; and the more strongly she favors continuing with the existing system that entailed a greater degree of income redistribution. However, no specific statistical test is possible given the categorical nature of the response variables in surveys used; respondents were not asked how intensely they felt about each alternative or their preferred option.

Electoral Appeal

In Poland, a rating of *Very High* requires that the group represent at least 10% of the population, twice the electoral threshold, in 41 or more of the electoral districts. Groups that did so in 31–40 of the electoral districts are rated as having a *High* electoral appeal. Groups that constituted at least 10% of the vote in 21–30 districts are deemed to have Moderate appeal. Groups possessing this voting bloc in only 11–20 of the electoral districts are deemed to have a *Low* electoral appeal; and groups who could potential muster at least 10% of the vote but do so in 10 or less of the 46 districts are deemed to have a very low appeal, as are all groups which could not as a bloc provide at least 10% of vote in any district.

In Hungary, with its more stringent voting rules and allocation formulas (see Chapter 4), the threshold for having a *Very High* level of electoral appeal is the ability of a group to account for at least 15% of the vote, or three times the electoral threshold, in 17 or more of the 20 electoral districts. Groups doing so in 13–16 of the electoral districts are deemed to have a *High* electoral appeal. Groups doing so in 9–12 districts are defined as having *Moderate* appeal while those who could provide at least 15% of vote in only 5–8 of the districts are coded as having a *Low* appeal. Finally, those capable of providing this support in 4 or less districts, or less than 15% of the vote at all, are deemed to have a *Very Low* electoral appeal.

In the Czech Republic, a group whose membership was capable of providing at least 10% of the vote, twice the threshold, in 6 or more of the 8 electoral districts is defined as having a *High* electoral appeal. If the group can do so in 4–5 districts, then it is coded as *Moderate*, if in 3 or less, or not at all, then it is coded as having *Low* appeal. All groups seeking to add mandatory private accounts are deemed to have a low electoral appeal as only 6.8% of the total population supported this alternative.

Nature of the Objective

Jointness of Supply

For those seeking to add a Universal, Flat-rate pension to the existing arrangement (in the Czech Republic only), the objective does (*Yes*) offer a benefit in joint-supply; the state was promising to provide it regardless of past employment or tax payments, and more importantly, to provide it to all retirees regardless of their number. A soft budget constraint is therefore assumed. For large groups, the effective is positive (+) while for small groups the effect is more muted, while still beneficial (0/+). Large groups are defined as representing at least 15% of the population.

For those groups seeking to reform the existing PAYG system, without the introduction of mandatory private accounts, the collective benefit does not (*No*) offer a benefit in joint supply. For large groups, the effect is negative (-) while it is more muted for smaller ones while still acting as a detriment as the group gets larger (0/-). A hard budget constraint is assumed as the PAYG systems under examination here were all formally separated from their respective state budgets in the early 1990s. Strictly speaking, benefits paid out are a purely a function of contributions paid in. While the firmness of this hard budget constrain can be questioned, the evidence suggests that governments more frequently cut benefits before they soften the budget constraint by transferring revenue from general taxation or other sources. One of the main reasons for undertaking pension reform in the first place, is for the government to avoid having to make this choice.

For those groups seeking to introduce new, mandatory private pension accounts, the issue of joint supply is moot. Private accounts are private goods, not public or collective ones.

Exclusive Benefits

None of the pension reform alternatives considered here offers exclusive benefits. As the reforms were either mandatory or universal for all, or would be in a matter of a few decades, it was always possible to free ride on the effort and contributions of others. If they were successful in bringing out the desired objective, the free rider could not be excluded from enjoying the fruits of their success. Therefore, all groups are coded No.

Increasing Returns

Those seeking the introduction of a universal flat-rate pension do not (*No*) gain the advantage of a benefit that offers increasing returns to scale, as the cost of the program rises with each new old person, and the demographic forecast for all countries in the region is unfavorable over the next several decades as the baby-boomers begin to retire. This out rightly negatively (-) effects larger groups while still posing a hindrance (0/-) for smaller ones.

Attempts to reform the existing PAYG system, without the adoption or introduction of mandatory private accounts do (Yes) entail an effort that offers increasing returns. This is due to the inclusion of provisions to increase the retirement age. The benefits (+) large groups while diminishing (-) the likelihood that smaller groups will overcome the challenges inherent in collective action. Large groups are defined as those representing at least 15% of the total population.

Efforts to introduce new, mandatory private pension accounts are capable (Yes) of taking advantage of increasing returns to organization, thanks to the mandatory nature of the proposal. Per-capita charges and management fees leveled against these accounts are minimized if the entire workforce is required to open such an account. This benefits large groups (+) and hinders smaller ones (-).

Environment

Other Actors

All groups in all countries had (*Yes*) the benefit of other actors seeking the same alternative. There was always a party, trade union or business group seeking the same objective. Individuals were never confronted with a situation where they had to organize without the presence of an institutional actor.

The Likelihood of Organizing

When Joint Supply is not moot

Very High	8–9 positive factors
High	6–7 positive factors
Moderate	4–5 positive factors
Low	2–3 positive factors
Very Low	0–1 positive factors

When Joint Supply is moot

7–8 positive factors
5–6 positive factors
4 positive factors
2–3 positive factors
0–1 positive factors

The Likelihood of Influence

This variable is coded according (equal) to the group's electoral appeal as coded above.

Appendix 3

Data for Figure 1.1

Poland and Hungary: 1950–2000

Year	Poland			Hungary		
	Pensioners	Employed Persons	System Dependency Ratio	Pensioners	Employed Persons	System Dependency Ratio
1950				526.6	4,254.2	0.124
1955				537.7	4,563.0	0.126
1960	1,369.0	12,401.0	0.110	796.0	4650.7	0.171
1965	1,792.0	13,521.0	0.133	1,156.0	4,780.6	0.242
1970	2,346.0	16,406.1	0.143	1,453.0	5,010.3	0.290
1975	3,192.0	16,572.2	0.193	1,802.0	5,093.2	0.354
1980	4,517.0	17,768.9	0.254	2,082.0	5,014.5	0.415
1985	6,173.0	17,914.7	0.345	2,299.0	4,892.5	0.470
1990	7,104.0	16,484.7	0.431	2,556.0	4,668.7	0.547
1995	9,085.0	15,485.7	0.587	2,983.0	3,615.0	0.825
2000	9,412.0	15,480.0	0.608	3,115.0	3,849.1	0.809

Sources: Statistical Yearbook of Poland, Statistical Yearbook of Hungary, various years.

Czech Republic: 1950–2030

	Pensioners [1]	Czech Rep. Employed Persons [2]	System Dependency Ratio
1950	1,339.0	5,577.0	0.240
1955	1,508.0	5,956.0	0.253
1960	1,750.0	4,530.0	0.386
1965	2,051.0	4,787.0	0.428
1970	2,502.0	5,026.0	0.498
1975	2,648.0	5,219.0	0.507
1980	2,747.0	5,148.0	0.534
1985	2,850.0	5,266.7	0.541
1990	2,951.0	5,351.0	0.551
1995	3,057.0	4,962.6	0.616
2000	3,210.0	4,731.6	0.678
2005	2,688.5	4,362.1	0.616
2010	2,919.0	4,340.0	0.673
2015	3,143.9	4,225.7	0.744
2020	3,278.4	4,079.6	0.804
2025	3,381.2	3,934.6	0.859
2030	3,481.8	3,756.3	0.927

Source: Statistical Yearbook of Czechoslovakia (the Czech Republic), various years.
1) Projected number of pensioners 2005–2030: Kral 2001, Table 6a.
2) 1950-1990: Average Employment in the National Economy (excluding trainees and women on maternity leave).
1995–2000: Employed Persons in the National Economy (over 15 years old).
2005–2030: Estimated size of the Economically Active Population, (Kral 2001, Table 6b) less a constant unemployment rate of 8.8% (Lasagabaster et al 2002).

Appendix 4

Sources of Data

Provided Data

CEPS/INSTEAD, PACO data project, Luxembourg

The data used in this study are from the public use version of the PACO datafiles, including data from the German Socio-economic Panel Study, the British Household Panel Study, the Lorraine Panel Study, the Panel Study of Income Dynamics, the Luxembourg Household Panel, the Hungarian Household Panel Study and the Polish Household Panel Study. The comparable variables in this datafile were created by the PACO project, coordinated through the CEPS/INSTEAD in Luxembourg.

Hungary   The data used in this study are from the public use version of the Hungarian Household Panel. These data were provided by TÁRKI (Social Research Informatics Center), Hungarian Central Statistical Office and the Department of Sociology of the Budapest University of Economics.

Poland   The data used in this study are from the public use version of the Poland Household Panel. These data were provided by the University of Warsaw, Department of Economics, using data from the Polish Central Statistics Office.

The Czech Sociological Data Archive, Prague

The data used in this study pertaining to the Czech Republic are drawn from the Survey of Economic Expectations and Attitudes and was provided by the Institute of Sociology, Sociological Data Archive, Jilska 1, 110 00 Praha 1, Czech Republic.

Purchased Data

The Roper Center, University of Connecticut

The data used here on Polish attitudes towards pension reform are drawn from the 1998 Government and International Relations survey (#9825) and was purchased from the Roper Center for Public Opinion Research; it was originally collected by CBOS, Warsaw, Poland.

TÁRKI (Social Research Informatics Center), Budapest Hungary

The Omnibusz 1996 survey was purchased directly from TÁRKI (Social Research Informatics Center), Budapest Hungary.

Bibliography

Achen, Christopher. 1986. *The Statistical Analysis of Quasi-Experiments*. Berkeley: University of California Press.

Ágh, Attila. 1998. *The Politics of Central Europe*. Thousand Oaks: Sage Publications.

--- and Sándor Kurtán, eds. 1995. *Democratization and Europeanization in Hungary: the First Parliament (1990–1994)*. Budapest: Hungarian Centre for Democracy Studies.

--- and Gabriella Ilonszki. 1996. *Parliaments and Organized Interests: the second steps*. Budapest: Hungarian Centre for Democracy Studies.

Akov, Ned. 1997. "The Privatization Process in Hungary, Czech Republic, Poland: principles and outcomes." Master's Thesis. Central European University.

Alchian, Armen. 1965. "Some Economics of Property Rights." *Il Politico* 30(4): 816–29.

Almond, Gabriel and Sidney Verba. 1965. *Civic Culture*. Boston: Little, Brown & Co.

Alston, Lee, Thráinn Eggertson and Douglass North. 1996. *Empirical Studies in Institutional Change*. New York: Cambridge University Press.

Alvarez, Michael et al. 1996. "Classifying Political Regimes." *Studies in Comparative Institutional Development* 31: 3–36.

Anderson, Richard et al. 2001. *Postcommunism and the Theory of Democracy*. Princeton: Princeton University Press.

Appel, Hillary. 1998. "Mass Privatization in Post-Communist States: ideas, interests and economic regime change." Doctoral Dissertation. University of Pennsylvania.

---. 2000. "The Ideological Determinants of Liberal Economic Reform: the case of privatization." *World Politics* 52(4): 520–49.

Arenas de Mesa, Alberto and Fabio Bertranau. 1997. "Learning from Social Security Reforms: two different cases, Chile and Argentina." *World Development* 25(3): 329–48.

Arrau, Patricio and Klaus Schmidt-Hebbel. 1995. "Pension Systems and Reform: country experiences and research issues." Policy Research Paper # 1470. Washington, DC: World Bank.

Audretsch, David. 1998. "Agglomeration and the Location of Innovative Activity." *Oxford Review of Economic Policy* 14: 19–29.

Balcerowicz, Leszek. 1995. *Socialism, Capitalism, Transformation*. Budapest: Central European University Press.

Baron, David and John Ferejohn. 1989. "Bargaining In Legislatures." *American Political Science Review* 83(4): 1181–1206.

Bartlett, David. 1992. "The Political Economy of Privatization: property reform and democracy in Hungary." *East European Politics and Society* 6(1): 73–118.

Bastian, Jens. 1998. *The Political Economy of Transition in Central and Eastern Europe: the light(s) at the end of the tunnel.* Aldershot: Ashgate Publishing.

Baylis, Thomas. 1996. "Presidents Versus Prime Ministers: Shaping Executive Authority in Eastern Europe." *World Politics* 48:297–323.

Becker, Gary. 1983. "A Theory of Competition among Pressure Groups for Political Influence." *Quarterly Journal of Economics* 98: 371–400.

Bendor, Jonathan and Dilip Mookherjee. 1987. "Institutional Structure and the Logic of Ongoing Collective Action." *American Political Science Review* 81(1): 129–54.

Berglund, Sten et al, eds. 1998. *The Handbook of Political Change in Eastern Europe.* Northampton: Edward Elgar.

Bernhard, Michael. 1993. "Civil Society and Democratic Transition in East Central Europe." *Political Science Quarterly* 108(2): 307–26.

Beveridge, William. 1942. *Social Insurance and Allied Service: report by Sir William Beveridge.* London: HMSO.

Blanchard, Oliver et al. 1994. *The Transition is Eastern Europe.* Chicago: University of Chicago Press.

Blaszczyk, Barbara. 1995. "Various Approaches to Privatization in Poland, their Implementation and the Remaining Privatization Potential." In *Privatization in Poland and East Germany: a comparison, Volume 1*, eds. Wolfgang Quaisser et al. Munich: Osteuropa Insitüt.

Bollen, K. and Robert Jackman. 1989. "Democracy, Stability, and Dichotomies." *American Sociological Review* 54: 612–21.

Bonoli, Giuliano. 2001. "Political Institutions, Veto Points, and the Process of Welfare State Adaption." In *The New Politics of the Welfare State*, ed. Paul Pierson. New York: Oxford University Press.

Brady, Henry and David Collier, eds. 2004. *Rethinking Social Inquiry: diverse tools, shared standards.* New York: Rowman and Littlefield.

Branyicki, I. et al. 1992. "The Back Door: spontaneous privatization in Hungary." *Annuals of Public and Corporate Economy* 53(2): 303–16.

Bromley, Daniel. 1989. *Economic Interests and Institutions.* New York: Basil Blackwell.

Bruszt, László and David Stark. 1992. "Remaking the Political Field in Hungary: from politics of confrontation to the politics of competition." In *Eastern Europe in Revolution*, ed. Ivo Banac. Ithaca: Cornell University Press.

Buchanan, James and Gordon Tullock. 1962. *The Calculus of Consent, Logical Foundations of Constitutional Government.* Ann Arbor: University of Michigan Press.

Busch, Marc and Eric Reinhardt. 1999. "Industrial Location and Protection: the political and economic geography of U.S. Nontariff barriers." *American Journal of Political Science* 43: 1028–50.

---. 2000. "Geography, International Trade, and Political Mobilization in U.S.

Industries." *American Journal of Political Science* 44(4): 703–19.

Cain, Michael. 2001. "Supplying Demand for Pension Reform in Central and Eastern Europe." Annual meeting of the Association for the Advancement of Slavic Studies.

--- and Aleksander Surdej. 1999. "Transitional Politics or Public Choice? Evaluating stalled pension reforms in Poland." In *Left Parties and Social Policy in Postcommunist Europe*, eds. Linda Cook et al. Boulder: Westview Press.

Chlon Agnieszka, Marek Góra and Michal Rutkowski. 1999. "Shaping Pension Reform in Poland: security through diversity." Social Protection Discussion Paper No. 9923. Washington, DC: the World Bank.

Churchill, Winston. 1947. House of Commons, Parliamentary Debates, November 11, 1947. *Hansard* 5th Series, Volume 444: Column 206f. London: HMSO.

Coalition Agreement of the Hungarian Socialist Party and the Alliance of Free Democrats. June 24, 1994. English translation. Budapest: Central European University.

Coase, Ronald. 1937. "The Nature of the Firm." *Econometrica* 4 (November): 386–405.

---. 1960. "The Problem of Social Cost." *Journal of Law and Economics* 3(1): 1–44.

---. 1988. *The Firm, the Market and the Law*. Chicago: University of Chicago Press.

Coffee, John. 1996. "Institutional Investors: the Czech experience." In *Corporate Governance in Central Europe and Russia*, eds. Roman Frydman et al. Budapest: Central European University.

Collier David. 1993. "The Comparative Method." In *Political Science: the state of the discipline II*, ed. Ada Finifter. Washington, DC: American Political Science Association.

---. 1995. "Translating Quantitative Methods for Qualitative Researchers: the case of selection bias." *American Political Science Review* 89(2): 461–66.

--- and Robert Adcock. 1999. "Democracy and Dichotomies: adapting categories in comparative analysis." *Annual Review of Political Science* 2: 537–65.

--- and James Mahoney. 1996. "Insights and Pitfalls: selection bias in qualitative research." *World Politics* 49(1): 56–91.

--- and Steven Levitsky. 1997. "Democracy with Adjectives: conceptual innovation in comparative research." *World Politics* 49(3): 430–51.

Comisso, Ellen. 1995. "Legacies of the Past or New Institutions: the struggle over restitution in Hungary." *Comparative Political Studies* 28(2): 200–38.

Commission on Social Security. 2001. *Strengthening Social Security and Creating Wealth for all Americans*. Final Report of the President's Commission on Social Security, December 2001. http://www.csss.gov/reports/Final_report.pdf.

Cook, Linda et al., eds. 1999. *Left Parties and Social Policy in Postcommunist Europe*. Boulder: Westview Press.

--- and Mitchell Orenstein. 1999. "The Return of the Left and Its Impact on the Welfare State in Poland, Hungary and Russia." In *Left Parties and Social Policy in Postcommunist Europe*, eds. Linda Cook et al. Boulder: Westview Press.

Coppedge, Michael. 1997. "Modernization and Thresholds of Democracy: evidence for a common path and process." In *Inequality, Democracy, and Economic Development*, ed. M. Midlarsky. New York: Cambridge University Press.

Cordes, Joseph and C. Eugene Steuerle. 1999. "A Primer on Privatization." Research Report, November 1, 1999. Urban Institute. www.urban.org.urlprint. cfm?ID=6441.

Cox, Gary. 1997. *Making Votes Count: strategic coordination in the world's electoral systems*. NY: Cambridge University Press.

---. 1999. "Electoral Rules and Electoral Coordination." *Annual Review of Political Science* 2: 45–161.

Cox, Terry and Andy Furlong, eds. 1994. Special Edition: "Hungary: the politics of transition." *Journal of Communist Studies and Transition Politics* 10:3.

Crawford, Beverly, ed. 1995. *Markets, States and Democracy: the political economy of post-communist transformation*. Boulder: Westview Press.

---. 1995. "Post-Communist Political Economy." In *Markets States & Democracy*, ed. Beverly Crawford. Boulder: Westview Press.

Crawford. Keith. 1996. *East Central European Politics Today*. New York: Manchester University Press.

Csaba, László 1995. "The Political Economy of Trade Regimes in Central Europe." In *Foundations of an Open Economy*, ed. L. A. Winters. London: CEPR.

---. 1998. "Privatization and Distribution in Central and Eastern Europe: theory from evidence." Kopint-Datorg Discussion Paper No. 38, Budapest.

---. 1998. "A Decade of Transformation in Hugarian Economic Policy: dynamics, constraints and prospects." *Europe-Asia Studies* 50(8): 1381–91.

Dahl, Robert. 1971. *Polyarchy: participation and opposition*. New Haven: Yale University Press.

---. 1982. *Dilemmas of Pluralist Democracy*. New Haven: Yale University Press.

---. 1989. *Democracy and Its Critics*. New Haven: Yale University Press.

Danics, Viktoria. 1998. "The Hungarian Pension Reform: how could the government do it in 18 months?: the politics of welfare state retrenchment in a post-communist country." Master's Thesis. Central European University.

Daviddi, Renzo. 1995. *Property Rights and Privatization in the Transition to a Market Economy: a comparative view*. Maastricht: European Institute for Public Administration.

Dawisha, Karen and Burce Parrott, eds. 1997. *The Consolidation of Democracy in East-Central Europe*. New York: Cambridge University Press.

De Alessi, Louis. 1980. "The Economics of Property Rights: a review of the evidence." *Research in Law and Economics* 2: 1–47.

Demsetz, Harold. 1967. "Toward a Theory of Property Rights." *American Economic Review* 57: 347–59.

---. 1972. "Wealth Distribution and the Ownership of Rights." *Journal of Law and Economics* 1(2): 13–28.

Devlin, Robert. 1989. *Debt and Crisis in Latin America*. Princeton: Princeton

University Press.

Diamond, Larry. 1996. "Democracy in Latin America: degrees, illusions, and directions for consolidation." In *Beyond Sovereignty: collectively defending democracy in the Americas*, ed. T. Farer. Baltimore: Johns Hopkins University Press.

---. 1999. *Developing Democracy: toward consolidation*. Baltimore: Johns Hopkins University Press.

Dion, Douglas. 1998. "Evidence and Inference in the Comparative Case Study." *Comparative Politics* 30: 127–45.

Duncan, G. 1984. *Years of Poverty, Years of Plenty*. Ann Arbor: Institute for Social Research, University of Michigan.

Earle, John et al. 1994. *Small Privatization: the transformation of the retail trade and consumer services in the Czech Republic, Hungary and Poland*. Budapest: Central European University Press.

--- et al. 1997. "Mass Privatization, Distributive Politics, and Popular Support for Reform in the Czech Republic." Edice Working Papers 97:4. Prague: Sociologický ústav.

Eckstein, Harry. 1975. "Case Study and Theory in Political Science." In *Handbook of Political Science, volume 7*, eds. Fred I. Greenstein and Nelson W. Polsby. Reading: Addison-Wesley.

Economist. 2002. "Half a billion Americans?," Special Report on Demography and the West. *Economist*, 364(August 24): 20–22.

Eggertsson, Thráinn. 1990. *Economic Behavior and Institutions*. New York: Cambridge University Press.

Ekiert, Grzogorz and Stephen Hanson. 2003. *Capitalism and Democracy in Central and Eastern Europe: assessing the legacy of communist rule*. New York: Cambridge University Press.

Elkins, Z. 2000. "Gradations of Democracy: empirical tests of alternative conceptualizations." *American Journal of Political Science* 44(2): 293–301.

Esping-Anderson, Gøsta. 1990. *The Three Worlds of Welfare Capitalism*. Princeton: Princeton University Press.

Estrin, Saul. 1990. "Privatization in Central and Eastern Europe: what lessons can be learnt from Western Experience?" Rusel Working Papers Series, No. 4. University of Exeter.

---. 1994. *Privatization in Central and Eastern Europe*. New York: Longman.

European Bank for Reconstruction and Development. 1995. *Transition Report: investment and enterprise development*. London: European Bank for Reconstruction and Development.

---. 1996. *Transition Register: Hungary 1995–1996*. London: European Bank for Reconstruction and Development.

---. 1999. *Transition Report Update: 1999*. London: European Bank for Reconstruction and Development. 1999.

European Forum. July 2000a. "Major Political Parties in Poland." http://www.

europeanforum.bot-consult.se/cup/poland/parties.htm.

---. July 2000b. "Social Democratic and Left Oriented Parties."
http://www.europeanforum.bot-consult.se/cup/poland/socdem.htm.

Fearon, James. 1991. "Counterfactuals and Hypothesis Testing in Political Science."
World Politics 43(January): 169–95.

Ferge, Zsuzsa. 1997. "The Actors of Hungarian Pension Reform." In *Small Transformations: the politics of welfare reform – East and West*, ed. Janos Matyas Kovács. New Brunswick: Transaction Publishers.

---. 1999. "The Politics of the Hungarian Pension Reform." In *Transformation of Social Security: Pensions in Central-Eastern Europe*, eds. Katharina Müller, Andreas Ryll and Hans-Jürgen Wagener. Heidelberg: Physica Verlag.

Filatotchev, Igor et al. 1996. "Buy-outs in Hungary, Poland and Russia: governance and finance issues." *Economics of Transition* 4(1): 67–88.

Fletcher, C.E. 1995. *Privatization and the Rebirth of Capital Markets in Hungary*. Jefferson: McFarland & Co.

Flora, Peter and Arnold Heidenheimer. 1981. *The Development of Welfare States in Europe and America*. New Brunswick: Transaction Books.

Fox, Louise. 1997. "Pension Reform in the Post-Communist Transition Economies." In *Transforming Post-Communist Political Economies*, eds. Joan Nelson, Charles Tilly and Lee Walker. Washington, DC: National Academy Press.

Fougerolles, Jean de. 1996. "Pension Privatization in Latin America – lessons for Central and Eastern Europe." *Russian and East-European Finance and Trade* 32(3): 86–104.

Freedom House. *Freedom in the World 2004: the annual survey of political rights and civil liberties*. New York: Freedom House.

Frieden, Jeffry. 1991. *Debt, Development, and Democracy: modern political economy and Latin America, 1965–1985*. Princeton: Princeton University Press.

Frohlich, Norman et al. 1975. "Individual Contributions for Collective Goods: alternative models." *Journal of Conflict Resolution* 19: 310-29.

--- and Joe Oppenheimer. 1970. "I get by with a little help from my friends." *World Politics* 23(1): 104–20.

---, Joe Oppenheimer and Oran Young. 1971. *Political Entrepreneurship and Collective Goods*. Princeton: Princeton University Press.

Frydman, Roman, Andrzej Rapaczynski and Joel Turkewitz. 1997. "Transition in the Czech Republic and Hungary." In *Economies in Transition: comparing Asia and Eastern Europe*, eds. Wing Thye Woo, Stephen Parker, and Jeffrey D. Sachs. Cambridge: MIT Press.

---, Cheryl Gray and Andrzej Rapaczynski. 1996. *Corporate Governance in Central Europe and Russia*. Budapest: Central European University Press.

--- and Andrzej Rapaczynski. 1994. *Privatization in Eastern Europe: is the state withering away?* New York: Central European University Press.

---, Andrzej Rapaczynski and John Earle. 1993. *The privatization process in Central Europe: economic environment, legal and ownership structure, institutions for state regulation, overview of privatization programs, initial transformation of enterprises. Volume 1.* New York: Central European University Press.

Geddes, Barbara. 1990. "How the cases you choose affect the answers you get: selection bias in comparative politics." In *Political Analysis, volume 2*, ed. James A. Stimson. Ann Arbor: University of Michigan Press.

---. 1996. "The initiation of new democratic institutions in Eastern Europe and Latin America." In *Institutional Design in New Democracies*, eds. Arend Lijphart and Carlos Waisman. Boulder: Westview Press.

---. 1999. "What do we know about democratization after twenty years?" *Annual Review of Political Science* 2: 115–44.

----. 2003. *Paradigms and Sand Castles: theory building and research design in comparative politics.* Ann Arbor: University of Michigan Press.

George, Alexander and Timothy McKeown. 1985. "Case Studies and Theories of Organizational Decision Making." *Advances in Information Processing* 2: 21–58.

--- and Andrew Bennett. 2005. *Case Studies and Theory Development in the Social Sciences.* Cambridge: MIT Press.

Gesell, Rainer, Katharina Müller and Dirck Süß. 1998. "Social Security Reform and Privatization in Poland: parallel projects or integrated agenda?" Discussion Paper. Frankfurt (Oder): Frankfurt Institute for Transformation Studies.

Goertz, Gary, ed. 2005. *Social Science Concepts: a user's guide.* Princeton: Princeton University Press.

--- and Harvey Starr, eds. 2002. *Necessary Conditions: theory, methodology, and applications.* New York: Rowman and Littlefield.

Gould, John. 1999. "Winners, Losers and the Institutional Effects of Privatization in the Czech and Slovak Republics." European Union Institute Working Paper RSC No. 99/11. Florence: Robert Schuman Center.

Gourevitch, Peter. 1978. "The Second Image Reversed: the international sources of domestic politics." *International Organization* 32(4): 881–912.

Gradstein, Mark and Branko Milanovic. 2000. "Does Liberté = Egalité?: a survey of the empirical evidence on the links between political democracy and income equality." Working Paper. Washington, DC: World Bank.

Greskovits, Béla. 1993. "Dormant Economy, Subordinated Politics: the absence of economic populism in the transition of East-Central Europe." Political Science Department Working Paper No.1. Budapest: Central European University.

---. 1998. "Brothers-in-Arms or Rivals in Politics? Top politicians and top policy makers in the Hungarian transformation." Discussion Paper No. 55. Budapest: Collegium Budapest.

Gryzbowski, Marian. 1998. "Poland." In *The Handbook of Political Change in Eastern Europe*, eds. Sten Berglund et al. Northampton: Edward Elgar.

Gunther, Richard et al, eds., 1996. *The Politics of Democratic Consolidation: southern Europe in comparative perspective.* Baltimore: Johns Hopkins University Press.

Habich, Roland and Zsolt Spéder. 1998. "Winners and Losers: transformational outcomes in a comparative context." Discussion Paper No. 56. Budapest: Collegium Budapest.

Haggard, Stephen and Robert Kaufman. 1995. *The Political Economy of Democratic*

Transitions. Princeton: Princeton University Press.

Hardin, Russell. 1982. *Collective Action.* Baltimore: Johns Hopkins University Press.

Hausner, Jerzy. 1996. "Models of the System of Interest Representation in Post-socialist Societies: the case of Poland." In *Parliaments and Organized Interests: the second steps*, eds. Attila Ágh and Gabriella Ilonszki. Budapest: Hungarian Centre for Democracy Studies.

---. 1997. "Conditions for a Successful Reform of Poland's Pension System." In *Small Transformations: the politics of welfare reform - East and West*, ed. Janos Matyas Kovacs. New Brunswick: Transaction Publishers.

---. 1998. "Security Through Diversity: conditions for successful reform of the pension system in Poland." Discussion Paper 49 (October). Budapest: Collegium Budapest.

Headey, B., R. Habich and P. Krause. 1994. "Long and Short Term Poverty: is Germany a two-third society?" *Social Indicator Research* 31: 1–25.

Heckman, James. 1976. "The Common Structure of Statistical Models of Truncation, Sample Selection and Limited Dependent Variables and a Simple Estimator for Such Models." *Annals of Economic and Social Measurement* 5: 475-92.

---. 1979. "Sample Selection Bias as a Specification Error." *Econometrica* 47: 153–61.

---. 1990. "Varieties of Selection Bias." *American Economic Association Papers and Proceedings* 80: 313–18.

Hirschman, Albert. 1970. *Exit, Voice and Loyalty: responses to decline in firms, organizations and states.* Cambridge: Harvard University Press.

Hellman, Joel. 1998. "Winners Take All." *World Politics* 50(2): 203–34.

Hujo, Katja. 1999. "Paradigmatic Change in Old Age Security: Latin American Cases." In *Transformation of Social Security: Pensions in Central-Eastern Europe*, eds. Katharina Müller, Andreas Ryll and Hans-Jürgen Wagener. Heidelberg: Physica Verlag.

Huntington, Samuel. 1991. *The Third Wave: democratization in the late twentieth century.* Norman: Oklahoma University Press.

---. 1996. "Democracy for the Long Haul." *Journal of Democracy* 7: 3–13.

Inglot, Tomaz. Forthcoming. *Historical Legacies, Institutions and the Emergence of Modern Welfare States in East-Central Europe: patterns of social policy transformation in Poland, Hungary, Czech and Slovak Republics, 1919–1999.* New York: Cambridge University Press.

James, Estelle. 1998. "The Political Economy of Social Security Reform: a cross-country review." *Annals of Public and Cooperative Economics* 69(4): 451–82.

---. 1999. "Mandatory Saving Plans: Are They the Answer to the Old Age Problem?" In *Foundations of Pension Finance*, eds. Z. Bodie and E. P. Davis. Northampton: Edward Elgar.

--- and Sarah Brooks. 2001. "The Political Economy of Structural Pension Reform." In *New Ideas About Old Age Security*, eds. Robert Holzmann and Joseph Stiglitz.

Washington D.C.: World Bank.

Jari, Zsigmond. 1993. "10 per cent already sold: privatization in Hungary." In *An Economy in Transition*, eds. Istvan Szekely and David Newbery. Cambridge: Cambridge University Press.

Jelinek, Thomas. 1997. "Political Strategy of Pension Reform." Presented to the Legislative Issues Service Project Policy Workshop on Pension Reform. Institute for East West Studies, Bucharest.

--- and Ondřej Schneider. 1997. "Time for Pension Reform in the Czech Republic." *Transition* (June): 77–100.

Kapoor, Michael. 1997. "Slow Death: the Polish privatization stalled." *Business Central Europe*, April.

Karsai J. and M. Wright. 1994. "Accountablility, Governance and Finance in Hungarian Buy-Outs." *Europe-Asia Studies* 46(6): 997–1016.

Kavan, Zdenek and Martin Palouš. 1999. "Democracy in the Czech Republic." In *Democratization in Central and Eastern Europe*, eds. Mary Kaldor and Ivan Vejvoda. New York: Pinter.

Kéri, László. 1998. "Hungarian State, Society, Politics: the political process." In *The Reliable Book of Facts, Hungary 1998,* eds. M. Bak et al. Budapest: Greger-Delacroix Kiado.

Kimura, Kunihiro. 1989. "Large Groups and a Tendency Towards Failure: a critique of M. Olson's model of collective action." *Journal of Mathematical Sociology* 14(4): 263–71.

King, Gary. 1990. *Unifying Political Methodology: the likelihood theory of statistical inference.* Cambridge: Cambridge University Press.

--- et al. 1994. *Designing Social Inquiry: scientific inference in qualitative research.* Princeton: Princeton University Press.

Kingdon, John. 1984. *Agendas, Alternatives and Public Policies.* Boston: Little Brown.

---. 1993. "How Do Issues Get on Public Policy Agendas?" In *Sociology and the Public Agenda*, ed. William J. Wilson. Newbury Park: Sage Publications.

Kitschelt, Herbert. 1995. "Patterns of Competition in East Central European Party Systems." Annual Meeting of the American Political Science Association.

--- et al. 1999. *Post-Communist Party Systems: competition, representation and inter-party cooperation.* Cambridge: Cambridge University Press.

Klvačová, Eva. 1996. "Czech Privatization: fast, delicate, for free (and a bit fictive)." Privatization Project Country Report No. 4/3. Budapest: Central European University.

Knight, Jack. 1992. *Institutions and Social Conflict.* New York: Cambridge University Press.

Körösenyi, András. 1995. "Forced Coalition or Natural Alliance? The socialist-liberal democrat coalition 1994." In *Question Marks: the Hungarian Government 1994–1995*, eds. Csaba Gombár et al. Budapest: Korridor.

Kotrba, Josef. 1994. *Czech Privatization: players and winners.* Prague: CERGE-EI.

Kiss, Yudit. 1994. "Privatization Paradoxes in East Central Europe." *East European*

Politics and Societies 8(1): 122–52.

Kral, Jiri. 2001. "Restructuring the First Pillar: the Czech pension reform." International Social Security Association, Seminar for Actuaries and Statisticians. Montevideo.

Król, Marcin. 1999. "Democracy in Poland." In *Democratization in Central and Eastern Europe*, eds. Mary Kaldor and Ivan Vejvoda. New York: Pinter.

Kuran, Timor. 1991. "Now out of Never: the element of surprise in the East European Revolutions of 1989." *World Politics* 44(1): 7–48.

Laitin, David. 1998. *Identity in Formation: the Russian-speaking populations in the near abroad.* Ithaca: Cornell University.

--- et al. 1995. "Review Symposium- The Qualitative-Quantitative Disputation: Gary King, Robert O. Keohane, and Sidney Verba's Designing Social Inquiry: scientific interference in qualitative research." *American Political Science Review* 89(June): 454-82.

Lasagabaster, Esperanza, Roberto Rocha and Patrick Wiese. 2002. "Czech Pension System: challenges and reform options." Social Protection Discussion Series Paper No. 0217. Washington, DC: World Bank.

Lawrence, Peter. 1993. "Selling off the State: privatization in Hungary." In *The Political Economy of Privatization*, eds. Thomas Clarke and Christos Pitelis. New York: Routledge.

Lawson, Kay, Andrea Römmele and Georgi Karasimeonov, eds. 1999. *Cleavages, Parties and Voters: studies from Bulgaria, the Czech Republic, Hungary, Poland, and Romania.* Westport: Praeger.

Leighley, Jan. 1996. "Group Membership and the Mobilization of Political Participation." *Journal of Politics* 58(2): 447–63.

Levush, Ruth, Ed. 1991. "Campaign Financing of National Elections in Foreign Countries." Project LL91-8, Washington, DC: Law Library of the United States Congress.

Lieberson, Stanely. 1991. "Small N's and Big Conclusions: an examination of the reasoning in comparative studies based on a small number of cases." *Social Forces* 70: 307–20.

---. 1994. "More on the uneasy case for using Mill-type methods in small-N comparative studies." *Social Forces* 72: 1225–24.

Lijphart, Arend. 1971. "Comparative Politics and Comparative Method." *American Political Science Review* 65(3): 682–98.

---. 1975. "The Comparative-Case Strategy in Comparative Research." *Comparative Political Studies* 8:158–77.

--- and Carlos Waisman, eds. 1996. *Institutional Design in New Democracies: Eastern Europe and Latin America.* Boulder: Westview Press.

Linden, Ronald, ed. 2002. *Norms and Nannies: the impact of international organizations on the Central and East European States.* Lanham: Roman and Littlefield.

Linz, Juan. 1975. "Totalitarian and Authoritarian Regimes." In *Handbook of Political*

Science, ed. F.I. Greenstein. Reading: Addison-Wesley.

--- and Arturo Valenzuela, eds. 1994. *The Failure of Presidential Government*. Baltimore: Johns Hopkins University Press.

--- and Alfred Stepan. 1996. *Problems of Democratic Transition and Consolidation: southern Europe, South America, and post-communist Europe*. Baltimore: Johns Hopkins University Press.

Lohmann, Susanne. 1993. "A Signaling Model of Informative and Manipulative Political Action." *American Political Science Review* 87(2): 319–33.

Long, J. Scott. 1997. *Regression Models for Categorical and Limited Dependent Variables*. Thousand Oaks: Sage Publications.

Lowery, David and Virginia Gray. 1998. "The Dominance of Institutions in Interest Representation: a test of seven explanations." *American Journal of Political Science* 42(1): 231–55.

Lowry, William. 1998. "Public Provision of Intergenerational Goods: the case of preserved lands." *American Journal of Political Science* 42(4): 1082–1107.

Maddala. G.S. 1983. *Limited-Dependent and Qualitative Variables in Economics*. Cambridge: Cambridge University Press.

Mahoney, James. 2000. "Strategies of Causal Inference in Small-N Analysis." *Sociological Methods and Research*, 28(4): 387–424.

Mainwaring, Scott. Guillermo O'Donnell, and J. Samuel Valenzuela, eds. 1992. *Issues in Democratic Consolidation: the new South American democracies in comparative perspective*. Notre Dame: University of Notre Dame Press.

Mair, Peter. 1996. "What is different about Post-Communist Party Systems?" Studies in Public Policy 259. Centre for the Study of Public Policy. Glasgow: University of Strathclyde.

Mansfeldová, Zdenka. 1998. The Czech and Slovak Republics." In *The Handbook of Political Change in Eastern Europe*, eds. Sten Berglund et al. Northampton: Edward Elgar.

Márkos, György. 1996. "Party System and Cleavage Translation in Hungary." Working Papers of Political Science, Institute for Political Science, No.3. Budapest: Hungarian Academy of Sciences.

---. 1999. "Cleavages and Parties in Hungary after 1989." In *Cleavage, Parties and Voters: studies from Bulgaria, the Czech Republic, Hungary, Poland, and Romania*, eds. Kay Lawson et al. Westport: Praeger.

Marshall, Monty and Keith Jaggers. 2005. *Polity IV Project: Political Regime Characteristics and Transitions, 1800–2003*. Center of International Development and Conflict Management, University of Maryland. http://www.cidcm.umd.edu/inscr/polity.

Marwell, Gerald and R.E. Ames. 1979. "Experiments on the Provision of Public Goods I: resources, interest, group size and the free rider problem." *American Journal of Sociology* 84: 1335–60.

Matesova, Jana and Richard Seda. 1994. *Financial Markets in the Czech Republic as a Means of Corporate Governance in Voucher Privatized Companies*. Prague:

CERGE-EI.

McGillivray, Fiona. 1997. "Party Discipline as a Determinant of the Endogenous Formation of Tariffs." *American Journal of Political Science* 41: 584–607.

Mesa-Lago, Carmelo. 1997. "Social Welfare Reform in the Context of Economic-Political Liberalization: Latin American Cases." *World Development* 25(4): 497–517.

Micklewright, John. 2000. "Education, Inequality and Transition." Innocenti Working Papers, ESP No.74. Florence: UNICEF Innocenti Research Centre.

Mihályi, Peter. 1993. "Hungary: a unique approach to privatization: past, present and future." In *Hungary: an economy in transition*, eds. Istvan Szekely and David Newbery. Cambridge: Cambridge University Press.

---. 1998. *A Magyar Privatizáció Krónikája, 1987–1997*. (A Chronicle of Hungarian Privatization, 1989–1997). Budapest: Közgazdasági és Jogi Könyvkiadó.

Milanovic, Branko. 1998. *Income, Inequality and Poverty during the Transition from Planned to Market Economy*. Washington, DC: The World Bank.

Mill John Stuart. [1843] 1974. *A System of Logic: ratiocinative and inductive*. Toronto: University of Toronto.

Miller, Gary. 1992. *Managerial Dilemmas*. New York: Cambridge University Press.

Ministry of Welfare and Ministry of Finance. 1996. "Proposal for a Compositely Financed Pension System and Conditions of the Introduction of the System." Report to Parliament, May 9, 1996. Budapest: Mimeo.

Moore, Barrington. 1966. *Social Origins of Dictatorship and Democracy: lord and peasant in the making of the modern world*. Boston: Beacon Press.

Mortkowitz, Siegfried. 1996. "Pension Showdown may prompt coalition to resign." *The Prague Post*, October 23. http://praguepost.newtonit.cz.

Muller, Edward and Mitchell Seligson. 1994. "Civic Culture and Democracy: the question of causal relationships." *American Political Science Review* 88(3): 635–52.

Müller, Katharina. 1999. *The Political Economy of Pension Reform in Central-Eastern Europe*. Northampton: Edward Elgar.

---, Andreas Ryll and Hans-Jürgen Wagener, eds. 1999. *Transformation of Social Security: Pensions in Central-Eastern Europe*. Heidelberg: Physica Verlag.

Myant, Martin. 2003. *The Rise and Fall of Czech Capitalism: economic development in the Czech Republic since 1989*. Northhampton: Edward Elgar.

Nelson, Joan. 1993. "The Politics of Economic Transformation: is Third World experience relevant in Eastern Europe?" *World Politics* 45(3): 433–63.

---. 1998. "The Politics of Pension and Health Care Delivery Reforms in Hungary and Poland." Discussion Paper No. 52 (November). Budapest: Collegium Budapest.

---, Charles Tilly and Lee Walker, eds. 1997. *Transforming Post-Communist Political Economies*. Washington D.C.: National Academy Press.

Nichols, Elizabeth. 1986. "Skocpol on Revolution: comparative analysis vs.

historical conjecture." *Comparative Social Research* 9: 163–86.

Noonan, Rebecca. 1998. "Pension Reform in Transition Socialist Economies." Draft Report. Budapest: East-West Institute.

North, Douglass. 1981. *Structure and Change in Economic History*. New York: W.W. Norton.

---. 1990. *Institutions, Institutional Change, and Economic Performance*. New York : Cambridge University Press.

--- and Barry Weingast. 1989. "Constitutions and Commitments: the evolution of governing public choice in seventeenth-century England." *Journal of Economic History* 49(4): 803–32.

Ockrent, Christine. 2005. "EU Constitution I: the price of arrogance." *International Herald Tribune*, Arpil 22, 2005. http://www.iht.com/bin/ print_ipub. php?file=2005/04/22/opinion/-edockrent.php.

O'Donnell, Guillermo et al., eds. 1986. *Transitions from Authoritarian Rule: comparative perspectives*. Baltimore: Johns Hopkins University Press.

--- and Philippe Schmitter. 1986. "Tentative Conclusions About Uncertain Democracies." In *Transitions from Authoritarian Rule: comparative perspectives*, eds. Guillermo O'Donnell et al. Baltimore: Johns Hopkins University Press.

OECD. 1995. *Economic Surveys: Hungary*. Paris: OECD.

Oliver, Pamela. 1993. "Formal Models of Collective Action." *Annual Review of Sociology* 19: 271–300.

--- and Gerald Marwell. 1988. "The Paradox of Group Size in Collective Action: the theory of the critical mass II." *American Sociological Review* 53(1): 1–8.

---, Gerald Marwell and Ruy Teixeira. 1985. "A Theory of the Critical Mass I: interdependence, group heterogeneity, and the production of collective action." *American Journal of Sociology* 91(3): 522–56.

---, Gerald Marwell and Ralph Prahl. 1988. "Social Networks and Collective Action: a theory of the critical mass III." *American Journal of Sociology* 94(3): 502–34.

---. 1988. Errata: "Social Networks and Collective Action: a theory of the critical mass III." *American Journal of Sociology* 94(4): 519–22.

Olson, Mancur. 1971. *The Logic of Collective Action*. Cambridge: Harvard University Press, 2nd Edition.

Orenstein, Mitchell. 1996. "The Failures of Neo-Liberal Social Policy in Central Europe." *Transition* (June 28): 16–20.

---. 1998. "Václav Klaus: revolutionary and parliamentarian." *East European Constitutional Review* 7(1), 46–55.

---. 1999. "The Return of the Left and its Impact on the Social Welfare State in Russia, Poland and Hungary." In *Left Parties and Social Policy in Postcommunist Europe*, eds. Linda Cook et al. Boulder: Westview Press.

---. 2000. "How Politics and Institutions Affect Pension Reform in Three Postcommunist Countries." World Bank Policy Research Working Paper 2310, March 2000. Washington D.C: World Bank.

---. 2001. *Out of the Red: building capitalism and democracy in Post-Communist*

Europe. Ann Arbor: University of Michigan Press.

--- and Raj Desai. 1997. "State Power and Interest Group Formation: the business lobby in the Czech Republic." *Problems of Post-Communism* 44(6): 43–52.

Ost, David. 1993. "The Politics of Interest in Post-Communist Eastern Europe." *Theory and Society* 22: 453–86.

Ostrom, Elinor. 1998. "A Behavioral Approach to the Rational Choice Theory of Collective Action." *American Political Science Review* 92: 1–22.

Palacios, Robert and Roberto Rocha. 1997. The Hungarian Pension System in Transition. Washington, DC: World Bank.

Panków, Irena. 1996. "The Main Actors of the Political Scene in Poland." In *Parliaments and Organized Interests: the second steps*, eds. Attila Ágh and Gabriella Ilonszki. Budapest: Hungarian Centre for Democracy Studies.

Pierson, Paul. 1994. *Dismantling the Welfare State: Reagan, Thatcher, and the Politics of Retrenchment*. Cambridge: Cambridge University Press.

---. 2000. "Increasing Returns, Path Dependence, and the Study of Politics." *American Political Science Review* 94: 251–67.

---, ed. 2001. *The New Politics of the Welfare State*. New York: Oxford University Press.

Pereira, Luiz et al. 1993. *Economic Reforms in New Democracies: a social-democratic approach*. Cambridge: Cambridge University Press.

Powell, G. Bingham. 1989. "Constitutional Design and Citizen Electoral Control." *Journal of Theoretical Politics* 1(2): 107–30.

Pridham, Geoffrey and Attila Ágh. 2001. *Prospects for Democratic Consolidation in East-Central Europe*. New York: Manchester University Press.

Przeworski, Adam. 1991. *Democracy and the Market: political and economic reforms in Eastern Europe and Latin America*. New York: Cambridge University Press.

--- and Henry Tune. 1970. *The Logic of Comparative Social Inquiry*. New York: John Wiley and Sons.

--- and Fernando Limongi. 1993. "Political Regimes and Economic Growth." *Journal of Economic Perspectives* 7(3): 51–69.

--- and Fernando Limongi. 1997. "Modernization: theories and facts." *World Politics* 49(2): 155–83.

---, Michael Alavarez, José Antonio Cheibub and Fernando Limongi. 1996. "What Makes Democracies Endure?" *Journal of Democracy* 7: 39–55.

Putnam, Robert. 1993. *Making Democracy Work: civic traditions in modern Italy*. Princeton: Princeton University Press.

Queisser, Monika. 1993. Vom Umlage- zum Kapitaldeckungsverfahren: die chilenische Rentenreform als Modell für Entwicklungsländer? (From Fully Funded to Pay-As-You-Go Financing: the Chilean pension reform as a model for developing countries?), ifo forschungsberichte der abteilung entwicklungsländer, No 79. Munich: Weltforum.

Riker, William. 1982. *Liberalism Against Populism: a confrontation between the theory of democracy and the theory of social choice*. San Francisco: W.H.

Freeman.

---. 1986. *The Art of Political Manipulation.* New Haven: Yale University Press.

--- and Itai Sened. 1991. "A Political Theory Toward the Origin of Property Rights: airplane slots." *American Journal of Political Science* 35(4): 951–69.

Robinson, Neil. 2001. "The Myth of Equilibrium: winner power, fiscal crisis and Russian economic reform." *Communist and Post-Communist Studies* 34(4): 423–46.

Róna-Tas, Ákos. 1997. "The Czech Third Wave: privatization and the new role of the state in the Czech Republic." *Problems of Post-Communism* 44(6): 53–62.

Rose, Richard, William Mishler and Christian Haerpfer. 1998. *Democracy and Its Alternatives: understanding post-communist societies.* Baltimore: Johns Hopkins University Press.

Rueschemeyer, Dietrich, Evelyne Huber Stephens, and John D. Stephens. 1992. *Capitalist Development and Democracy.* Chicago: University of Chicago Press.

Sachs, Jeffrey. 1993. *Poland's Jump to the Market Economy.* Cambridge: MIT Press.

---, ed. 1989. *Developing Country Debt and the World Economy.* Chicago: University of Chicago Press.

Salisbury, Robert. 1984. "Interest Representation: the dominance of institutions." *American Political Science Review* 78(1): 64–76.

Samuelson, Paul. 1954. "The Pure Theory of Public Expenditure." *Review of Economics and Statistics* 36(1): 387–89.

Sartori, Giovanni. 1962. *Democratic Theory.* Detroit: Wayne State University Press.

---. 1970. "Concept Misinformation in Comparative Politics." *American Political Science Review* 64(4): 1033–3.

---. 1987. *The Theory of Democracy Revisited.* Chatham: Chatham House.

---. 1991. "Comparing and Miscomparing." *Journal of Theoretical Politics* 3: 243–57.

Savolainen, Jukka. 1994. "The Rationality of Drawing Big Conclusions Based on Small Samples: in defense of Mill's methods." *Social Forces* 72: 1217–1224.

Schamis, Hector. 1999. "Distributional Coalitions and the Politics of Economic Reform in Latin America." *World Politics* 51(2): 236–68.

Schedler, Andreas. 1998. "What is Democratic Consolidation?" *Journal of Democracy* 9(2): 91–107.

Schelling, Thomas. 1978. *Micromotives and Macrobehavior*, 1st Edition. New York: Norton.

Schiller, Wendy J. 1999. "Trade Politics in the American Congress: A Study of the Interaction of Political Geography and Interest Group Behavior." *Political Geography* 18(7) 769–89.

--- and Fiona McGillivray. 1996a. "The Political Geography of Lobbying: Forming Coalitions to Maximize Influence in Trade Politics." Annual meeting of the American Political Science Association.

---. 1996b. "The Political Geography of Lobbying: How Industries Maximize

Their Influence in Congress." Annual meeting of the Midwest Political Science Association.

---. 1998. "Political Geography, Counter-Coalitions, and Interest Group Influence in U.S. Trade Policy." Annual meeting of the Midwest Political Science Association.

Schmitter, Philippe. 1996. "Organized Interests and Democratic Consolidation in Southern Europe." In *The Politics of Democratic Consolidation: southern Europe in comparative perspective*, eds. Richard Gunther et al. Baltimore: Johns Hopkins University Press.

---- and Terry Lynn Karl. 1991. "What Democracy is ... and is Not." *Journal of Democracy* 2(3): 75–88.

Schneider, Ondřej. 1996. "Pension Reform in the Czech Republic: gradualistic Czechs." Central European Banker (December): 22–6.

Schofield, Norman. 1975. "A Game Theoretic Analysis of Olson's Game of Collective Action." *Journal of Conflict Resolution* 19: 441–61.

Schumpeter, Joseph. 1950. *Capitalism, Socialism, and Democracy, 3rd edition.* New York: Harper.

Sen, A.K. 1967. "Isolation, Assurance and the Social Rate of Discount." *Quarterly Journal of Economics* 80: 112–24.

Shepsle, Kenneth and Barry Weingast. 1984. "Uncovered Sets and Sophisticated Voting Outcomes with Implications for Agenda Institutions." *American Journal of Political Science* 28(1): 49–74.

Skocpol, Theda. 1979. *States and Social Revolutions: a comparative analysis of France, Russia, and China.* Cambridge: Cambridge University Press.

---. 1986. "Analyzing Causal Configurations in History: a rejoinder to Nichols." *Comparative Social Research* 9: 198–94.

--- and Margaret Somers. 1980. "The Uses of Comparative History in Macrosocial Inquiry." *Comparative Studies in Society and History* 22: 174–97.

--- et al. 1993. "Women's Associations and the Enactment of Mothers' Pensions in the United States." *American Political Science Review* 87(3): 686–701.

Spéder, Zsolt. 1998. "Poverty Dynamics in Hungary during the Transition." *Journal of Economics of Transition* 6(1): 1–21.

Stark, David. 1994. "Path Dependency and Privatization Strategies in East Central Europe." In *Transition to Capitalism? the communist legacy in Eastern Europe*, ed. Janás Mátyás Kovács. New Brunswick: Transaction Publishers.

--- and László Bruszt. 1998. *Post-Socialist Pathways: transforming politics and property in East Central Europe.* Cambridge: Cambridge University Press.

State Property Agency. 1994. *Annual Report on the Activities of the State Property Agency.* Budapest: Hungarian Privatization and State Holding Co.

Stepan, Alfred and Cindy Skach. 1993. "Constitutional Frameworks and Democratic Consolidation: parliamentarianism versus presidentialism." *World Politics* 46: 1–22.

Stiglitz, Joseph. 2002. *Globalization and Its Discontents.* New York: Norton.

Stopler, Wolfgang and Paul Samuelson. 1941. "Protection and Real Wages." *Review of Economic Studies* 9: 58–73.

Szulc, Adam. 2000. "Economic Transition, Poverty and Inequality: Poland in the 1990s." Institute of Statistics and Demography, Warsaw School of Economics.

Tanner, Michael. 2002. "The Third Rail is Dead." Fox News, November 20. http://www.foxnews.com/story/0,2933,70981,00.html.

TÁRKI . 1996. "Changes of Attitudes and Attitudes to the Pension Reform." Report No. 1/5 for the Ministry of Finance. Budapest: Social Research Informatics Center (TÁRKI).

Tetlock, Philip and Aaron Belkin, eds. 1996. *Counterfactual Thought Experiments in World Politics*. Princeton: Princeton University Press.

Tilly, Charles. 1997. "Democracy, Social Change, and Economies in Transition." In *Transforming Post-Communist Political Economies*, eds. Joan Nelson, Charles Tilly and Lee Walker. Washington D.C.: National Academy Press.

Tóka, Gabor. 1998. "Hungary." In *The Handbook of Political Change in Eastern Europe*, eds. Sten Berglund et al. Northampton: Edward Elgar.

Triska, Dusan. 1991. "Privatization: Czechoslovakia." *Eastern European Economics* 27 (Fall).

Tsebelis, George. 1990. *Nested Games: rational choice in comparative politics*. Berkeley: University of California Press.

---. 1995. "Decision Making in Political Science: veto players in Presidentialism, Parliatmentarianism, Multicameralism, and Multipartyism." *British Journal of Political Science* (25): 289–326.

---. 1999. "Veto Players and Law Production in Parliamentary Democracies: an empirical analysis." *American Political Science Review* 93: 591–608.

---. 2002. *Veto Players: how political institutions work*. Princeton: Princeton University Press.

Valenzuela, J. Samuel. 1992. "Consolidation in Post-Transitional Settings: notion, process, and facilitating conditions." In *Issues in Democratic Consolidation: the new South American Democracies in Comparative Perspective*, eds. Scott Mainwaring et al. Notre Dame: Notre Dame University Press.

Van Evera, Stephen. 1997. *Guide to Methodology for Students of Political Science*. Ithaca, Cornell University Press.

Vittas, Dimitri. 1995. "The Argentine Pension Reform and Its Relevance for Eastern Europe." Mimeo. Washington, DC: The World Bank.

Weimer, David, ed. 1997. *The Political Economy of Property Rights: institutional change and credibility in the reform of centrally planned economies*. New York: Cambridge University Press.

Wellisz, Stanislaw et al. 1993. "The Polish Economy 1989–1991." In *Stabilization and Structural Adjustment in Poland*, eds. Henryk Kierzkowski et al. New York: Rutledge.

Wilensky, Harold. 1976. *The New Corporatism, Centralization, and the Welfare State*. London: Sage Publications.

--- Charles Lebeaux. 1965. *Industrial society and social welfare; the impact of industrialization on the supply and organization of social welfare services in the*

United States. New York: Free Press.

Williamson, John. 1993. *Democracy and the Washington Consensus*. World Development 21(8): 1329–36.

---, ed. 1990. *Latin American Adjustment: how much has happened?* Washington, DC: Institute for International Economics.

Williamson, Oliver. 1979. "Transaction-Cost Economics: the governance of contractual relations." *Journal of Law and Economics* 22 (October), 233–61.

Wolchik, Sharon. 1994. "The Politics of Ethnicity in Post-Communist Czechoslovakia." *East European Politics and Societies* 8(1): 155–56.

Woo, Wing Thye, Stephen Parker, and Jeffrey D. Sachs. 1997. *Economies in Transition: comparing Asia and Eastern Europe*. Cambridge: MIT Press.

World Bank. 1994. *Adverting the Old Age Crisis: policies to protect the old and promote growth*. Oxford: Oxford University Press.

---. 1996. *World Development Report 1996: from plan to market*. New York: Oxford University Press.

---. 1997. *World Development Report 1997: the State in a changing world*. New York: Oxford University Press.

---. 2000. *World Development Indicators*. Washington, DC: The World Bank.

Zielonka, Jan, ed. 2001. *Democratic Consolidation in Eastern Europe, Volume 1*. New York: Oxford University Press.

--- and Alex Pravda, eds. 2001. *Democratic Consolidation in Eastern Europe, Volume 2*. Oxford: Oxford University Press.

Index

For Product Safety Concerns and Information please contact our EU
representative GPSR@taylorandfrancis.com Taylor & Francis Verlag GmbH,
Kaufingerstraße 24, 80331 München, Germany

Batch number: 08158427

Printed by Printforce, the Netherlands